COMBAT READY

Tim Satchwell

Published by Earth Island Books
Pickforde Lodge
Pickforde Lane
Ticehurst
TN5 7BN

www.earthisland.co.uk
© Copyright Earth Island Publishing Ltd

This edition printed April 2022 by Earth Island Books.

First Published in Great Britain 2016 by Stay Free

Reprinted 2016, 2021

Text © Tim Satchwell except where credited

All Rights Reserved

No part of this book may be reproduced in any form or by any electronic or mechanical means, including information storage and retrieval systems, without written permission from the publisher, except a reviewer who may quote passages in a review.

The author endeavors to ensure that information in this book is correct, but does not accept liability for error or omission.

Front cover incorporates the "Combat Rock" illustration by Nob Suzuki used with his permission. Clash logo created by Mark Wyatt and enhanced by David Ashby

Back cover "heavily influenced" by the work of Jules Balme and his design on the back of the "Combat Rock" album cover.

Photographs and artwork are credited wherever possible, product pack shots taken by the author from his own collection except where credited. We have made every effort to credit all sources of text and images.

Special Thanks to Junko and Ant for their enthusiasm and assistance, who have pulled me up when I was down. Huge thanks to David Ashby at Cambridge Printers for his time and patience and Joe Streno for his faith in me.

ISBN 9781739795559

Printed and bound by IngramSpark

"Do what you wanna do, if you wanna paint, paint. If you wanna do music, do music!"
Paul Simonon (2015) His advice to a young Paul Simonon from the current Paul Simonon.

"It's your life son, you do what you want with it"
My Dad - His advice to me probably from the age of 18 until his passing in 2003

"Please make use of all facilities"
Mick Jones (1998) - to me via fax

"Thanks from me for all your support"
Joe Strummer (1997) - to me on a birthday greeting

"Why has this book taken longer than it took for "Combat Rock" to be recorded, mixed and released?"
The Author (2016)

1. INTRODUCTION
2. WHAT IS MY NAME?
3. STOP THE WORLD 1981
4. THE RECORDINGS
5. THE RECORDIT
6. ALBUM REVIEWS
7. ALBUM SLEEVE AND
8. ALBUM PROMOTION
9. LONG HAUL 1982
10. MARKETING AND TRACKS
ALBUM FORMATS

1. INTRODUCTION

There is a famous/infamous book in Clash Circles, which appeared around the time that *Combat Rock* was released in 1982. It was released as a promotional device by the record company. The book had the *Combat Rock* album cover picture on the front, and the "Poster" image on the back with the track listing. It's what is inside that was controversial…nothing!

All the pages are blank…now maybe you could say that it backs up Joe's "The Future is Unwritten" tag line…but for me…it is a book waiting to be written…I want so much to fill those pages and do it justice.

I remember a few of my mates not really "getting it"…they thought it was the "Great Combat Rock N' Roll Swindle". But here we are 30 years on…and it was really saying something to me.

Photographs – Pennie Smith Design – "Devices" Jules Balme Book – Epic USA

My confession…I am a huge fan of The Clash…I didn't see them until *The Give 'Em Enough Rope* tour, but as with other Clash fans…it was enough to make quite an impact. "Life Changing" is a popular quote, but I wanted to avoid saying that outright as I think they have had a greater impact in my later life than when I was in my teens. I understand and have read so much more, and I was charging around listening to a whole lot of other stuff in those years.

The band has been an obsession for a long time now…well a man needs a hobby right?

So…why choose *Combat Rock*…well…The Clash's fifth studio album…depending on how you look at the wealth of releases and compilations. It was their biggest and most successful…and broke them as a truly International act…and broke the band as well.

The more I researched for this book, the more I realized what an amazing story it was. A whole lot of drama crammed in to a relatively short period of time. How on earth did this album ever get written, recorded, remixed, released and promoted!! I hope to shed light on this amazing set of events. There are many fantastic Clash books out there...and I have read all the English language versions, absorbed and ingested, and paged through the ones I can't read the language of! What is interesting, is the different approaches and in some cases factual differences in the content. Some written by journalists, others friends of the band (and often journalists!!!)...

I am neither and can't pretend to be...but hell I wish I had been their friend!

The material in the book comes from a wide range of resources, the many books I have already mentioned, Music Press over the years from past to the present, DVD and TV documentaries, websites, blogs, friends and acquaintances.

I have no direct interviews with the band members. I feel that they have all probably said what they want to say about this time period, and are happy to move on.

In my internet trawls, I also came across an incredible source of live recordings which covers the period I am looking at. I am truly thankful to the similarly obsessed individual or individuals as this reveals some early outings of some of the tracks that make it to *Combat Rock*...and a couple that don't!

The outline of the book is to look at what I consider some of the background period before the band started writing and recording the album in earnest. With the aid of my trusty gaffa taped timeline and my customized tiger stripe camouflage notebooks I will be looking at some of the key and defining moments that led the band down the path to World recognition, and in some cases notoriety.

I will look at the cast of characters involved and try and introduce them into the turn of events. There will be a fairly comprehensive look at what was going on in Clash World in the run up to release, the tours, the tantrums, side projects and issues. Then moving along to the writing and rehearsal of the new material, the recording and mixing, and more mixing and remixing of the tracks.

I take a look at the album tracks themselves, gathering opinions from reviewers, fans and other musicians. I want to look at the Album sleeve design and execution which seems to have created a whole debate on the symbolic nature of the cover photo and the song content and the title change from *Rat Patrol From Fort Bragg* to *Combat Rock*.

More generally...Was the album "All Killer and No Filler" and what Creem magazine really thought about it! I make an attempt to gather opinions of the album both from the release date the past, and the present, because the album and songs are still influencing musicians and artists today.

This will be followed by a look at the album formats and releases in various territories and how they may have been marketed. Then a look at various "Alternative Versions" which have appeared along the way in some depth and then return to the time line for the "Post Apocalypse" chapter on some of the events post album up to the present day. This will include a look at the cover versions of album tracks that have appeared over the years and in some cases the controversy surrounding them.

By way of conclusion, I look at the cultural effect that the album has had over the years and is still having now.

What is important to consider, is that many views and opinions are gathered from sources after the initial release. Many people now look back, knowing what they know now...seeing things in some of the events as symbolic and significant. At the time...it was just another event or comment...or photo shoot.

So...what have a bottle of R-Whites lemonade and a toilet cleaner advertisement got to do with the most commercial Clash album produced?

2. WHAT'S MY NAME...?

I wanted to include some of the people involved in the release of *Combat Rock*. Obviously, the band members go without saying. I'm sure you are by now familiar with the life and times of Joe, Paul, Topper and Mick, but if you are not, take time out to read one or more of the excellent books in the reading list provided. I also look at where The Clash were historically.

The Artists

Ladies first…

Ellen Foley

Ellen Foley is listed on the mighty internet, as a singer and actress. Musically her debut album was released in 1979 and called *Night Out*. The album was produced by Ian Hunter and Mick Ronson. Prior to this, she had in particular, sung the duet with Meat Loaf *Paradise by the Dashboard Light* which was released as a single from the multi award winning, Jim Steinman produced *Bat Out Of Hell* album

The working relationship with Ian Hunter led to her providing backing vocals on a 1980 Mick Ronson produced album. She also recorded a duet with Ian Hunter in 1980 *We Gotta Get Out Of Here*.

In yet another Clash connection, she sang the title track on The Blue Oyster Cult album *Mirrors*, also in 1980. In the same year she contributed to the *Sandinista* album, *Hitsville UK*, *Corner Soul* and a never officially released track called *Blonde Rock 'N Roll*, available on a couple of Clash Bootleg albums. The strongest Clash connection is the *Spirit of St. Louis* album which was partly written by Strummer/Jones, and all members of The Clash appeared on, along with various Blockheads and Tymon Dogg. The album wasn't a huge success, but is I would say, a vital part to The Clash catalogue, considering the amount of input they had on the writing, recording and production. (Mick at the helm here). She provided backing vocals on *Combat Rock* (more later) and may or may not have provided the inspiration for the *Should I Stay or Should I Go* Mick Jones written track.

Acting roles have seen Foley with a small part in *"Fatal Attraction"* (1987), and bit parts in *"Cocktail"* (with Tom Cruise and some outrageous 80's hair) and *"Married to the Mob"* (with more outrageous hair).

She also appeared for that brief snippet in *"The King of Comedy"* when the camera pans onto to the "Street Scum", aka Foley and The Clash plus entourage. Pause it and you can just about make them out. Ellen is still singing and acting in the US.

MORE INFO

en.wikipedia.org/wiki/Ellen_Foley/
www.imdb.com/name/nm0284129/bio?ref_=nm_dyk_trv_sm#trivia

Pearl Harbour

Pearl was the daughter of an army major and a "strict stylish" Filipino mother. At 17, she moved alone to San Francisco to get into music. In 1976 she entered and won a contest to dance with "The craziest rock band in the world"…at that time The Tubes! She went on to tour with them as a dancer. She also performed with a kind of cabaret rock act called Leila and The Snakes. In 1978, she formed Pearl Harbour and the Explosions, and had some success with the single *Drivin* in 1980 and their self titled album which came out in the same year. They toured with British acts like Elvis Costello, Nick Lowe and Graham Parker as well as The Clash. In 1980, Pearl left the Explosions and went to live in London where she recorded the *Don't Follow Me I'm Lost Too* "solo" album. This actually had contributions from a number of musicians including Topper, Mick and Paul, Nigel Dixon from Whirlwind (Later in Havana 3am with Paul Simonon), Wilko Johnson, and Steve New from the Rich Kids. It was produced by Mickey Gallagher of the Blockheads.

Paul and Pearl were married at some point around 1983, from my research, this was a very low key affair, and Paul didn't tell anyone or invite the band members it seems. She accompanied The Clash on the Far East Tour and performed *Fujiyama Mama* with the band in Tokyo. Well worth watching the DVD of the shows and the track can be found on YouTube, complete with witty introduction from Topper. At some point in 1989 Paul and Pearl were separated and divorced. She moved back to San Francisco later moving to LA in 1997 and pursued a career in the performing arts. She made a very moving and honest appearance in both *"The Rise and Fall of The Clash"* (Garcia, 2012) and the Julian Temple Strummer film *"The Future is Unwritten"* (Temple, 2007).

MORE INFO

en.wikipedia.org/wiki/Pearl_Harbor_and_the_Explosions/
www.pearlharbourmusic.com/

Futura 2000

"Futura is my name and I say graffiti is where I got my fame" the opening rap from the single *The Escapades Of Futura 2000*. Futura was and still is a graffiti artist who started out painting street art on the subways of New York in the early 1970's. As well as graffiti art, he also worked as a graphic designer and illustrator. His first involvement with The Clash was in the design of the *Radio Clash* single cover. He was also involved in the *Combat Rock* sleeve, more of which later. He accompanied The Clash on the 1981 European tour to do a spot of stage decoration, producing back-drops live for the band as they played the shows. As we will see he contributed artistically in other ways to the *Combat Rock* album.

Probably best known among Clash fans for the 12" single, on which The Clash backed him and Mick co wrote with him, the afore mentioned *Escapades of Futura 2000*, which was released on the independent Celluloid label as opposed to an official Clash release through CBS. According to dangerousminds.net the track was recorded during The Clash Bonds residency at Electric Lady. The Clash laid down the backing track, and Futura, Fab 5 Freddy and fellow graffiti artist, Dondi White were in attendance. Futura took the main rap with Joe, Fab 5 and Dondi backing. Dangerous minds author didn't rate his rapping abilities too highly, but recognised the importance of the "Hybridization of punk and black street culture" and the subsequent avalanche of rap from both black and white artists. Futura is still very active in art and design today, putting on exhibitions around the world, and works on designs with some big multinational companies like Nike, North Face and Levis.

MORE INFO

en.wikipedia.org/wiki/Futura_2000d/
dangerousminds.net/comments/the_clash_meet_futura_2000_and_a_riot_they_didnt_own/
www.discogs.com/Futura-2000-The-Escapades-Of-Futura-2000/release/81886

Allen Ginsberg

Ginsberg was a New York based poet who was a "leading figure" in the poet scenes of the "Beat Generation" of the 50's, and later in the next decade. He met and "bonded" with a number of writers during the "beat" era, including William Burroughs and Jack Kerouac.

Ginsberg it could also be said straddled the beat and hippie generations of the 1960's and he became friends with a number of high profile artists and creative people, including Bob Dylan and Timothy Leary. He became involved in Buddhism and Krishnaism. On numerous occasions at political rallies, he chanted "OM" over sound systems for hours at a time.

His views were to some, pretty controversial at the time, opposed to militarism, and materialism economically, at a time when both were on the rise in the US. He also stood strongly against sexual repression. He was a very visible figure in a number of non violent political protests including the Vietnam War. Protesting in particular against "Imperial politics and the persecution of the powerless" He had become a controversial figure since the 1960's, largely because he was always willing to talk about subjects that were considered "taboo". In 1954, Ginsberg met and fell in love with his future lifelong partner Peter Orlovsky. (Also a poet)

You can certainly see a connection between The Clash (particularly Joe) and the "alternative" views of Ginsberg. His involvement and knowledge of the Vietnam War could have provided Joe with much stimulation for his own writing. As Edward Shannon pointed out in "Don't call me Woody" (Harrsion, 2014)(*Punk Rock Warlord*), Joe was older than the other members of The Clash. Being 16 in 1968, he would have been more aware of the Vietnam protests, and Ginsberg may have been of more interest to him. Ginsberg died in 1997. In a Melody maker news feature (Harrigan, 1982),the writer referred to Ginsberg as "The John Cooper Clarke of the Acid Generation"

MORE INFO

en.wikipedia.org/wiki/Allen_Ginsberg/

Tymon Dogg

Tymon was a long time Joe collaborator and played with Joe in the last configuration of the Mescaleros. He is a multi instrumentalist and songwriter who began his musical career at 15 in Liverpool. He was signed to his first record label when still only 17 and played and wrote with some of the big names of the late 60's and early 70's. He became disillusioned with the "commercial music industry" and sought refuge in the more underground music scene. Tymon squatted in West London, where Joe (then as "Woody") was also living. The two busked together, Joe initially collecting the money for Tymon, and then branching off on his own as his confidence built. As Joe developed the 101ers, Tymon would play at the gigs in "The Charlie Pig Dog Club" Tymon also shared a house at one point with the Slits (All of them apparently!!)

In 1980 he moved to New York, and fell in with Joe and Mick who were recording there for the *Sandinista* album. Here he made his contribution to the triple album adding his own *Lose This Skin* track and taking lead vocals, and adding violin and harmonium to a number of other tracks.

In 1981, he was also involved with the Ellen Foley album, contributing "tunes and lyrics, and violin" on a number of tracks. To follow the Mick connection, he also played violin on the Ian Hunter album *Short back and Sides*, which Mick produced in the same year. On his Wikipedia biography page, he is credited with both the playing and composition of the piano part of the *Combat Rock* track *Death is a Star*. Tymon is still very a very active musician, writing recording and producing, both for himself and others.

MORE INFO

en.wikipedia.org/wiki/Tymon_Dogg
www.tymondogg.net/

Gary Barnacle

Gary Barnacle is session man supreme. He played saxophone and flute on *Combat Rock*, but must have played with every major music star you can think of. As well as playing, he is an arranger, composer and producer. He is still actively playing today. Back in the 1980's, his clients included Level 42, Visage, Tina Turner, Kim Wilde, Soft Cell, David Bowie, Pet Shop Boys, Paul McCartney, Stock Aitkin and Waterman, and even that honking saxophone on the Stray Cats album!

His family were, and are noted musicians, his father Bill, and his brothers Steve and Pete. They were based around Dover, and so were acquainted with Topper and his drumming skills. Around 1976, the three brothers moved to London and started to get work as session musicians. Gary played on Clash recordings *1-2 Crush on You* and their version of *Time Is Tight*. The Topper connection was a useful introduction to the band. Gary had also been to school with Topper. He may or may not…have been involved in the *Guns on the Roof* pigeon shooting incident which saw Paul and Topper being asked some questions by the law!, no surprises for guessing who won.

Gary played on *Sandinista* and the *This Is Radio Clash* single that followed in November 1981, and returning to album duties on *Combat Rock*. Take a look at his CV on the wiki page, you will be amazed!!

MORE INFO

en.wikipedia.org/wiki/Gary_Barnacle/
www.allmusic.com/artist/gary-barnacle-mn0000737851/credits/

Joe Ely

Joe Ely is a Texan musician and song writer, who according to Wikipedia, has had a "genre crossing" career. Ely spent some years in Lubbock Texas…birth place of Buddy Holly!

Chiefly guitarist and singer, Ely has played with Bruce Springsteen, Uncle Tupelo, the Chieftains, as well as The Clash. In 1970 he formed the Flatlanders with a country fanatic, a folk lover, and Ely as the "Kinda Rock 'n Roll guy". "We almost had a triad" said Joe, they just seem to hit it off and played together. This sounds like a familiar scenario, players from diverse musical background, meeting and creating a little something from their different influences. Ely met The Clash around

1978, after Ely had gone "solo", and they seemed to be "impressed with each other's performances". The two bands toured with each other, including an appearance in Lubbock.

He came along for the ride on *Combat Rock*, assisting Joe with the Spanish back up vocal parts on *Should I Stay or Should I Go*. Also responsible in part for putting the shits up Mick while he was recording the vocals on *Should I Stay or Should I Go*, the reaction wasn't enough for them to need to re take the track.

Ely was asked to write some songs for the film "*The Horse Whisperer*". The consequence was the reformation of the Flatlanders, and subsequent album releases as that band.

MORE INFO

www.ely.com/
en.wikipedia.org/wiki/Joe_Ely

Poly Mandell aka Tommy Mandell

Tommy Mandell is a New Yorker. He studied music from a very early age, and played in a number of bands in the sixties. He played keyboards on a staggering number of albums, most famously with Bryan Adams throughout his career, starting with *You Want It You Got It*. He contributed keyboards to Dire Straits live album *Alchemy*, played with David Johansen, Bon Jovi member Richie Sambora, John Waite, The Pretenders and making The Clash connection through Ellen Foley association with Ian Hunter and Mick Ronson. Mandell had played on the Mick Jones produced *Short Back and Sides* album.

His contribution to *Combat Rock* is pretty impressive, particularly on *Overpowered by Funk*, which although worked as a live track, as can be heard on bootlegs from the later end of 1981, certainly gains "attack" and full on funkiness on the album mix. His own website biography makes no mention of his appearance on *Combat Rock*. Despite a collapse on stage in 1981 with a cerebral aneurysm, and the surgery that followed, he continues to be active in music today, touring, producing soundtrack and TV Work, preferring to stay close to home in New York with his family.

MORE INFO

en.wikipedia.org/wiki/Tommy_Mandel/
www.tommymandel.com/

The Business

CBS Records

I think it's important to consider who potentially was paying for the forthcoming album, and what their relationship was like with the band.

CBS had signed The Clash in 1977, back in the days when maybe more bands were treated as a going proposition, not a tax loss. Also there was an intention to try and build a career for artists over a longer period of time, and not be in such a mad rush to recoup their money in the shortest possible time. But maybe this is me looking at the music business through rose tinted spectacles.

Although Joe in an early interview believed that they had been signed to "keep them quiet" (Audio interview with John Tobler, available on a couple of Bootleg albums) In *The Last Gang In Town*, Gray said that Maurice Oberstein had signed them, not because he saw punk as a threat to the label or the already established artists, but he saw it as a money making proposition. Mark Perry of Sniffing Glue famously said that punk died the day The Clash signed to CBS.

At the time of signing, CBS was one of the largest of the Six Major multinational labels who pretty much controlled the music business. Oberstein it seems had another agenda also according to Gray. He was American, but wanted to prove himself better than the American label, by signing acts and then "selling" them to the US Company. So in many ways, it was in Oberstein's interest to push and develop the new bands he signed.

The record industry was littered with Huge Egos, and none of the directors or presidents would like to see themselves lose face. Oberstein had absolutely backed The Clash; it was a bold move to sign The Clash when he did, especially in the light of the Sex Pistols EMI fiasco. Depending on whose theory you believe, Joes that "the band were signed to keep them quiet, while the label carried on selling their ABBA records" or that Oberstein saw an opportunity and a talent that was worth investing in.

In the trade paper Music and Video Week dated February 19th 1983, the Market Shares from 1981 and 1982 appear, revealing that CBS (which was the overall company name, including the CBS label) had an 11.8% share of the UK Singles market in 1982, a fall from 1981 when it was 15.3%. In terms of albums, 1982 the label had 14.1% of the market down from 15.8% the previous year. The actual label CBS, to which The Clash were signed had the largest share of the UK albums market in 1982 with 7.4%. Sales of *Combat Rock* had contributed to this success. Singles wise, CBS label had a 3.8% of the market.

In the same edition of Music and Video Week, in the UK, the CBS label had done extremely well in the annual "Music Week Awards", with a Top Sales Team award along with the Albums "Top Company".

When asked at the Press conference in Australia if the band "hated their record company", Mick responded by telling the press that they had just been in Japan, and had met "This really tasty geezer, he looked just like one of the band". He worked for EPIC/Sony, and that he was dead fantastic. Mick added that "Sometimes I think I hate the top floor of the record company".

Pete Winkelman

Pete Winkelman was the CBS product manager for the *Combat Rock* album. In my interview with him, he explained that he had worked in record shops when he was younger. After school he studied for a Business Degree, and on a year's work placement, had landed a job as an EMI Sales Rep. When his qualification was complete, he moved to London and secured a job at CBS as a Product Manager at the tender age of 22. He worked with lots of artists and their releases, juggling perhaps as many as 50 acts releases albeit not simultaneously. Around the same time as *Combat Rock*, he recalled working on US AOR Stars Journey, a bizarre twist as The Clash certainly didn't rate that band or the genre very highly! First Class executive travel to New York for him to see the band live went some way to getting him "with the program". He also remembered working on the latest Eurovision Song Contest winner *A Little Peace* by Nicole. Pete described CBS as "Music Machine", which successfully turned out records through a great team effort.

Shortly after the *Combat Rock* release, around July 1982, Pete left CBS to join the A&M label in a similar role, and shortly moved on to Arista Records. Pete was and still is an ideas man, very focused. While at CBS, he came up with the idea of compiling an album for Julio Iglesias of more well known songs. This was then TV advertised in different territories. It gave the label a huge album hit, and helped promote the artists back catalogue, much of which was sung in Spanish. In the interview, he recalled receiving a reprimand from his bosses over a sampler compilation album he had manufactured for retailers, not the general public. The 10" album drew together some of Frank Zappa's more "well known" tracks, and was designed to remind the record dealers that he was still around, and there was a catalogue available. Mr. Zappa was apparently not amused! Pete went on to work for and then for a short time, own Bronze Records, and managed the re-release of the Motorhead album *Ace Of Spades*, based around a "Dance Remix" of the title track. Certainly enough to get Lemmy on Top Of The Pops in the UK. He was also involved in the career of The Wildhearts and Ginger Wildheart.

Today, Pete is the Chairman on the football team MK Dons in Milton Keynes, an extraordinarily successful man, also property developer and until fairly recently a recording studio owner, with Skunk Anansie, The Sugarbabes and Nigel Kennedy amongst his clientele.

Bernie Rhodes

Bernie was in league with Malcolm McLaren in the early stages of the Sex Pistols, and according to him and others was responsible for getting John Lydon into the band.

According to his biography, he grew up in Stepney, East London, never knew his father, and spent his childhood in an orphanage in South London, as his mother was unable to support him. He began designing and printing "radical" t-shirts and reacquainted himself with Malcolm and Vivienne Westwood (He previously knew Malcolm). More T shirts followed and were sold in "Sex". He had wanted to joint manage the Pistols after he acted as caretaker while Malcolm was away in the US trying to manage the floundering New York Dolls.

Bernie then began to work with The Clash, some say he manufactured the band, others would disagree, and that he was a vital co-coordinator, fixer and motivator. Whatever your view, he was absolutely crucial to the development of the band. He found them "Rehearsals Rehearsals" which gave them free, unlimited access to practice rooms.

Joe told Caroline Coon in 1977, that Bernie "had a load of influence, especially at the start" and that he had put the group together, and had put them on "the Right Track", mainly about song content". Always stirring things up amongst the band and crew, he was never popular. He was "ousted" as manager in 1978 (principal mutineer was probably Mick). Bernie managed other bands, Subway Sect, Dexys Midnight Runners and famously The Specials, and later the JoBoxers.

As we will see, he returned to manage The Clash in 1981, and depending on your point of view actually became "The Clash" with the release of the *Cut The Crap* album in 1985. Again depending on your point of view, Bernie was instrumental in the sacking of Mick Jones in 1983, perhaps partly as revenge for being ousted first time round in 1978.

Always confrontational and controversial, I witnessed his outburst in May 2007 at St Martins College, and I know what he said. He was accused of making a statement about crime, and referenced Peckham and its inhabitants. The atmosphere became pretty tense, and the event was brought to a fairly abrupt end. The event was actually to discuss the clothes/fashion element of The Clash, and the work of Alex Michon in the design of the clothing ranges. This covered the very first zips all over jacket up to the *Combat Rock* era cut offs. Bernie was along I thought to talk about this, and give his point of view from his business angle. What we got was a state of the nation address, which in some parts was absolutely spot on. (The country is screwed!!). But, he was living in the States now, and was possibly more of an outside commentator now.

Clash longtime roadie "The Baker" on his website, thought that Bernie "adopted the role of surrogate adopted father figure" for Joe. "He could also have been the elder brother to Joe, to replace the one he had lost." It was Joe who had "demanded" the return of Bernie after the relationship with Blackhill their then management seemed to go sour. Bringing back Bernie would certainly stir things up again, create that more "out of control" environment which the band seemed to thrive on, but ultimately add to the causes of the Joe/Mick relationship breakdown. For more insights into the complicated mind of Bernie Rhodes, I would recommend the 2012 film documentary "*The Rise and Fall of The Clash*" for some pretty honest straight forward opinions. In a Zig Zag article (Banks, 1981), Robin Banks commented that "Bernie was back, and certainly keeps them on their toes, despite the fact that his methods can sometimes be devious". He added that "I like him, but no longer respect him"

Bernie runs a website from which he puts over his views on "Social and Political issues". He managed to put in a controversial appearance at the funeral of Malcolm McLaren in 2010, and gave an unscheduled speech. You can read more in the Viv Albertine autobiography *Boys, Music, Clothes* (Albertine, 2014)

Bernie is still keeping his hand in with T Shirt design, in 2014, he teamed up with Lewis leathers to produce a range of "Biker" orientated T Shirts.

MORE INFO

bernardrhodes.com/
en.wikipedia.org/wiki/Bernard_Rhodes/
clash.wikia.com/wiki/Bernie_Rhodes/
thebaker77.wordpress.com/tag/bernard-rhodes/
www.lewisleathers.com/

Kosmo Vinyl

In a *Rolling Stone* article "The Year of The Clash" (Hall, 1982), Kosmo was described as being a "Brash, shrewd, Aide de camp for the past few years, now settled in to the Public relations spot". Johnny Green former roadie and road manager described him as a "Loud Mouthed Cockney". Mick in the same *Rolling Stone* article said that his job "involved protecting us from Bernie as well as the press". Kosmo (real name Mark Dunk) was also known as a Consigliore (Italian term for advisor to the Godfather). He was a spokesman, press officer and aid to the band. Contrary to one source I read, he was not brought in when Bernie returned to manage The Clash.

Kosmo started getting involved with The Clash when they were being managed by The Blackhill Agency, who also managed Ian Dury and The Blockheads. There has always been a close link between the Blockheads musicians, in particular Mickey Gallagher who joined the band as "The Fifth" as keyboard player on their 16 Tons tour. Gallagher played on the *London Calling* album, and *Sandinista*. Norman Watt Roy bass player extraordinaire, along with Mickey did session work for the band, certainly on *Sandinista* and some of the off-shoot projects.

Previously, Kosmo had been involved with Stiff Records, hence the Ian Dury connection. In *The Last Gang in Town*(Gray, 1995), Gray wrote that he became the labels PR and Package Tour MC. (Live Stiffs tour). Again Gray pinpointed the time around June 1979 that he first started casually turning up at Vanilla Studios, eventually breaking down some defences and striking up a friendship with Mick.

When asked By Danny Baker in a radio interview on 23rd April 2013, he believed that his first "work" with them was to be on hand a press conference for the *Give 'Em Enough Rope* album.

There seemed to be a split among The Clash crew and associates about Kosmo, while on tour in the US later in 1979, as Ray Lowry described in *The Last Gang in Town*, "He turns up in California, a loud mouthed cockney retard, wearing a bomber jacket emblazoned with a map of Vietnam". Johnny Green as you can tell from his earlier comment was also not impressed. He did note that "other members did fall in love with Kosmo very quickly". Joe told Creem magazine in 1980 that they needed someone to keep your spirits up when they were flagging, and that he was "All razzle dazzle and no downs". In *Zig Zag* magazine (Banks, 1981), Robin Banks called Kosmo "The Andrew Loog Oldham of the eighties"

In the radio interview with Danny Baker, Kosmo was asked exactly what his job was. His reply was that it was making sure that nobody knew what it was so that he couldn't take any flak for anything. Baker commented that Kosmo seemed to dominate the room as a "ring master for an entire period". While working for Ian Dury ("For £50 a week for making him a Household Name"), Dury named him the "Fromage De Pompadour". Kosmo did bring in a certain "Sartorial" influence to the band. He had been a noted "snappy dresser" who wore Johnson's suits. The band certainly became more "suited and booted" as a result. In the same Radio interview, he believed that what he brought to The Clash was that he "Gave them the will to go for it", this referring to his belief that they could be the greatest rock and roll band ever. Whatever his good or bad points, Kosmo was still with The Clash in 1982 when *Combat Rock* was released, and worked for, or alongside and at some points managed the band when the need arose. His role was certainly pretty vital in the forwarding of their career, particularly seizing opportunities to make the bands presence known in New York during the Bonds dates in 1981. In his *NME* article "*How The Clash Fed the Wonderbread Generation*" (Farren, 1981a), the writer said that Kosmo was "Their conscience and their greatest Psychic Projector"!

MORE INFO

en.wikipedia.org/wiki/Kosmo_Vinyl/
www.youtube.com/watch?v=x5Ma7lra0ws/

The Magicians

Glyn Johns

Glyn Johns is a musician, recording engineer, as well as a very successful Record producer. He has worked with some of the biggest names of particularly the 70's, but not exclusively. Johns played in The Presidents in the 1960's, but also began working as an engineer in IBC studios in London. His first "production job" was his own band.

His first "rescue mission" was to try and recover The Beatles *Get Back* sessions. Despite several versions being made, eventually the honours went to Phil Spector, and the album became *Let It Be*. According to "*The Record producers File 1962-1984*"(Muirhead, 1984), from 1971, his production credits included The Faces *Ooh La La*, three Eagles albums (1972,73 and 74). He also produced four Joan Armatrading albums from 1976-'79), and even a couple of Eric Clapton albums *Slowhand* and *Backless*. He also recorded and mixed The Who *Who's Next* album, again in 1971.

He has continued to work with the likes of Blue Oyster Cult, Midnight Oil, New Model Army, and Belly to name a few. Like The Clash, he was enrolled in the Rock and Roll Hall of Fame (in 2012) More recently he has worked with Ryan Adams and The Band Of Horses (2011 and 2012 respectively)

In *Redemption Song* (Salewicz, 2006) the author wrote that he was not your "typical rock and roller". Preferring regular hours, and getting on with the job.

In an online interview (*Talks At Google - Glyn Johns in Conversation*, 2014), accessed 2/1/2015, it was revealed that Production ran in the family, brother Andy Johns is also in the production game with a list of high profile names including Led Zeppelin and Bon Jovi to name just two. His son Ethan also building and impressive CV with the likes of Ryan Adams, and The Kings Of Leon. So here we have another set of "Three Johns"!

In *Squat City Rocks* (Dudanski, 2014) Richard Dudanski wrote that Joe had put up some money for an album to be recorded by Tymon Dogg and himself with Glyn Johns in the Production chair. As yet to be released. This was confirmed by Johns in his Autobiography *Sound Man* (Johns, 2014)

MORE INFO

en.wikipedia.org/wiki/Glyn_Johns/
www.glynjohns.com/about-glyn-johns/

Jeremy "Jerry" Green

Jeremy was a "Staff Engineer" at Wessex studios as opposed to a freelance engineer. Bill Price when interviewed about the studio mentioned that Jeremy was on the staff, "But as the decade progressed, it became the era of the freelance engineer. It was very hard to get a band to work with a house engineer when they could go and hire their own"

Wessex was used by an incredible roster of artists, and The Clash connection is strong with both Jeremy Green and the studio. With Bill Price, he engineered on *London Calling* album, engineered on some of *Sandinista* album. He also engineered on the Theatre Of Hate album *Westworld* which Mick Jones produced, as well as the Ian Hunter album *Short Back and Sides*, again with Mick producing.

MORE INFO

www.digitalprosound.com/Features/Interviews-Discuss/Pt1BillPrice5.htm
www.philsbook.com/wessex-studio-1.html

Joe Blaney

Joe Blaney is a New York City man, from birth to work. He started playing guitar and tinkering with electronics from the age of 10 and through his teenage years. He went on to study how to repair electronic equipment such as radios, TV's and stereos.

In the same way that Jeremy Green was an "in house" engineer, it would seem that Joe Blaney was brought in to The Clash fold by the same means. Joe was hired by Electric Lady Studios in 1979 as a technician. The studio saw some pretty heavyweight names both in terms of artists and producers, including the Rolling Stones, AC/DC, producers Mutt Lange, Bob Clearmountain, and Chris Kimsey.

In July 1981 he was engineer/mixer on The Clash *Radio Clash* single which was recorded at Electric Lady. When The Clash returned later in the year to work on *Combat Rock*, Joe was chosen as Engineer for the recording and mixing. You can catch some video footage of Joe, with Joe and Mick in the studio on YouTube.

Joe has done recording and mixing for an impressive list of artists, including Prince, The Ramones, Tom Waits, Dennis Leary, the Def Jam label, Keith Richards, World Party and the Waterboys. Later in the 1990's he moved more emphasis on to producing artists, but still with a firm base in mixing and engineering.

MORE INFO

www.joeblaney.net/
www.allmusic.com/artist/joe-blaney-mn0000141431/
www.worldsend.com/clients.asp/

The Visual Image

You may or may not consider anything except the music as important when looking at reviewing or analyzing an album. But the fact is that The Clash were also about "visuals", not just the music.

Whether it was artwork, posters, t-shirts, customizing their instruments with stickers or paint, it all went in to the mix. The "artistic" element was always in the band, from the spray painted boiler suits, Pollack style splattered clothes, through to backdrops, video shoots, the visual image has always featured very strongly…you can't ignore it.

Pennie Smith

"I don't take pictures of bands, I take pictures of people"

In "Clash circles", Pennie Smith is the "Clash Photographer", with Bob Gruen possibly in second place. She has photographed many rock musicians over her long career, from Led Zeppelin, The Rolling Stones, The Who, Iggy Pop, and then punk artists The Slits, Siouxsie, Debbie Harry, The Jam and The Clash. Later she covered; The Stone Roses, Morrissey, Radiohead and The Manic Street Preachers and The Strokes. She works as a freelance photographer.

Trained at Art School, Pennie revealed to Steve Bateman in an interview in 2003 that she didn't intend to be a photographer; she did it for half a day a week, but hated it. She worked on a magazine called "Friendz" with Nick Kent and Barney Bubbles from 1969 until 1972. Her first "Commission" was to cover the Led Zeppelin tour in the 1970's. Portrait photography is only part of her work, as she has attended a number of band tours, including The Clash. Much of the work she produced appeared in the NME, as well as on Album sleeves and associated promotional material.

With Nick Kent writing the interviews, and Pennie taking pictures, often these were informal shots off stage, not the usual music paper style shots. Although officially "Freelance", the pair were taken on by the NME to provide material for the paper.

Dating back to 1972, she designed the album sleeve for the Pink Fairies album *What a Bunch of Sweeties* and photography on sleeves for the likes of The Slits "Cut", The Jam "All Mod Cons".

The Clash Before and After (Pennie Smith, 1980) book put together a visual record in Black and White of some of her pictures of the band. Her specialty is the Black and White image, but as we will see later, not exclusively! Her photography work with the record sleeves of The Clash included *London Calling*, *Sandinista* and of course *Combat Rock*. The now iconic picture of Paul Simonon, trashing his bass on stage that was used on the *London Calling* album, was in 2002, awarded "Greatest Rock 'N Roll Photograph of all time" by Q magazine.

Looking through the amazing portrait shots she took of the band, there are many that really stand out for me, which as Steve Bateman pointed out in his interview with her in 2003, "Show the real person behind the rock star". Of particular relevance to the book I am writing here, there is one that sticks firmly in my mind. This is a shot of Joe Strummer in his hotel room, just prior to leaving Japan before flying to the Australian/New Zealand Leg of the Far East Tour. It was Joe in his tiger stripe camouflage shirt and samurai sword which he had received as a gift from a fan, hair slicked back, and bandana round is neck. It was like he was ready to take on the next territory. The picture was published in the Christmas edition of the NME in 1982, in black and white. It is quite stunning. But let's not forget, as Pennie Smith told Steve Bateman (Bateman, 2003), "When Joe died, people kept wanting mug shots of Joe, and I kept trying to explain, that he wasn't the singer with the band, The Clash were a unit". Pennie added that "With The Clash, the reason I stuck with them, is that they just left me completely alone". Interestingly, in the same Bateman interview, Pennie talked about photographers she admired. Although not really acknowledging she was herself a "photographer", more a person who "Took Photographs", she said that she liked the pictures taken by photo journalist Don McCullin in Vietnam. It is well worth looking at some of his work, much of it in black and white, and much of it taken in "Combat Zones". You might even spot a Killing Joke album cover while you are browsing. Pennie is still producing and providing photographs for Albums, more recently Babyshambles, Paul Weller, The Good The Bad and The Queen and Oasis.

MORE INFO

en.wikipedia.org/wiki/Pennie_Smith/
www.repeatfanzine.co.uk/Rants/Penniesmith.htm
www.allmusic.com/artist/pennie-smith-mn0001220927/

Alex Michon

Alex Michon was involved in designing of clothes for The Clash between 1977 and 1983. Today she is involved heavily in the arts. In partnership with Cathy Lomax, she runs the Transition Art Gallery in London. She still exhibits her drawings and paintings, and writes for and edits art magazines.

In an interview in "Arty" Magazine (Michon, 2004), Alex explained that she was originally from Nottingham, but in her imagination, lived in a small estate 150 miles south of Moscow? When asked in the same interview who inspired her, we were told that among the list were The Slits, Patti Smith, Joe Strummer, Rockabilly Rebels and Paris 1968.

In late 1976 according to *The Look* (Gorman, 2006) Bernie Rhodes "recruited" Alex Michon , then a 19 year old art student, to produce clothes for The Clash. His statement was "There's gonna be fighting in the streets, Things are gonna' get rough, so we're gonna' need clothes which are tough".

With very little experience in fashion, she came up with as Gorman says "repeated waves of hard wearing militaristic designs that would define the look of one of the most visually exciting rock bands of all time". Bernie wanted to create an image and in the same way Westwood and McClaren had used the Sex Pistols to display his clothing, possibly build a fashion business for himself at the same time. Bernie had originally approached fashion students, and Alex just happened to be sharing a house with a fashion student at the time. Her house mate took Bernie to their house after meeting him at a party.

In the great punk tradition of just getting up and giving it a go, Alex despite her lack of real expertise, jumped at the chance to work with Bernie, even though as she admitted in The Look "I couldn't really sew". With assistance from fellow art student Christina Kolowska, they spent the weekend making a zippered jacket in petrol blue material.

Later, Alex lived at the home of Sebastian Conran, where Joe also lived for a while, and there was an office in the building set up for the "Upstarts" company, which was going to produce mass market Clash clothes.

When Bernie was ousted as manager in 1978, Alex was doing other things, a degree at Goldsmiths and band member in The Blue Cats. She produced a one off shirt design for The Clash in 1979 of "rockabilly" influence. When Bernie returned in 1981 prior to the release of *Combat Rock*, he asked Alex to come back, they were going to America! She was asked to come up with some designs for their forthcoming tour, and this was the era of the epaulettes, braided stripes and those suitcase fasteners instead of buttons.

As Alex said in The Look, "It was flash, but still tough. They were on parade, but as Generals not foot soldiers". As Gorman said, these clothes formed the basis of the range worn by The Clash on the 1982 *Combat Rock* album, and in videos and on the American Who support dates.

A later addition to the line was what Alex called "The Boxer", cowl-collared shirts and tops. Joe can be seen wearing one on some of the US Tour dates. The tops were also worn by Bananarama!!.

Bernie was keen to open an office in New York, which was part of his "International Vision". He found a loft space in New York on West 26th Street, from where he wanted to create The Clash Clothes range. In a way it is strange for me to think that even back in 1982, artists were involved in the fashion business. The McClaren/Westwood and Sex Pistols fashion connection was strong, but I felt that this was a much later trend, particularly with millionaire US Rappers and bored footballers wives, but Greenday have even dabbled in this. In *The Clash – The Only Band That Mattered* (Egan, 2015) the author expressed some surprise that there was a plan to produce and market a range of "Clash clothes", which seemed to go against their non commercial stance. These based on their "militaristic look". But the *Combat Rock* fatigues as we have already seen was not the first time a clothing range had been proposed. Apparently when questioned about this, Kosmo had made the comment that if anyone should make money from their image, it should be The Clash.

According to Gilbert, the clothes were made with input from Paul, using camouflage designs and Vietnam era styling. Materials included webtex webbing which allowed for ventilation. As Bernie and Alex looked for a suitable outlet in New York, and Alex had completed plans for a whole range of clothing, everything fell apart for the band and the future, as after returning to London, the band and organisation started to disintegrate.

www.transitiongallery.co.uk/htmlpages/girl_on_girl/alex_michon.html
en.wikipedia.org/wiki/Alex_Michon/

Julian "Jules" Balme

"Jules" Balme was the creative eye of the sleeve designs on a number of Clash and Clash related album sleeves. According to the Discogs website, he is credited with the design of a staggering number of album sleeves. This includes the Adam and The Ants and Adam Ant solo albums and singles sleeves, Psychedelic Furs *Talk Talk Talk* and Julian Cope *World Shut Your Mouth*. There are so many albums that I recognize, particularly from my "record shops days", it is hard to take in. Madness *One Step Beyond*, Tears For Fears *The Hurting*, Texas, Transvision Vamp, Big Country and Mari "Beehive" Wilson

From a Clash point of view, his credits include *Black Market Clash*, *Sandinista*, *Super Black Market Clash*, *The Story of The Clash*, *Live At Shea Stadium* and the *Revolution Rock* DVD. He was also designer of the painstakingly put together Singles Box Sets of 7" vinyl and CD, with the reproduction sleeves and that beautiful box. "Essential Clash" and the record store day single of *London Calling Remix* also received his attention.

Clash related covers include the Ellen Foley Album *Spirit Of St Louis* and the great Havanna 3AM album.

Julian started his career as a designer working for Stiff Records in 1979, the "Clash Connection" developing through the Kosmo/Blockheads relationship. In my interview with Jules, he recalled that the first "job" for The Clash was to design the front cover of the sheet music for the *London Calling* single. He went on to design the "Bank Robber" 7" sleeve.

After leaving Stiff, Jules became a freelance designer, and through his reputation for getting the job done, continued to get work from The Clash and other bands and record labels. Jules did not work for any one record label, but there was quite a strong CBS connection, amongst others.

Jules recalled how he had been asked to design the *Black Market Clash* sleeve with input from Paul Simonon and using the iconic shot of Don Letts facing the wall of Police at the Notting Hill Riots. The sleeve has a very distinct style, Retro is how Jules described it, which is as he said his style of choice "if left to his own devices". The influence of this can be seen on a 2005 album by Swedish punk band Topper called *Once a Punk, Always a Punk*.

Sandinista and singles design work followed, and as mentioned the Ellen Foley album and also the Pearl Harbour albums followed. *The Call Up* adverts came from a postcard presented to him by Mick. *Mag 7* followed and an extra request for some "Stickers" to be included in the 12" sleeve. Jules, who was continually battling with a heavy workload passed on the sticker design to Eddie King, fellow Stiff Designer, who painstakingly drew up the range of stickers like "Wave Goodbye To The Boss" and "Ring Ring It's 7AM" This was the first work Jules had got "post Bernie return".

Jules was also picking up work from the Phonogram record label and work was coming in thick and fast. His relationship was as he put it a "conduit between The Clash and the Record Company". He would get a brief, and go away and produce the work.

For *Radio Clash*, Jules confirmed that Futura had supplied the graphic of the Transistor Radio, and the rest of the design fell to him. Jules was around in New York at the time Alex Michon and Bernie were developing the "Clash clothing range", and during my discussion with him remembered that they even had a shop designated to sell the clothes from.

Jules also designed the captions for the Joe produced film "*Hell W10*" which was filmed in early 1983 and finally saw the light of day on the DVD release of "*Essential Clash*".

As The Clash (1) developed into The Clash(2) with just Paul and Joe and additional hired hands, a position became available for what sounded to me like an "artist in residence"…although more like an "Artist on The Road". Perhaps, in some way, a combination of the skills of Pennie Smith and Ray Lowry. The new Clash wanted an "Art Man" full time. Jules was offered the position but felt unable to commit to one project. Eddie King was suggested as a candidate, and he took up the role, touring the US and Europe and contributing designs for the "Out of Control" t-shirts and other promotional material. Eddie had done the majority of the work on the *Cut The Crap* album, but left before the release. Jules' services were called upon again to wrap this up.

Jules later went on to create his own company called Vegas Design Associates. Currently he takes on a variety of commissions, but as his website says, his early work was creating packaging, advertising and marketing campaigns for the music industry. He has also produced some great "Spoken Word" covers including James Bond Books and a series of "Carry On" film spoken word series.

In a YouTube interview for www.rockhistory.co.uk Julian explained how he "blagged" his way into getting a couple of days work at Hipgnosis the album sleeve designers while he was in effect still training as a graphic designer. Although he was in effect "rumbled" by the owners as never having done "Art Worker" duties before, he stayed the term of the job, recalling that he worked on the Bethnal Album *Crash Landing* and a Todd Rundgren *Back To The Bars* album. He had been so impressed with the early Roxy Music albums, as a youth, and wanted to "do" album sleeves.

It seems that "Classic Cars" have become a big part of his life and he has branched out into books about the subject, including "Kustom Graphics: Hot Rods, Burlesque and Rock 'n' Roll" that's quite a combination if you want to check it out.

Jules was involved in a number of The Clash re-issue projects and compilations. *The Story Of The Clash* design was heavily influenced by Joe. Always concerned to keep the quality high, even the budget priced reissues were tended to with care, unlike some other record companies releases which are produced as "budget" in every way. Jules also did the design on the re-issues of *London Calling*, *Should I Stay Or Should I Go* and *Rock The Casbah* in their various formats. He also did the design for the solo Joe Strummer single *Trash City* The memorable logo which adorns Joes Fender Telecaster still when it was on display at the "*Blackmarket Clash*" popup exhibition in 2013, was designed by Derek Stewart, who was working for Jules at the time.

In 2013, Jules co-curated along with Kosmo and Jemima Dury, an exhibition of some of the art from the late, great Ian Dury called; "Ian Dury: More Than Fair – paintings, drawings and artworks 1961-1972". He was also involved in the exhibition of Kosmo's "Football Related" art in 2013.

In the time old tradition of a "Top Ten", we will deviate from the norm and list Jules's Top Four favourite Clash designs.

1. *Black Market Clash*
2. The hardback book version of *The Clash at Shea Stadium*
3. The (If I may say) "Stunning" *Singles Box Collection*.
4. *The London Calling 25th Anniversary Edition* CD and DVD

So, with the connection made, Jules Balme was responsible for the design of the *Combat Rock* album sleeve, more of which later.

MORE INFO

www.discogs.com/search/?q=julian+balme/
www.vegasdesign.co.uk/
www.rockhistory.co.uk/
www.youtube.com/watch?v=cGekJwjRyNQ

The Boys in the Band

The life and times of the members have been covered many times by a number of authors, critics and journalists, and I urge you to read them if you want to get a balanced view of our four main characters.

In relation to *Combat Rock*, I think a summary of where the band were "at" around the period 1981-1982, the main time period I look at would be in order.

The band had finished recording and released their fourth contractual album for CBS, *Sandinista*. The triple record set that really split the critics and fans, and kicked off a storm of controversy in those same groups of people, as well as their record label both in the UK and US. In an attempt to shorten their commitments to CBS, the triple album only counted as one album, and in the time honoured tradition of The Clash, they wanted the release to be VFM (Value For Money). And in the time honoured Clash tradition of "making things very difficult for themselves", they would receive no performance royalties from the record until they had sold 200,000 copies.

1980 and 1981 were incredibly creative times for The Clash. There was the material written for the Triple *Sandinista* album, material written for the Ellen Foley album, Mick was producing work by not only Ellen, but an Ian Hunter solo album, and working and producing with the breaking new act Theatre Of Hate. It is quite staggering how busy their lives must have been.

With regards to management of the band, they had been with the Blackhill Agency for a couple of years, but the relationship seemed to be going downhill, and the old time honoured "Making life difficult for themselves" came in to play again. In between having an "Official Manager", that is between Bernie and when he left and when Caroline Coon (may or may not have been acting in that capacity), Mick it seemed had stepped up and been the driving force in the day to day activities. There was then a power balance which shifted as the band developed. As the Blackhill deal came to an end, back came Bernie Rhodes to stir it all up again. Within the band then, the dynamic changed. In a *Smash Hits* article (Silverton, 1982), Mick had admitted that "Although he had been in charge until the beginning of the year (Bernie's return). Joe had now taken over. "It's partly ego, partly "me, me, me", Joe had said."As long as the music's good", said Joe, "I don't give two tosses who is in charge". He also talked about how after *Sandinista*, he was "looking for the opposite really" He felt that Mick had "had his fling" with *Sandinista*, and that it was someone else's turn.

Internally, there were increasing issues with Topper and his drug use. This was causing problems with the other band members. Although, it did not seem to have no real affect on his playing abilities or stamina. The band were starting to notice some erratic behavior. As the band were so close and had already been through so much together, maybe they tried to turn a blind eye, as long as Topper was there and bashing the drums at the right times.

It seemed that as Joe took charge more, he needed to take the Topper situation in hand, as ever a conflict between his loyalty to the person, and the future of the band and the bitterness he felt as Topper could drag them down.

In retrospect, Joe and others admitted that they didn't really know very much about heroin and its effects and treatments. But incidents were occurring which might jeopardize the bands future as well as the personal relationships within the group.

In The Australian issue of *Rolling Stone* magazine (McSporran, 1982) There was a comment made by a named Tour manager (Jerry) which was quite succinct. "The Clash have grown up. Before we had four boys, now we have four world-weary hardened men. You can't tell them anything"

So…enter Bernie Rhodes…for the second time.

3 - STOP THE WORLD 1981

It would be difficult to look at *Combat Rock* without getting some of the background and looking at the events prior to the release in May 1982. So…I'm taking my starting point as the previous year, 1981 with the return of Bernie Rhodes as manager of The Clash.

On 12th December 1980, the band had released the much debated *Sandinista* Triple album, and had been busy also with writing recording and in the case of Mick, producing The Ellen Foley Album *Spirit of St Louis*. Later in April, Mick was credited as producer of the Theatre Of Hate single *Rebel Without A Brain*.

In 1981, Ronald Reagan had become the President of the US, In terms of world events, 1981 was a year of violence and nuclear tests, and some good things too.

January

IN THE UK, PETER SUTCLIFFE, "THE YORKSHIRE RIPPER" WAS ARRESTED.

IN SALVADOR, THE FMLN GROUP OPENED WHAT IT CALLED A "GENERAL OFFENSIVE".

THE US HOSTAGES HELD IN IRAN WERE FREED.

RONALD REAGAN (FUTURE CLASH SINGLE COVER STAR) WAS INAUGURATED AS PRESIDENT OF THE USA.

AND IN GALVESTON BAY, TEXAS, THERE WAS A HUGE OIL SPILLAGE AFTER A TWO SHIP COLLISION.

February

WAS A LITTLE MORE CIVILIZED, AS IN THE UK PRINCE CHARLES ANNOUNCED HIS ENGAGEMENT TO LADY DIANA SPENCER.

PAUL MCCARTNEY AND STEVIE WONDER LIVED TOGETHER IN PERFECT HARMONY,

IN THE US, GRAMMIES WERE AWARDED TO BILLY JOEL AND CHRISTOPHER CROSS.

THE US PERFORMED A NUCLEAR TEST IN NEVADA AND SET THE TONE FOR THE YEAR.

March

THIS MONTH SAW THE IRA MEMBER BOBBY SANDS BEGIN A 65 DAY HUNGER STRIKE IN THE MAZE PRISON.

THE FRENCH PERFORMED THEIR NUCLEAR TEST.

IN CHILE, PINOCHET BEGAN A SECOND TERM IN POWER.

AND IN THE US, AN 18 YEAR OLD WAS STABBED AT DISNEYLAND.

PRESIDENT REAGAN WAS SHOT AND WOUNDED BY ONE JOHN W HINCKLEY II.

...BUT HEY! ROBERT DENIRO GOT AN ACADEMY AWARD FOR "ORDINARY PEOPLE".

THE USSR, NOT WISHING TO BE LEFT OUT ALSO PERFORMED NUCLEAR TESTS.

April

IN THE UK "RACE RIOTS" BROKE OUT IN THE BRIXTON AREA OF LONDON. AS THE BRIXTON RIOTS SPARKED UP, THIS LED TO MORE UNREST IN TOXTETH, LIVERPOOL LATER IN THE SUMMER. LONDON WAS INDEED BURNING.

IN A BIZARRE TURN, THE IMPRISONED IRA HUNGER STRIKER WAS ELECTED TO THE BRITISH PARLIAMENT.

IN THE US RONALD REAGAN WENT HOME AFTER HIS SHOOTING.

THE FIRST SPACE SHUTTLE WAS LAUNCHED.

IN CHILE, COPPER MINERS WENT ON STRIKE AND IN GERMANY, ONE MILLION STEEL WORKERS WENT ON STRIKE TOO.

IBM-PC INTRODUCED THE PERSONAL COMPUTER, AND XEROX PARK RESEARCH INTRODUCED A COMPUTER MOUSE.

May

IN ANOTHER SHOOTING, POPE JOHN PAUL II WAS SHOT AND CRITICALLY WOUNDED IN VATICAN CITY.

FASCISTS IN BARCELONA TOOK 200 HOSTAGES AT THE CENTRAL BANK.

ANDREW LLOYD WEBBERS "CATS" PREMIERED IN THE UK.

June

JUNE 1981 SAW THE FIRST REPORTS FROM THE CENTER OF DISEASE CONTROL ABOUT A FORM OF PNEUMONIA AFFECTING THE GAY POPULATION. THE AIDS EPIDEMIC WAS OFFICIALLY RECOGNISED.

IN THE US, MAYA YANG LIN WON THE COMPETITION TO DESIGN THE VIETNAM WAR MEMORIAL.

THERE WAS A US THIRD BASEBALL STRIKE...AND TOM SNYDER INTERVIEWED CHARLES MANSON ON THE "TOMORROW SHOW".

THE SUPREME COURT UPHELD THE "MALE ONLY" DRAFT REGISTRATION AS CONSTITUTIONAL.

MARK CHAPMAN PLEADED GUILTY TO THE ASSASSINATION OF JOHN LENNON THE PREVIOUS DECEMBER.

IN THE UK, A TEENAGER FIRED SIX BLANK BULLETS AT THE QUEEN.

AND JOHN MCENROES "CANNOT BE SERIOUS" AT WIMBLEDON, WAS DESCRIBED AS A "DISGRACEFUL ACT OF MISBEHAVIOR".

July

JULY SAW ISRAELI BOMBERS DESTROY PLO HQ IN BERUIT.

SUMMER MADNESS SET IN WITH NUCLEAR TESTS BEING CARRIED OUT BY THE FRENCH, USSR, USA AND INDIA.

IN THE US NEW YORK THE TRANSIT FARE ROSE TO 75 CENTS.

August

AUGUST 1981, BROUGHT THE MTV PREMIERE AT 12:01 AM IN THE US.

PRESIDENT REAGAN SACKED 11,500 AIR TRAFFIC CONTROLLERS WHO WENT ON STRIKE FOR 2 DAYS.

COCA COLA IN THE US AGREED TO PUMP $34 MILLION INTO BLACK BUSINESS.

THE IBM PERSONAL COMPUTER WAS RELEASED.

THE VERY LAST EPISODE OF THE WALTONS WAS AIRED ON US TV ..."GOODNIGHT GRANDPA".

IN THE UK, IAN BOTHAM SCORED A CENTURY AT OLD TRAFFORD.

September

WE WERE TREATED TO MORE NUCLEAR TESTS.

IN THE US, "MIAMI VICE" PREMIERED ON US TV.

...AND SIMON AND GARFUNKEL WERE REUNITED IN CENTRAL PARK.

October

SAW A NEW PRESIDENT ELECTED IN IRAN.

IN FRANCE, CAPITAL PUNISHMENT WAS ABOLISHED.

IN THE US, PRINCE, THEN A VIRTUALLY UNKNOWN ARTIST, OPENED FOR THE ROLLING STONES IN LA.

THERE WERE MORE "POLICE AND THIEVES" IN COP SHOW CAGNEY AND LACEY WHICH PREMIERED ON TV.

THE US NATIONAL DEBT HIT $1 TRILLION!!

A RUSSIAN SUBMARINE RAN AGROUND OFF THE COAST OF SWEDEN,

WHILE IN BRUSSELS, 200,000 PEOPLE DEMONSTRATED AGAINST CRUISE MISSILES.

THERE WAS A BOMB ATTACK ON A SYNAGOGUE IN ANTWERP.

November

OF 1981 SAW A SECOND SPACE SHUTTLE LAUNCHED.

THERE WERE MORE NUCLEAR TESTS. NASA ALSO LAUNCHED "INTELSAT".

AND THE "AIDS" VIRUS WAS OFFICIALLY RECOGNISED.

IN AMSTERDAM, 400,000 DEMONSTRATED AGAINST CRUISE MISSILES, BUT AIR LAUNCHED CRUISE MISSILES WERE BEING TESTED.

IN GENEVA, THE US AND USSR NEGOTIATED ARMS REDUCTIONS IN EUROPE.

THE SPANISH GOVERNMENT REQUESTED TO JOIN NATO, THE POLISH GOVERNMENT DECLARED MARTIAL LAW, AND ARRESTED SOLIDARITY ACTIVISTS.

IN THE NETHERLANDS, UNEMPLOYMENT HIT A RECORD 475,000. MEMBERS OF THE RED BRIGADE KIDNAPPED GENERAL JAMES DOZIER.

BACK IN EL SALVADOR GUERILLA GROUP FMLN OPENED "A LIMITED OFFENSIVE".

THE ARGENTINE PRESIDENT FLED THE COUNTRY, AND GENERAL GALTIERI WAS SWORN IN AS THE NEW PRESIDENT.

December

AS THE YEAR DREW TO A CLOSE...THERE WERE MORE NUCLEAR TESTS.

Source: Wikipedia 2014

Musically, 1981 was a mixed bag, perhaps more so in the UK than the US, where the order of the day was "mainstream". In the UK, the competition for The Clash's Singles success went from the sublime to the utterly ridiculous. *There's no one quite like Grandma* had captured the country at the end of 1980, with its cutting edge vocal style. Joe Dolce wooed everyone with his sensitive ballad *Shuddup Ya Face*, Shaky (Shakin Stevens) kept folks rockin' in the aisles with *This Ole House* and *Green Door*. Bucks Fizz were still *Making Their Mind Up*. Two John Lennon songs hit Number one *Imagine* and *Woman*. Roxy Music hopped on the Lennon Train with their version of *Jealous Guy*. Adam and The Ants were Charming their way into people's hearts with *Stand and Deliver*.

On the more serious side of music, The Specials nailed it with *Ghost Town*, Soft Cell covered *Tainted Love*, and The Human League *Don't You Want Me?* put electro pop firmly up there at the end of the year. *Under Pressure* by Queen and David Bowie made quite an impression.

In the States, those favourites, REO Speedwagon, Hall and Oates, Rick Springfield made their presence known. Kim Carnes and her *Bette Davis Eyes* took the number one spot for nine weeks. At the end of the year, in a blur of lycra and headbands, Olivia Newton John encouraged us to get *Physical*.

Possibly the scariest trend was the *Stars on 45* release which spawned a thousand similar atrocities. Then again, I can remember one of my mates bands (The Abusive Dolls) performing *Abuse on 45*, a megamix of Punk Rock classics, so, maybe not such an atrocity after all.

Album Chart wise, *Sandinista* was never going to take on the might of ABBA, Cliff Richard and Shaky in the popularity stakes. And even an album of Stars on 45, is enough to make you want to dive into Joe's spliff bunker and stay there until the coast is clear. In the US, the likes of Styx, Journey, Reo Speedwagon (Oh Yes) and Foreigner dominated, hardly *Mensforth Hill* was it?

Looking back through the releases in 1981, perhaps through rose tinted glasses, there was some tremendous music released. Certainly more of the interesting stuff came from the UK. Some of the now established "Punk/New wave" bands produced some sterling work, The Jam, The Pretenders, Psychedelic Furs, The Cure and Billy Idol hitting solo artist status. The Slits disbanded in this year, The Buzzcocks (but not forever!!) and Generation X. "Synth Pop" hit the mainstream with the likes of Ultravox, Depeche Mode, OMD and the earlier mentioned Human League.

Album releases in 1981 reveal a broad range of genres, a little wider than the many encompassed by *Sandinista*. Elvis Costello was well into his album career with *Trust*, The Pretenders excellent second album *II*, and the Stray Cats hit us with some Rockin' Tunes. In the US, yes it was Styx, Toto, Foreigner and Journey. The Exploited hit us with *Punks Not Dead* and Pil confirmed this by releasing their *Flowers of Romance* album!!

The Beat *Wha' Appen* and Killing Joke *What's This For?* also hit the shops.

Mick produced Ian Hunters album *Short Back and Sides* (more on this later), Bow Wow Wow released *See Jungle…* complete with controversial sleeve, The Stranglers *La Folie* and Joan Jett *I Love Rock 'N Roll*.

Joe had produced (or co-produced) an album in 1980 by the Little Roosters, who were according to various sources, a "Glammy Pub Rock" band. The band was formed from the ashes of the band Cock Sparrer. As payment for his work, Joe had been on the receiving end of some long overdue dental work, which was arranged by the Little Roosters manager. The album was released in 1981, but only saw release in France. More Information at these two links, accessed December 2014.

www.clashcity.com/boards/viewtopic.php?f=6&t=4969
dangerousminds.net/comments/the_little_roosters_lost_album_produced_by_joe_strummer

1981 also saw the loss of two what could be called "Pioneers" in music, Bill Haley (Heart Attack) and Bob Marley (Cancer). In the UK, the BPI (British Phonographic Institute) Chairman at the time, Chris Wright, unveiled the "Home Taping is Killing Music" slogan which we will come across later in the book.

Source: Wikipedia/Music Week/ Billboard/Authors own collection

The Clash 1981

So, how did The Clash fit in to this pretty traumatic year? In *Mojo Magazine* August 1994 (Salewicz, 1994), the author wrote, that at the beginning of the year (1981), The Clash were self managed. "After falling out with Blackhill, Jenner and King". Joe had been playing again with the 101ers. He ran into Bernie in a Wimpy Bar and invited him to a band meeting".

Bernie returned as manager around February 1981, according to Marcus Gray, (Gray, 1995) the band had become disillusioned with their current management company Blackhill. Joe put his foot down "I'm not doing anything else with them". Paul Simonon was quoted "Joe wanted Bernie back because there was no excitement in the situation" During the period of management by Blackhill, "everything had been running smoothly...perhaps too smoothly for the band" (Needs, 2005)

In *The Clash – Punk Rock Band* (Bowe, 2011), the author reported that "In February 1981, The Clash rehired Bernie as manager at Joe's insistence and against Mick's wishes". In the Edgehill *Rock Milestones* DVD *The Clash's London Calling* (Unknown, 2006), Micky Gallagher identified that Bernie was back, and that Mick was overruled possibly for the first time. Mick had been behind the dismissal of Bernie first time round in 1978. As Kris Needs noted in *Q Classic The Clash Special* (Needs, 2010). Back in '78 when Bernie had tried to replace Mick with Steve Jones from The Sex Pistols, The Clash bonded together and ousted Bernie instead.

In the 2012 Documentary and accompanying book, "*The Rise and Fall of The Clash*" (Garcia, 2012) Robin Banks explained "There was conflict in late 1978, particularly with Mick, led to his sacking. Bernie was reinstated, but while he was away, they had produced some great work, *London Calling* and *Sandinista*."

In *Clash City Showdown* (Knowles, 2003), It reported that "Despite Joes front man status, Mick ran The Clash with his own iron fist after Bernie was fired. Rhodes compared The Clash to a Classic Car...'it was a rusty wreck, and I had to do it up and put my updated engine back in them'".

In Rolling Stone (Gilmore, 2011)*The Fury and The Power of The Clash* it stated that "Rhodes returned with big ideas and big assertations. When a reporter asked him how his role in the band had changed, Rhodes snapped, "I own this group".

In an article in Australian Rock magazine *RAM* (Du-Noyer, 1981), Joe made it clear that "There's a lot of people would like to see us take a dive". He also talked about how the band had done loads of tours, and that they just couldn't do that anymore. Commenting that he didn't mind the physical stresses and strain, but that financially it made no sense and that "We're gonna have to work something else out". Du Noyer asked the question "Are The Clash innovative musically?", and Joe answered by saying that they were learning to be, and were not afraid to play around, and he would only put it on record if it was interesting! Joe added, "I hate music that's so concerned with being new, that it forgets to have any soul. We experiment, but with these limitations, it's gotta be worth listening to". One last quote which paves the way for *Combat Rock*, although it refers to *Sandinista* in this interview, "We've really fused some stuff, we are interested in mixing it up."

In June 1981, it was reported in *Melody Maker* (Hewitt, 1981)"They have claimed their territory and are sticking to it. But that resilience was so nearly broken after the release of *Sandinista*. It's no big secret that they came close to splitting up". In the same article, Hewitt also noted that with the release of *Sandinista*, that the band were now "International", and that their music now "incorporated all kinds of styles for all kinds of people"

He also noted that *Sandinista* was far removed from The Clash debut album, and that there was only one way for The Clash to be treated, "not as failed punks, or saviours, but are they a good band?"

In *The Clash – The Only Band That Mattered* (Egan, 2015) the writer made an interesting comment about *Sandinista*, and how the release must have affected the fans and critics. He felt that at the time it was "ludicrous beyond belief". The band had their roots in punk, and were releasing a triple album.

In a Sounds article (Lewis, 1981) Joe was quoted as saying "A few months ago, it seemed like The Clash were on the verge of breaking up. I think every group goes through that, whether you are tiny or big, but you just got to have enough humour to get through when it's rocky". When asked what pressure had led to that? Joe replied "Just not getting anywhere, that's how it felt anyway".

In Uncut Magazine in a "Combat Rock Special" (Martin, 1999), Joe was quoted as saying "We were drifting and I saw my chance. We wanted some direction to the thing because *Sandinista* had been a sprawling six sided "Masterpiece". You gotta get out there and fight like sharks, it's a piranha pool, and I wanted to reunite the old firm, like in the wild bunch. Get the old gang together and ride again. We didn't know anything about anything. We were buffoons in the business world, even Mick wanted him back, because he's not stupid, and he had to admire Rhodes ability to make things happen"

In *The Clash, A Visual Documentary* (Miles/Tobler/Peachy, 1992) Miles stated that "In the early part of 1981 The Clash reunited with Bernie (March 1981). The Clash had made progress but felt vulnerable in business terms" and that Bernie was the only person that they could trust. This does seem to contradict one of the reasons given for Bernie being sacked first time round, as there were potentially issues about how the bands earnings and money were being administered! Again from *The Rise and fall Of The Clash* Garcia quoted "On returning"…Bernie had said, "They were half a million pounds in debt, I had to pull them out of a hole."

In *The Clash Visual Documentary* (Miles/Tobler/Peachy, 1992) stated that "Soon after coming back, Bernie announced that at the end of April there would be an extensive European tour *Impossible Mission*, then USA and then the UK in Autumn. So with Bernie back "At The Controls", The Clash undertook *The Impossible Mission* tour of Europe, taking in dates in Spain, Portugal, France, Switzerland, Holland, Belgium, Germany and Scandinavia and finishing off towards the end of May in Italy.

During this period, Joe ran the London Marathon, Topper hit the news charged with possession of heroin and cocaine. They released the *Magnificent 7 /Magnificent Dance* in early April. The European tour was a great success; the highlight was a gig in Lyons to 8000 people.

As Miles explained again "Support from Europe may have motivated Bernie to suggest they should spend and extended period, perhaps 9 months away from Britain. The proposed US tour was not funded by Epic, and so they could not do the tour as planned. Probably not helped by the *Sandinista* "Low Price" policy. (Which was also a condition laid down by The Clash for the US Territory).

In *Redemption Song*, (Salewicz, 2006) "After the European tour The Clash were back in financial shape. Bernie only got a percentage of profit, so it was in his interest to earn wads of cash." On paper, a six night stint at one venue would be cheaper than transporting band, crew and gear across America. Joe had referred to this as "Making the mountain come to Mohammed".

In *The Clash, A Visual Documentary* (Miles/Tobler/Peachy, 1992) it was reported "So they settled on Bonds in Times Square venue. This did not involve long tedious journeys between venues. They also said that no press tickets would be issued. As Kosmo said (Farren 20th June 1981) "The original idea was to tour the US, but their US Label Epic would not underwrite the tour financially. The only alternative was to play an expanded season in a city like New York. Bring the fans to the show. It's like the fans are going out on tour instead of us". Bonds, was also known as Bonds Casino, and was formally a Department Store (Called Bonds) which had been converted.

In *Clash On Broadway* (Salewicz, 1994), Salewicz reported that "Bonds was chosen by Bernie and Kosmo, a former disco to replicate the sleazy venues booked earlier in their career." And that "A lot of New Yorkers were confused by the idea. Why had they turned down Madison Square Gardens, they could have made more money for less effort". "Making more money for far less effort was not only not the point, it was more like the anti-point."

According to the NME Article *How The Clash Fed The Wonderbread Generation…* (Farren, 1981), Bonds was situated "Slap in the middle of Times Square, pretty much America's epicenter of vice, culture shock, sleaze and dark doorway vampirism".

In *The Clash Punk Rock Band* (Bowe, 2011), Bob Gruen (Photographer and Bugle Blower) was quoted "Bonds was a big thing because it seems the bigger a group gets, the more distant they get from their audience. But the bigger The Clash got, the more they wanted to give back. They played twice the number of shows. What band does that for the same money?"

On the radio in New York, *The Magnificent 7* was being played by WBLS Radio station. It was an instrumental version with dialogue added. (Available on numerous Bootlegs – more on this later).

In the New Musical Express dated 18th April 1981, on page 4, (Unknown, 1981) an interesting competition was presented to the readers. "Win A Week in New York With The Clash" "The Magnificent Insult". The paper gave readers an opportunity to "Insult The Clash In Public", before they added "You're seen Dancin' to their latest record".

The paper encouraged you to "Sharpen Up Your Wit, and hurl no less than 7 Magnificent insults in the direction of The Clash". They added "And then be prepared to leave the country double quick". The competition form gave you space to write down the insults, and announced that if they were not "unprintable rubbish" you and a companion could win an expenses paid trip to New York City with The Clash at the end of May / start of June.

The whole idea is fascinating, it is almost like the band are taking the criticism that was being aimed at them generally, and taking it all on the chin, and actually turning it around in their favour. The winner was promised "Action packed days on Broadway with Joe, Paul, Mick and Topper", and warned that "After you have insulted The Clash, you've got to spend the week with them in the same hotel!". The condition was that on the winner's return, they had to "Spill The Beans" to the NME.

The deal was two return flights, seven nights in the Hotel, back stage passes for "All Seven" of the Broadway shows, and "A Fistfull of Dollars as Pocket Money".

According to *The Last Gang In Town* (Gray, 1995) The band was booked in for seven nights originally. Joe thought that someone had called up the Fire department and "others". There was a big demand for tickets and it was oversold. They ended up doing 15 shows in a row. (17 Shows in Total). In the *Westway To The World Documentary* (Letts, 2001) Joe said "15 Nights nearly killed us".

In the New Musical Express dated 6th June, (Farren, 1981) the writer reported on the initial "Riot" in New York as the shows were cancelled and that the band were "Forced" to play a "16 Date Season, after the ticket fiasco".

The band stayed at the Iroquois Hotel (where James Dean used to stay) which was at Gramercy Park (Times Square / Greenwich Village) and was popular with musicians. It became as Salewicz said "Clash Central".

Joe Strummer told Chris Salewicz "We went out all guns blazing" and when asked how the bands morale was when they got to New York he said "Well we had great morale because we were a great group, we knew we wrote great songs and played great live".

So as the series of shows at Bonds started, (Miles/Tobler/Peachy, 1992) "Tickets were selling for five times face value. After the first night, the fire department announced that they would enforce the legal capacity set at 1750 people. So that everybody could get out if there was a fire. On the first night the crowd was believed to have been 4000."

In the NME, 20th June 1981, Mick Farren wrote that "Bonds had a legal limit was 1750, but had sold more. The fire department got a tip off."

Farren reported in the *NME* 20th June that other clubs also oversold tickets, but Bonds "Got caught". Firemen arrived just before the end of the first set. The fire chief wanted to pull the plug. But Kosmo pointed out that if they did the crowd would rip the place apart." The band did an encore and the lights went on. For the next 24 hours, Bonds was shut down. As the news spread, there was confusion amongst the many fans who had travelled to Mohammed!

In *The Clash - A Visual History* (Miles/Tobler/Peachy, 1992) "Once it was announced that the club would have to be closed, the crowd on the pavement outside went berserk. Mounted police were brought in. It was eventually agreed that they could do the shows, which were extended another 16 shows to accommodate all the ticket holders".

In *"The Rise and Fall of The Clash"* film (Garcia, 2012), it was reported that in New York they ended up playing 17 shows. Pearl Harbor explained "There were screaming fans, Police, nothing like this had happened before. It brought New York to a standstill". What ensued was a mass of publicity that Malcolm McClaren would have been proud of. But, as with the great Bill Grundy incident which catapulted The Sex Pistols into the media spotlight in the UK, the "stunt" was not intentionally planned.

In the same *NME* article (Farren 20th June 1981), Kosmo was quoted saying "I got the news on every channel, I conned them all. Told them all I would give them an exclusive, and then I stitched them all up. Seven major NY Channels have run a substantial Clash item on early evening shows." As Farren said "The Clash by a sweet combination of ignorance, arrogance, deviousness and plain blind luck have become if not a cause, at least a major talking point. The Clash turned up, created two mini riots on Times Square got themselves four solid days of media coverage". In the same article, Farren explained that "With the full glare of the media, it was agreed that the shows could go ahead, but with the safety maximum of 1750 attending. As the shows had all sold around 4,000 tickets each, this left a lot of potentially unhappy fans who in some cases had driven hundreds and hundreds of miles to New York." At a press conference given by the band, one journalist asked the band to comment on a Paul Weller quote along the lines that The Clash had "Sold Out" Mick took the lead by explaining that a sellout is when tickets go on sale, and when there are none left, that constitutes a sellout. This is Mick at his most entertaining and eloquent. You can catch this clip on a number of Unauthorized DVD's, and yes even YouTube.

The band decided that the ethical course was to honour all the tickets sold, although there was concern about the strain on Joe's voice as they had just done a European Tour. The extra dates also meant that the tour expenses would be doubled, and so the dates would be a financial loss. The extension also meant that Bonds had to blow out some forthcoming gigs by The Stranglers and Gary Glitter!

In the same NME article 20th June, Farren also pointed out that The Clash were "Jerking around the whole of New York", in the middle of a "Mini British Invasion", which included other bands such as PIL, The Jam, U2, The Teardrop Explodes and The Fall", but that nobody had really made the same impact. PIL, thought Farren, had come close after their bottling off at the Ritz, and had been asked to go back and play again. The writer also felt that the "Riots" were the "biggest New York fiasco since Sid stuck a knife in Nancy".

As a small piece of light entertainment, in the same issue of NME, the "Results" of "The Magnificent Seven Insults" competition were published as promised. The light hearted winning insults came from a "Scottish tauntress" called Louise Bolloton, who listed among the seven, that she had "seen better dressed wounds than Topper", and "their physical defects would be tolerable if they had a modicum of talent". Paul, Joe and Mick all come in for an insult. Louise and companion Liz seemed to have a good time, and Louise well and truly "spilt the beans". Amongst their adventures were "wizzing around" with Don Letts as he filmed areas of New York for a documentary (presumably *Clash On Broadway*), and a trip to some less secure parts of town with Ray Jordan. The Ladies got to see the first six nights of the Bonds Shows, not the full compliment. Louise also pointed out that nobody really liked Bernie except Joe and Gaby, and that he was "really obnoxious" to both her and friend Liz.

In *The Fury and Power of The Clash* (Gilmore, 2011), he noted "Things seemed to misfire almost every inch of the way. Fire Marshalls, audience abuse of support acts, and riots" and "yet overall, the event had a tremendous effect, it hoisted The Clash to headline news repeatedly in one of the most important cities in the world."

In a Sounds Article 20th June (Lewis, 1981) the writer pointed out that "The band were on the brink of major success in America. In a scene dominated by overweight bozos and fancy dress poseurs, it's great to be reminded what a real rock band should look like, Lean and hungry, all anger and sinew, and restless energy. They tore through about 25 songs". From the NME article (Farren 20th June 1981) the journalist reported that "Four days in, and The Clash are finding their feet. The thing that's most noticeable is the stature they have acquired. They have matched and acquired a definite authority, where there was once enthusiasm and raggedness and all over the place. They are now tight tough and confident."

With the additional dates, that meant additional support act slots were available, and in keeping with their eclectic tastes….these acts included Grandmaster Flash, Funkapolitan and the Slits. In *A New Documentary* (Miles/Tobler/Peachy, 1992) it was noted that the support acts experienced "difficulties".

This was confirmed by (Farren 20th June 1981) when Joe was quoted as saying that "We play music that hopefully not only gets people dancing, but makes them think while they are dancing. Unfortunately, America isn't thinking". Farren added that "First and worst victims are Grandmaster Flash… the rap talk over is too much for three quarters of the crowd. They depart after 15 minutes after hails of rubbish and paper cups". Grandmaster Flash was quoted saying "We've played a lot of places to a lot of faces, but we've never seen shit like this!"

This was perhaps a similar reaction, in some cases, to Mikey Dread, being on the last tour. Support acts ESG, Funkapolitan and the Slits also had a hard time. According to the Farren NME report, the band that went down best were *Siren*, an all girl band who verged on heavy metal. The NME Competition winner also confirmed that the Audiences attitude towards the support bands was "crap, really very bad".

Farren in his 20th June NME report, also believed that the "hardcore" of the audiences saw The Clash as a "Macho Rock band".

In *Clash On Broadway* (Salewicz, 1994) confirmed that on opening night, Grandmaster Flash got pelted off by "Out Of Towners" who travelled to New York." These were the "Ticketron" ticket holders who were given first dibs on the show because of the distance some of them had travelled. In a later interview in the same article, Mick was upset by this "It's so fucking narrow minded. The Clash were always more than just a Rock band". "It's an insult in a way" said Mick. "We picked bands to open for us, so supposedly, we liked them. They are too narrow minded to open up to anything new".

Mick expanded further in the June 20th Farren NME article (1981) by saying that "They're like little kids with roller skates and Walkmans on their heads", and how he didn't think the bands influence was really getting through to them, and that they were the result of "Mass Hypnotism".

And this quote seems to hit the nail on the head, "They were a musical distillery!" And as Salewicz confirmed, "dub reggae, rockabilly and the new rap music were hungrily absorbed into their BREW!!" Salewicz also reported that "The group was tight, and immeasurably confident. This group was a powerhouse."

In his NME article (Farren 20th June 1981) the writer said that "Jones has become a passingly nifty guitarist with a pleasing eclectic style that spans from JA to Rockabilly, as well as straight ahead Chuck Berry knocking it out. In addition he has gained a number of electronic toys, including a pair of heavily "Gizmoed Rototoms" to keep us amused."

Farren also wrote that "Topper lays down the foundation rhythm for The Clash, with a dependability that can't be beat", and that he was "rock steady". He also reported that the shows were just under two hours long, quite a taxing experience. Again from Rolling Stone Magazine (Gilmore, 2011), the writer stated that "The Clash themselves delivered some off centre performances" (Owing in part to Headon's drug use), so, a little contradiction in reports. Farren had noted that some songs seem to go "Dubwise", some interesting, and some dull. He overheard a comment from someone saying "Jesus, they want to be the Grateful Dead when they grow up".

In *Last Gang In Town* (Gray, 1995) the author quoted Mick "We were really together, our playing was pretty hot, and we were confident" Joe said "Topper had the most physical job of the unit, to beat the drum kit. He had no help from beat boxes, just him on the skins"

Looking at the film of Topper being interviewed in the back of a cab after a show in *Clash On Broadway* video (Letts, 2011), you can see it has taken its toll physically on Topper. He looked exhausted, and a little out of it. Topper said "17 shows is easy compared to being on the road," And that he wasn't enjoying the long tours. He met Billy Cobham and he had told him if he didn't enjoy drumming without having a drink… he should have a drink, and enjoy it. When asked "Where do The Clash go from here?" he replied "Physically we go to Japan… musically we go further on… financially we go down".

Interestingly during this period, there was much made about "The New Rolling Stones", and how The Clash were possible contenders. The critics believed that The Stones had lost the plot and had become "disco heavy", and there was a need to find a "replacement". Farren again from the NME 20th June had approached Mick about The Clash taking the old Rolling Stones slot of "global bad boys", which it seemed the Americans were "anxious to slide them in to". Mick had replied "We don't really want it". A similar scenario will make an appearance later in this book!

So how does this all tie in with *Combat Rock*? In *Redemption Song* (Salewicz, 2006) the author made an important point. "The career of The Clash was definitely pre and post Bonds. This was the springboard; *Combat Rock's* success can be traced back to this point." The Clash had already spent time in New York during the recording of *Sandinista* and had taken to it both culturally and musically. Mick in particular was absorbing the music scene, particularly Hip Hop. *The Magnificent 7* had been played on "black music radio stations" in New York. During an incident with Pearl Harbor being taken to a hospital casualty department by Paul, (Someone had spiked her drink with acid), as she was being wheeled in, a black hospital porter walked past, took one look at Paul and rapped *Ring Ring Seven AM* with a laugh. As The Clash "Took New York" and their base became the Iroquois Hotel, the bar in which some of the scenes from "*Raging Bull*" were shot also became a Clash hangout. In a Radio Interview date unknown, The Clash were interviewed by Radio Station WCBN, and as a parting shot request that they play out with *YMCA* by The Village People. After some pretty ropey sing along, Mick starts to get people to ring in to Saturday Night Live and get them on the programme. As Mick added "and this time, we'll have America". This track appears on a few Clash bootlegs.

New additions to the "Clash camp" were rapper Fab Five Freddy (as name dropped in Blondie's *Rapture*) and graffiti artist Futura 2000. While they were there, Paul, Mick and Pearl threw a Birthday party for Ellen Foley, Mick's then girlfriend.

Mick recalled (Gray, 1995) "It was the start of the rap thing in New York, and we fell in with some graffiti artists who made a big banner for us" (As seen in *Radio Clash* Video) Futura 2000 would be an important part of the stage show with his graffiti art backdrops and rapped contributions. In the NME (Lewis, 1981) the author wrote that after one show, Bernie, the band and journalists went out to the South Bronx, home of the phenomenon that is The Clash current craze "rapping". The Clash have done their own *The Magnificent 7*. The added advantage to the Bonds Residency, was that as Joe said, (Martin 1999) "It gives you a chance to hang out and get a feel for the place" In *Last Gang In Town* (Gray, 1995) Mick said "We got to see some of New York and feel part of it for the first time, I quite wanted to stay."

All this helped consolidate their campaign, and cement their influences particularly New York and their strong interest in films. Scorcese and De Niro had attended Clash shows and the Vietnam story was a strong influence in reading matter and the "big screen" Vietnam. Again from *Last Gang In Town* Paul said that "Scorsese had some ideas about making a film with us. He suggested a film about the gangs of New York, and that he wanted us to be included in, but by the time he got round to it, we had split up". As their profile grew in the USA, back home in the UK there was an interview with Chris Salewicz in 1994 "*On Broadway*". Mick commented "We haven't played England for a long time. I think when we do; everyone will see that there are plenty of people who still want to see us. I think there are some writers saying 'fuck you, you abandoned your roots'".

In the 20th June NME article (Farren, 1981), the writer makes an interesting observation on the position of the band. "US Fans may want The Clash, but don't understand them". He also added that "But if the mix of rumour and media is anything to go by, there is at least a part of the English audience that seems to understand The Clash, and not want them anymore.

In *Home on The Range* (Salewicz, 1981) in The Face magazine, Paul was interviewed. "It's funny though, everyone seems to be out to get us these days. We're definitely the most fashionable group to have a go at". Most intriguingly, Paul added "And we've got a lot more surprises up our sleeves too. We're going to keep a lot of people on their toes". How right he was…!

The NME Magnificent 7 Insults Competition winner, Louise had a view on the band themselves, saying that they got a "lot of stick" from punks in Britain, but they had stuck to a lot of their principles, like not going on Top Of the Pops. Louise mentioned the fact that people felt the band had "sold out", but that when the band toured in Britain "Every night is always completely packed".

So, can you blame The Clash for taking the opportunities placed before them? After several years of being held in high regard by the UK Music Press, suddenly they were being slagged off. So what would you do? Bang you head against a brick wall and fade away into obscurity? or continue your mission. In *The Fury and the Power* (Gilmore, 2011) Joe said, "We're trying to be the biggest group in the world, and radical at the same time. Maybe the two can't co-exist".

And so by way of summary, The Bonds shows did push The Clash into the limelight, more by accident than design, in the Music Capital of the USA. It allowed the band to fine tune their live performance (even if it did nearly kill them). It introduced them to and allowed them to introduce to the fans, new genres and styles of music. Working closely with Futura 2000 allowed them an "in" to the rap scene, and immerse themselves into the music, art and films of the city.

The residency also qualified the idea of playing a series of several nights residency in a capitol city. I leave this section with a great passage from a Mojo Magazine article (Salewicz 1994) *The Clash On Broadway*.

"If there was one pivotal event in the history of The Clash assault on the USA, it was the 17 shows they played at Bonds" They had, said Salewicz "Already achieved cult status, *London Calling* had made the US Top 30". He also felt that "After these shows, large scale American stardom was there for the taking". Rather darkly ending with "The top 5 placing of *Combat Rock* the following year can be traced back to this springboard, and therefore we might say the beginning of the end." Interestingly, in *The Clash – The Only Band That Mattered*, Egan pointed out that the Bonds Episode had "no resonance" in Britain, a "Little reported incident in a Faraway land". The New Musical Express did cover the shows and the ticket issues in the best part of a page on 6th June, and again over two pages on the 20th June. From the 20th June edition, Farren made some pertinent observations. He felt that it was fairly certain "Barring an accident", that the band were on the verge of some sort of major breakthrough in the USA. He talked about the fact that the US was still the "land of big money and big exposure". He also felt that they would always be the target of the "bad guys", but also under attack from "some who are supposed to be their allies". Farren added that they may find themselves "at war" with their record label (no change there), "at odds" with the major section of the music media, "who will never be satisfied with their efforts". Farren wrote that the band may have difficulties maintaining their "Real World perspective, while being seduced and massaged by the trappings of stardom". In a final remark, Farren believed that of all the then contemporary rock and roll bands, The Clash had "gone further in using the medium on a mass politically based level".

According to *Redemption Song* (Salewicz, 2006). In April 1981, they had laid down early versions of *Car Jamming*, *This is Radio Clash* and *Sean Flynn* at Marcus Music in London. Then did *Know Your Rights* at Ear Studios in Notting Hill, along with *Inoculated City*, *Should I Stay or Should I Go* and *Ghetto Defendant*. The Author also stated that "After the Bonds shows, the band stayed in New York and started to record *Radio Clash* to be completed later in London. According to Big Cheese magazine (Ogg, 2008) "In April they recorded *Radio Clash*, with lines inspired by Michael Herr *Dispatches* book (Herr, 1977).

Following the Bonds Residency, the trend was continued as in late September 23–30th, The Clash played a series of shows at the Theatre Mogador, Paris. This was a seven night stand as part of the *Radio Clash Tour*. The Single *This is Radio Clash* was not released until November after the tour had started. It was here that the band debuted material from their next album. The live tapes from these shows reveal that some of the future *Combat Rock* material got an airing.

In August 1981, prior to the Paris shows, Guy Stevens died of an overdose and complications trying to get himself "cleaned up". In September, the band were rehearsing for the upcoming UK tour as well as "cooking stuff up" in terms of new material, and recorded the tribute *Midnight To Stevens*.

According to *Joe Strummer and The Legend of The Clash* (Needs, 2005) "In late September 1981 The Clash took a break from recording to tour Europe. They played seven nights at the Theatre Mogador in Paris. The stage set reported by Robin Banks consisted of two 12 foot barriers painted black and yellow. Futura 2000 spray painted a mural during the two hour show. The set list included *Should I Stay or Should I Go*, *Ghetto Defendant*, and "Escapades of Futura" (also known as *Graffiti Rap*), when he joined them on stage.

"The band got three encores a night" reported Robin Banks in his reviews for *Zig Zag* Magazine. (Banks, 1981) He also reported a row over Toppers "condition". This seemed to involve Bernie. Perhaps trying to deflect rumours of addiction in the music press, Banks spoke of "Topper doing

50 push-ups before each show." In the same review, Banks said that "On a good night, they are the greatest rock and roll band in the world". He also spoke about the new material being as powerful as any they have made, and that the lyrical content was "as bitingly sarcastic or as poignant as they have ever produced". He also felt that Strummer and Jones were at their artistic peak.

Banks maintained that the seven nights had all sold out, and there were probably 500 extra people inside the venue more than the official 2000 limit. In the same Zig Zag review, he enhanced the description of the stage set and barriers which had flashing lights. Robin Banks also felt that the inclusion of *The Escapades of Futura* "baffled the French punters". On the various nights, new songs were "added at random" said Banks, *Know Your Rights*, *Long Time Jerk* and *Inoculated City*, and on the strength of these "it's gonna be some album".

The Paris shows followed the pattern of "taking over a city" for a string of dates and in true Clash tradition…the theatre was due for demolition after the shows were completed. These and later shows were criticized heavily by the press, some noticed and "improved professionalism".

From my six CD set Bootleg from these shows, the future *Combat Rock* tracks that are aired are: *Should I Stay or Should I Go*, *Ghetto Defendant*, *Overpowered By Funk* and *Know Your Rights*. *Graffiti Rap* …or *The Escapades of Futura 2000* as it would eventually be released as was also a feature of the shows …and *This Is Radio Clash*. While the shows were going on, it appeared that there was a siege going on in the Turkish Embassy, hostages taken, police, and a whole area cordoned off. As Banks pointed out, "The Clash use a gentler and hopefully more persuasive method of projecting their own ideals"

On 5th October, the UK Dates of *The Radio Clash Tour* began, and ended with seven nights at the Lyceum in London. These were the first UK dates in 18 months. The NME panned the gigs; Barney Hoskins dismissed the latest two albums (*Sandinista* and *London Calling*) as "piffle".

In *The Clash Ultimate Listening Guide* (Thompson, 2013) the author wrote that the UK Media "Hammered Sandinista", and that the band had been "unable or unwilling to explain their motives" Accused of selling their soul to the highest bidders, Thompson rightly pointed out that *Sandinista* and been a "virtual albums worth of reggae and dub" which the States had proved to be "Inexplicably resistant to". But it seems that *Sandinista* actually fared better in the US than in the UK.

In *The Clash Visual Documentary* (Miles/Tobler/Peachy, 1992) in a section called "On The Road Again", it was noted that "The British Tour was announced with 7 out of the 13 nights being at The Lyceum in London and just six provincial dates. *Redemption Song*(Salewicz 2006) reported that "On October 5th the Tour shifted to the UK, opening in Manchester. It was the first time they had played in their own country for fifteen months. Two weeks later they hit London and the tour concluded with seven nights at the Lyceum. He went on to say that "The audience received the "Bonds Treatment". A similar format, the set included a rap by Futura 2000 to be called *The Escapades of Futura 2000*. "It was a 2 hour show; Futura would spray paint a graffiti mural backdrop and then leap off his step ladder to deliver the rap.

As with the Paris dates, the band aired *Know Your Rights*, *Should I Stay or Should I Go*, *Ghetto Defendant* , and *Graffiti Rap*.

Again in *The Clash Visual Documentary* (Miles/Tobler/Peachy, 1992) "The Paris and London shows were widely criticized in the Press. Some writers had again noticed an "increase in professionalism". The shows had Futura spray painting the stage set, transforming it as one reviewer noted into something representing a border post between two countries." (Probably with reference to the black and yellow barriers, reported by Robin Banks.

In a Melody Maker article (Sweeting, 1981) "The Clash and Cocktail Culture", Sweeting wrote that "Their sin had been survival" and that "A lot of people think The Clash should not be here" After the first Lyceum show the NME headline was "The Parody Lingers On". Sweeting wrote that he saw three of the week long shows, and was convinced he was witnessing an event. Sweeting raised some interesting points in the article, how The Clash (and others) could "keep moving in the narrow corridors of pop" and that their options might be to break into megastar status (like The Police) or to keep on making records that some people like, but are generally ignored…or give up! He also added that if they had been committed to "selling out", they could have made a more "lucrative job out of it".

In Kris Needs' book he said "The shows were eclectic and long, very different from the gigs of '77 and '78. The dates had sold out, and Joe commented that "That's another bum steer the NME gave me, I believed them when they said we weren't liked".

One writer noted that "The Clash's music had lost a lot of its abrasive power; the short sharp volatile statement had been replaced by the long meandering and convoluted. It seemed that The Clash fans were glad to have them back on the British stage. Plans were being made for the next album".

The Clash then were back in the UK after an extended break. They had received a lot of criticism for being away in the States, and not being around for the Riots in Brixton. The press were not kind with their reviews. After the real High of the Bonds Shows and New York, perhaps they were wondering why they had bothered! Even with the bad press, the Lyceum shows had sold out. After *The Radio Clash Tour* ended, the band flew to New York to record for the next album, more about this in the next chapter.

In November, *This Is Radio Clash* was released as a single… bizarrely… as the *Radio Clash Tour* was over by then. It was "not the big single that was needed". In his analysis in *The Only band That Mattered* Egan believed that the single release was "not helping" with it's very "in your face" mix with heavy handclaps and a very "rap" sound. The new album should have been ready and released in December, but recording was still in progress.

An important element in 1981 was that of the "Topper" situation. His dabbling and addiction to heroin and other drugs is well documented. But in relation to the *Combat Rock* album writing and recording it is relevant. Certainly, there had been no real sign of "the engine room" not coming up to par on the live shows and creatively, Topper was contributing to the new material.

In *The Clash – The Only Band That Mattered* Egan made some interesting and valid remarks. He noted that both The Clash and The Jam "sat out" as he put it, the year of 1981 in terms of an album release. The Jam had to an extent taken over the role of press darlings, both commercially and critically, and the two bands had become as Egan described, "Clear leaders of what remained of the punk movement". I'm sure there are a lot of opinions on this. He also felt that it was The Clash that had become "The Joke", and the Jam "the most beloved band in the world". In terms of the Bonds shows, which personally I believe were pivotal in the bands career, Egan also mentioned that it could have been another example of how they may have been seen to be neglecting their "home fans".

4. THE LONG HAUL 1982

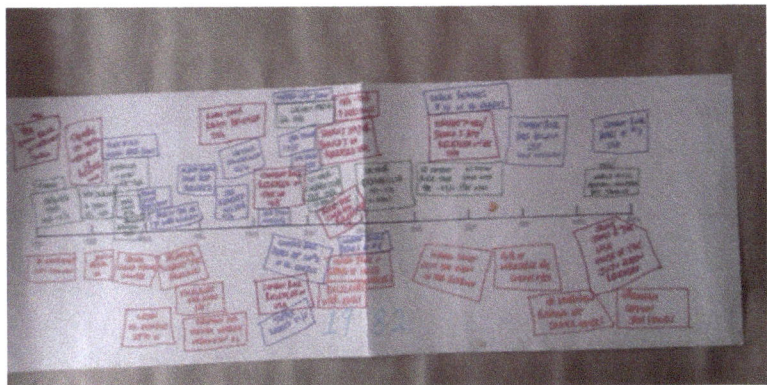

As we move into 1982, my trusty gaffa taped timeline becomes a mess of colour coded text! This is an extraordinary year for The Clash! But I'll start first with some more "World Events"

January

SAW THE RELEASE OF THE UK UNEMPLOYMENT FIGURES, WHICH TOPPED 3 MILLION.

IN NEW YORK, THERE WAS A FIVE YEAR PLAN TO UPGRADE THE NYC METRO. 75% OF THE USA WAS COVERED IN SNOW.

THE "FAME" TV SERIES PREMIERED ON US TV AND "JOHNNY CASH PARKWAY" OPENED IN TENNESSEE.

February

THERE WERE MORE NUCLEAR TESTS IN THE US AND USSR.

WALL STREET WAS BOMBED BY THE FALN. (A PUERTO RICAN PARAMILITARY ORGANISATION)

THE SYRIAN GOVERNMENT ATTACKED HAMA, KILLING THOUSANDS.

IN FLORIDA, NICARAGUAN EXILES WERE TRAINING FOR WAR AGAINST THE SANDINISTA GOVERNMENT ON PRIVATE OWNED LAND IN THE FLORIDA EVERGLADES.

IN THE UK THERE WERE MORE RIOTS, THIS TIME IN BRISTOL. I KNOW, BECAUSE I WAS THERE.

IN IRELAND THE DELOREAN CAR COMPANY CLOSED AFTER BEING BAILED OUT BY TAX PAYERS MONEY.

March

MARCH SAW A RUSSIAN SPACECRAFT LAND ON VENUS.

AND NOT TO BE OUTDONE, THE US LAUNCHED THE THIRD SPACE SHUTTLE.

PRESIDENT REAGAN ANNOUNCED ECONOMIC SANCTIONS AGAINST LIBYA.

FREDDIE LAKER'S CUT PRICE AIRLINE COLLAPSED, AND SO THERE WERE NO MORE CHEAP FLIGHTS FOR ROCK BANDS TRYING TO BREAK THE US. HE OWED 270 MILLION POUNDS!

NICARAGUA SUSPENDED CITIZEN RIGHTS FOR 30 DAYS

A DUTCH TV CREW WAS SHOT IN EL SALVADOR.

THE ARGENTINEANS LANDED ON SOUTH GEORGIA ISLAND IN A BID TO RECLAIM THE FALKLAND ISLANDS FROM THE UK.

ONE HUNDRED AND FIFTEEN ENGLAND CRICKETERS PLAYED IN SOUTH AFRICA, AND WERE SUBSEQUENTLY BANNED FROM PLAYING AS THE ANTI APARTHEID AGREEMENT WAS BREACHED. THIS WAS SEEN AS A SANCTIONS BREAKER, WITH VERY FEW NON WHITES IN THE CROWDS.

April

THE SOUTH ATLANTIC STARTED HOTTING UP AS ARGENTINE TROOPS INVADED THE FALKLANDS IN FORCE. OVERNIGHT THE ISLANDERS WERE UNDER NEW RULE. FROM THE UK, HMS INVINCIBLE WAS DISPATCHED TO THE AREA. PEOPLE CHEERED THEM OFF. PRINCE ANDREW WAS ON BOARD. HMS HERMIES, A LARGE AIRCRAFT CARRIER WAS ALSO SENT.

THE U.N. SECURITY COUNCIL DEMANDED THAT THE ARGENTINES WITHDRAW FROM THE FALKLANDS.

BRITAIN ALSO WAVED GOODBYE TO THE POUND NOTE AS POUND COINS CAME INTO SERVICE.

THE QUEEN ENDED COLONIAL TIES WITH CANADA.

THE ZX SPECTRUM COMPUTER WAS RELEASED.

ROD STEWART WAS MUGGED AND HAD HIS PORSCHE STOLEN.

THE USSR PUT A SPACE STATION INTO ORBIT.

May

MAY SAW MORE ACTION IN THE SOUTH ATLANTIC, WITH THE ARGENTINE CRUISER "BELGRANO" SUNK BY A UK SUBMARINE. HMS SHEFFIELD WAS HIT BY AN EXOCET MISSILE. AND "THE ATLANTIC CONVEYER" AND HMS COVENTRY WERE ALSO HIT. BRITISH TROOPS LANDED ON THE FALKLANDS AT SAN CARLOS. THE CRUISE LINER CANBERRA WAS USED AS A TROOP CARRIER. THE ARGENTINES WERE NOT REALLY AWARE OF THE TASK FORCE. THE BBC WARNED THAT ARGENTINA ITSELF MAY BE BOMBED. THERE WERE SHIPS LOST, CASUALTIES ON BOTH SIDES, WITH HEAVY LOSSES OF ARGENTINE PLANES.

THE POPE VISITED THE UK WHICH WAS CONTROVERSIAL AS THE UK WAS AT WAR WITH CATHOLIC ARGENTINA.

PRESIDENT REAGAN BEGAN WEEKLY 5 MINUTE RADIO BROADCASTS.

IBM RELEASED OS-DOS 1.1 FOR THE PC.

June

AFTER THE ASSASSINATION OF ISRAELIS IN THE UK, ISRAEL ATTACKED SOUTH LEBANON, AND LATER INVADED WITH 30,000 TROOPS.

LEBANON WAS ALSO BOMBED AFTER.

RONNIE REAGAN ADDRESSED THE UK PARLIAMENT AND HE AND NANCY MET THE QUEEN, AND WENT HORSE RIDING WITH HER TOO.

LADY DIANA GAVE BIRTH TO A SON, WILLIAM.

IN THE US, JOHN HINKLEY WAS FOUND NOT GUILTY OF THE 1981 ATTEMPT TO ASSASSINATE PRESIDENT REAGAN, BY REASON OF INSANITY.

AIR ATTACKS CONTINUED ON UK SHIPS IN THE FALKLANDS. THE "SIR GALAHAD" WAS BADLY HIT. ARGENTINA EVENTUALLY SURRENDERED TO BRITAIN ON THE FALKLANDS AFTER 74 DAYS OF CONFLICT. RIOTS FOLLOWED IN ARGENTINA, AND GALTIERI RESIGNED AS PRESIDENT.

POPE JOHN PAUL II VISITED ARGENTINA.

ON THE MOVIE FRONT, ET WAS RELEASED (THE HIGHEST GROSSING FILM) AND STAR TREK II THE WRATH OF KHAN OPENED IN THE US...ILLOGICAL.

July

IN THE UK RAIL DRIVERS WENT ON STRIKE OVER ROSTERING, BUT THIS WAS CALLED OFF AFTER THREE WEEKS.

IRA BOMBS EXPLODED IN HYDE PARK AND REGENTS PARK IN LONDON. GUARDSMEN AND HORSES WERE HIT BY THE CAR BOMBS WITH ADDED NAILS.

RONNIE AND REGGIE KRAY WERE LET OUT TO ATTEND THEIR MOTHER'S FUNERAL.

MARGARET THATCHER BEGAN HER SECOND TERM AS PRIME MINISTER...AIDED AND ABETTED BY THE FALKLANDS "VICTORY".

IN THE MIDDLE EAST, ISRAEL AND LEBANON WERE STILL FIGHTING.

ARGENTINA HAD A NEW PRESIDENT SWORN IN.

THE BOLIVIAN GOVERNMENT RESIGNED!

THE US LAUNCHED THE FOURTH SPACE SHUTTLE AND THE LANDSAT 4 SATELLITE TO MAP THE EARTH...OR SO THEY SAID!

August

THE ISRAELIS CARRIED OUT AN AIR BOMBARDMENT ON BEIRUT. US MARINES LATER ENTERED BEIRUT AND ISRAELI LEADER SHARON URGED PALESTINE TO DISCUSS PEACE.

THE USSR CARRIED OUT NUCLEAR TESTS.

IN JAPAN, THERE WAS AN AMENDMENT TO ALLOW PROPORTIONAL REPRESENTATION IN THEIR GOVERNMENT.

IN GERMANY, THE FIRST MUSIC COMPACT DISCS WERE RELEASED TO THE PUBLIC.

September

SAW THE COMMONWEALTH GAMES HELD IN AUSTRALIA. IN BRISBANE THERE WERE DEMONSTRATIONS BY AUSTRALIAN ABORIGINES AT THE EVENT, DEMANDING RIGHTS TO THEIR LANDS. ARRESTS WERE MADE. QUEENSLAND WAS SLOW AT GIVING RIGHTS BACK.

FIFTY PEOPLE DIED IN A PLANE CRASH FROM MALAGA AIRPORT IN A DC-10 JET.

THE ISRAELI AND PALESTINIAN CONFLICT STILL RAGED. THE POPE MET PALESTINIAN LEADER YASSER ARAFAT.

IN THE US, STREET CARS IN SAN FRANCISCO STOPPED RUNNING FOR A 2 YEAR REPAIR PROGRAM.

NASA LAUNCHED ANOTHER "INTEL" SATELLITE.

BOTH THE USSR AND US CARRIED OUT MORE NUCLEAR TESTS.

OH, AND IN THE UK, KEITH RICHARDS HOUSE BURNED DOWN.

October

IN THE UK, FALKLANDS TROOPS WERE WELCOMED BACK TO THE UK OFFICIALLY IN CENTRAL LONDON.

IN TEHRAN, A BOMB ATTACK KILLED 60 AND INJURED 700.

POLAND BANNED SOLIDARITY AND ALL LABOUR UNIONS. THE US LATER IMPOSED SANCTIONS ON POLAND FOR BANNING THE TRADE UNION.

PRESIDENT REAGAN DECLARED WAR AGAINST DRUGS, AND THE BUDGET DEFICIT REACHED $110 TRILLION FOR THE 1982 FISCAL YEAR.

"CATS" OPENED ON BROADWAY, RUNNING FOR 18 YEARS.

CHINA ANNOUNCED THAT ITS POPULATION HIT ONE BILLION.

AND IN JAPAN, THE FIRST COMMERCIALLY AVAILABLE CD PLAYER WAS RELEASED.

November

IN THE US, HONDA BECAME THE FIRST ASIAN CAR COMPANY TO PRODUCE CARS IN THE US.

THE VIETNAM VETS MEMORIAL OPENED.

NASA LAUNCHED SPACE SHUTTLE NUMBER 5.

ELIZABETH TAYLOR (IN A FOUL MOOD) WENT FOR HER 7TH DIVORCE; IT MUST HAVE BEEN A BAD HAIR DAY AGAIN.

THE IMF LENT MEXICO $3.8 BILLION. SOLIDARITY LEADER LECH WALESA WAS FREED IN POLAND.

AND JAPAN GOT A NEW PRIME MINISTER.

IN THE UK, UNEMPLOYMENT WAS MENTIONED IN THE QUEEN'S OPENING OF PARLIAMENT SPEECH.

AT GREENHAM COMMON, HOME OF THE US CRUISE MISSILES, WOMEN PROTESTED. THERE WERE PEACE DEMONSTRATIONS, AND THE BASE WAS SURROUNDED BY PEOPLE AS THEY JOINED HANDS IN A CANDLELIT VIGIL.

IN WALES, THERE WAS A VOTE ON WHETHER PUBS CAN OPEN ON SUNDAY OR NOT, AFTER HUNDREDS OF YEARS.

December

```
AT YEAR'S END, IN THE US, THE HIGHEST
TEMPERATURES FOR DECEMBER WERE RECORDED,
AND RECORD RAINFALLS.

POLICE AND RACIST DEMONSTRATORS CLASHED IN
ANTWERP.

A PUB BOMBING IN IRELAND KILLED 11 SOLDIERS
AND 6 CIVILIANS.

SPAIN RE-OPENED THE BORDER WITH GIBRALTAR.

THE US MAGAZINE "TIME" ANNOUNCED "THE MAN
OF THE YEAR", WHICH WAS A COMPUTER!

JAMAICA ISSUED A STAMP FEATURING BOB
MARLEY.
```

Source: Wikipedia 2014

Musically 1982

In the UK, the music charts were as eclectic as ever. The chart action included electronic hits from The Human League and Kraftwerk. There was the usual haul of "Pop Trash" from the likes of Bucks Fizz, Tight Fit, Shaky, and the Goombay Dance Band! Captain Sensible went all South Pacific with *Happy Talk*. The Jam got two number ones in a year which I guess fueled even more "The Clash vs. The Jam" debate. Madness scored a hit with *House Of Fun*, and rightly so! From the States, we were given *Fame* and *Eye Of The Tiger*… thanks for that. Culture Club hit the charts with their *Do You Really Want To Hurt Me* single and Dexys Midnight Runners got the best single of the year award with *Come On Eileen*… I swear.. The UK celebrated the end of the year with Renee and Renata *Save Your Love*.

Album wise, the "Competition" for *Combat Rock* came from Barbra Streisand *Love Songs*, *The Kids From Fame* soundtrack album and a Madness *Greatest Hits* album (already!!)

Electro Pop got a good look in, Duran Duran *Rio*, Human League's *Dare*, Yazoo *Upstairs at Eric's* and Soft Cell and Japan. ABC hit us with their *Lexicon of Love* in gold lamé suits, The Jam *Gift* and Dire Straits all topped the charts, and the *John Lennon Collection* topped off the end of the year.

1982 saw the loss of James Honeyman Scott… guitar whiz from the Pretenders, actor and comedian John Belushi was found dead after a drug overdose, and Ozzy Osbourne bit the head off a live bat and was also arrested for pissing on the Alamo. He made amends by marrying manager and future X factor judge Sharon. (Obviously she had an eye for "talent" even back then) Christians…that's the faith…not the band, burned Iron Maiden and Ozzy albums because of their "Satanic lyrics", so I guess they really did burn in hell!

Journalist and author Lester Bangs, also died from an overdose of prescription drugs.

There was the first mass production of Compact discs in Hannover, Germany. The first "US" festival was held in the US featuring The Police, Tom Petty, Fleetwood Mac and The Grateful Dead. Later in the year The Jamaican World Music Festival got underway with Squeeze, The Grateful Dead among others, and of course The Clash

The Who announced their first "farewell tour" which began in Washington, there were more to follow. Madonna released *Everybody* as her debut single. In the UK there was the first edition of *The Tube* on TV, The Jam made their last TV appearance in support of their *Beat Surrender* single. Michael Jackson *Thriller* was released…. and there isn't too much more I can say about that. ABBA released their final original single, but no official split was announced.

Among the other album releases of the year, Shalamar, and Sugarhill Gang released albums. Hanoi Rocks and Girl on the "rock" front, live albums from Simon and Garfunkel ,Talking Heads and the Rolling Stones. US AOR MOR or whatever you like to abbreviate it to… Asia, Toto, Hall and Oates, REO Speedwagon, Supertramp, John Cougar and Donald Fagan all made their mark in the UK and US.

Laurie Anderson hit us with BIG Science, largely off the back of *Oh Superman* single. More notable releases from The Cure *Pornography*, Roxy Music *Avalon*, Kid Creole and The Coconuts *Tropical Gangsters*, a Pete Townsend solo album, Dexys *Too Rye Aye*, Simple Minds *New Gold Dream*, Prince *1999* , and an interesting solo album from Phil Lynott!

In the US, the singles charts began the year still working out, with Olivia Newton John. J Geils *Centrefold* Joan Jett *I love Rock N Roll* held the top spot for seven weeks. Stevie Wonder and Paul McCartney were "Living Together In Perfect Harmony", and *Eye of The Tiger* Survived at number one for six weeks.

Theatre Of Hate released their *Do You Believe in The Westworld* single produced by Mick Jones, the twelve inch airing some incredible mixes of the A and B sides… drum effects, samples, dubs… not what you got when you saw the band live. I would flag this up as a very brave move on their part, and I recommend that you check this out; you can certainly see where Mick is headed. The previous year, Ronald Regan had become the US President, and could well be "The Cowboy turned his gun on himself and sang No Ones Alive". February saw the release of the *Westworld* album, again produced by Mick Jones… and again revealing some pretty groundbreaking "sounds", including some Spanish read out over the phone by band member John Boy Lennard's Spanish Tutor from the US / Canada, used on the *Conquistador* track. John Lennard would later pop up in the early incarnation of Mick's Big Audio Dynamite called TRAC

In a *Word* magazine article entitled "Once Upon a Time in the West End", (Kelly, 2005) Kelly praised the production of the single in particular, where Mick had "welded bubbly bass to martial drums" and how it seemed incredibly powerful as at the time, Britain was at war with Argentina, and the US had a "gung ho" president in power. My feelings are backed up in *The Clash - The Ultimate Listening Guide* (Thompson, 2013). "The seeds of his eventual dismissal from The Clash were as apparent in his contributions to *Combat Rock* as the roots of his next project, Big Audio Dynamite, already existed in the manic throb of the Theatre Of Hate album he'd been working on."

At some point in 1982, Mick also found time to produce a single by a band called BIM. There is some mystery surrounding the release which came out on a small label called Swerve and distributed by one of the then "Big Five" record labels, WEA. Some Clash pundits believe that Mick is singing on the single, although the three known members were Andy Harley, Cameron McLey and Stephen Wright according to the Discogs website. The band had previously released singles in 1980 and 1981, so I am not convinced this is purely "Mick in disguise". It does bear some Mick style production trademarks.

According to an online article *Turning Rebellion Into Money* by John Deeth (archive.today/k0Ob, saved from jdeeth.home.mchsi.com/clash.htm) (accessed March 2014), In 1982, The Clash "renegotiated their contract with CBS, earning themselves a higher position in the company's promotion plans, but ending their budget pricing policy". I was not aware of this from any previous reading and research, but it does make sense now. It would put the band in a stronger financial position in terms of royalties, especially after the *Sandinista* royalty payment situation. If true, I would imagine it was a "Bernie" move and as it turned out a very shrewd business move on his part, bearing in mind the later success of *Combat Rock*.

Source: Wikipedia/Music Week/ Billboard/Authors own collection/Credited References

The Far East Tour

In The Clash World, they were about to undertake a groundbreaking tour of the Far East. The album was still not finished, but they needed to crack on with it. As Salewicz noted (Salewicz, 2006), "The new record was still work in progress, it was not to meet the end of January deadline delivery date"

The "Topper Situation" reared its ugly head again at the start of the year, after Topper was busted at Heathrow for possession of heroin, in his underpants. There was a court case at Uxbridge Magistrates Court. After some heart-felt pleas on his behalf, he received a £500 fine and a condition that he accepted help and treatment for his addiction.

This did have implications on the upcoming tour, both for his own health, and the possibility of having work permits rescinded in the particularly "drug intolerant" Japan. All this added to the pressure on the band and management team, with a heavily behind schedule album still not mixed and ready, and a full scale assault on new territories. The Japanese "drug laws", also had an impact on the whole band, Mick and Joe were unable to get any weed, as Salawicz noted, "They were virtually "splifless" for the eight days they toured the country", and they "apparently burst into tears in the hotel lobby when they found out they had none."

So, where are we now, a band exhausted from recording sessions in New York, with a still unfinished album, tensions amongst band members; artistic, creative and personal, and one member with a serious drug addiction.

The Far East tour kicked off in Japan on January 24th. The reception they received from the fans pretty much freaked Joe out, Salewicz explained that Joe felt they were "treated like Western Gods, and showered with gifts".

The band arrived on January 23rd, and there were reportedly crazy scenes at the airport and again at the train station in Osaka. According to Kris Needs, Joe was uncomfortable with being involved in the "westernisation" of Japan. As the author noted, "the people loved The Clash, and The Clash loved them back". Mick recalled that the visit was "one of the most wonderful times we had together"

In *A Bit of a Blur* (Alex James, 2007) the Blur bass player experienced a similar reception. He also wondered why British "pop" was so revered by the Japanese, and that he had no idea they were "Big In Japan". He noticed that they were followed everywhere, and "treated like princes".

In *The Clash In Japan* article in *Sounds* (Minakami, 1982)the writer reported that Paul and Pearl were already in Tokyo before Joe and Mick arrived on the 23rd, the day before the first show. The last minute dash to for the flight from the New York studio, and the jet lag seemed to have left Joe exhausted.

In Japan, according to Record Mirror, the audience were given the honour of being able to stand up during the show. Although this meant that they could stand on their seats, which was a compromise. The Clash had never played there before, largely as Salewicz mentioned "because of a Clash edict, that they would not play Japan unless the audience could stand up, which wasn't allowed." Kosmo believed that they got a lot of TV coverage out of this, and the band were respected for sticking to their principles. In the Sounds article, Minakami talked about this, and the rumours that had gone around about The Clash refusing to play unless a promoter was able to make venues available without seats. Minakami pointed out that the venues were largely controlled by Local Councils and the Government, and that little could be done. The tour, he said was a compromise on behalf of The Clash.

The shows in Japan, nine in all, ran from 24th January until 2nd February, and were well received. In the Sounds article "The Clash in Japan", Minakami noted that Joe was pouring water over his head to keep himself going, and that he did not appear to be in great shape. All the reviews that were published the next day "praised them with one accord" as "The Only Real Band" (Possibly that mattered!!)

The nine shows consisted of seven in Toyko of which one according to Minakami was a matinee. The other two were in Osaka, (via the bullet train).

At the opening show, Joe wore the "Rising Sun" shirt which features on some of the press shots from the Tokyo dates. This according to the Sounds article sparked some controversy, perhaps in the same way as the "Brigade Rosse" t-shirt which Joe wore at The Ant Nazi League Carnival show. Minakami did not know what it meant, and that there were disputes between journalists and fans. Minakami had to ask his mother what it was about. He asked Joe if he knew the meaning, and Joe believed that the Rising Sun flag used to mean good luck for soldiers going off to war. Minakami pointed out to Joe that his mother had told him that during wars, people were forced to encourage their troops to die for their Emporer and Japan. He also felt that there might be a misunderstanding amongst the "right wing" people, who may have thought they were being insulted, or may think that Joe was on their side, praising the war and imperialism. Joe had asked if he should continue to wear it, and Minakami told him that if he was brave enough to wear it to "provoke our kids" who did not know too much about it, perhaps they would try and find out about it themselves. Joe had said he would keep wearing it, but after the second show, he stopped. Joe had also had some slogans painted on his arms with special pens. One read "Kill Mickey Mouse" and the other "The World Is One". The second in particular seemed to have resonance to Joe years later with his BBC World Service radio shows and the Festival Campfire Flags of the world philosophy. The "Mickey Mouse" reference reinforcing Joe's objection to the Americanisation of Japan and how it was destroying the Japanese culture. By way of contrast, Joe had visited Harajuku where in a blocked off street, kids danced to rockabilly music and wore 50's fashion.

At the last show in Tokyo, Minakami reported that Joe's voice was cracking due to a bad throat and flu, and that Mick was trying to help out by choosing songs that he could sing to save Joe's voice.

There are a number of bootleg albums in circulation from the dates, and a DVD from a Japanese TV Broadcast of good quality, not the full show, and none of the *Combat Rock* tracks are included. The Bootleg albums include a *Combat Rock* track here and there, *Should I Stay or Should I Go* and *Know Your Rights*

The shows at Osaka were again well received, the audience according to the *Sounds* article *The Clash in Japan*, went wild. It was here it appears that the fans were allowed to watch "standing up in their places", without being forced to sit down by the security staff. In the same article, Minakami retold how three girls had approached Joe complaining that they had to pay £50 for tickets from a street tout, Joe made a point of getting them in free for the next show to compensate.

Prior to the dates in Japan, in an interview reproduced in *Crossbeat*, (Hayashi, 1981) Mick responded to a question about one of the songs being recorded sounding like reggae, and would the style of the new album be like *Sandinista*. Mick replied that "The Clash is The Clash", and didn't like styles, as that tended to categorise people. The Clash were "Creating unique and interesting rhythms that are connected with reality".

The interviewer also said, that in Japan, "fans are waiting for you like they are waiting for a hero". Mick's response was "We're not Heroes. We want people to know what we have experienced through our music, but we don't want them to overrate it" He added, "The Clash is just a band, above all we want them to dance to our songs and enjoy them".

The writer also brought up the criticism from the UK Press, and was it because they toured and recorded in the States, and that the English were jealous? Mick replied by saying that he didn't feel that they had been in the States as long as they thought, and that they were still an English band. Mick was also asked why they were recording in New York. It was revealed that because after the Bonds shows and the Don Letts documentary over running, they decided to stay in New York until filming finished and record the album there.

When asked about the tour of Japan, and the problems of the venues (sit down only), Mick explained that he was really looking forward to it, and when in Japan he wanted to go on the bullet train. As mentioned earlier, he got his wish! The same writer interviewed Paul Simonon, and was asked about The Clash members loving films, and that Paul looked like James Dean. Paul preferring Marlon Brando, who could play different roles well. Paul also commented that he liked the actors in "*The Harder They Come*" and "*Taxi Driver*", and that he sympathized with them. Would Paul be interested in starring in a movie? "Yeah I would be interested; a movie is a very powerful tool to communicate, like Rock and Roll".

After the shows in Japan, the audiences did not want to leave after the band had finished.

At this stage, the *Combat Rock* album was not released. In Japan, journalist Yuji Konno was trying to get an interview with Joe. (Konno, 1982). He had been following him closely, and after a number of aborted attempts, finally got an opportunity. Joe seemed evasive about the album, suggesting that maybe they went for a beer before going any further. Joe talked about who was on the album, and he mentioned Paul Shrader alongside Tymon Dogg and Ellen Foley. This was a reference to the "*Taxi Driver*" speech that Kosmo reads in *Red Angel Dragnet*. Joe added that they hadn't properly asked him for permission to use it, and wouldn't be surprised if he sued them. Ironic then, that they did later face legal action over some of the content of *Combat Rock*. He also added that it was 99% completed, and took about three months to record. The title was going to be *Rat Patrol From Fort Bragg*. It would include a 12" rap version (of what was not specified) and that it was produced by themselves, Jeremy Green and engineer Joe Blaney. In Japan, the tour was called *Rat Patrol*.

I am deeply grateful to Akito Watanabe, guitarist in Japanese band The Strummers www.thestrummers.com who took considerable time to answer some questions for me about the Japanese dates and *Combat Rock*. Watanabe attended three of the shows at Nakano Sun Plaza in Tokyo, which unlike other venues The Clash played at remains standing today, not demolished shortly after their appearance! The shows and tour had been announced on News6 TV channel, and information was also made available on radio programs and then newspapers confirmed the schedule.

Watanabe attended 27th, 29th January and 1st February. Remembering the shows vividly, he recalled his body "trembling" before the curtain was raised. He had been waiting so long for The Clash to visit Japan, but missed the opening night. There was a Live review of the show on 24th January in the evening edition of a Tokyo Newspaper. He also talked about the issue of playing a seated venue, and that being allowed to stand on your seats was a compromise for both sides, The Clash and the "traditional way". There were no unseated venues in Japan that would be able to support the demand. He also remembered that his and other eyes were "glued to every move of the performance", and that the venue became "one". The band were "full of energy and charisma". Of the performance, he remembered Mick bouncing across the stage, Paul looking "cool and earnest"! and Topper playing happily. During one of the shows, he recalled that Joe's voice "collapsed" because of the overburdening schedule they were on. Everybody in the band sang a song, Joe and Mick obviously, with Paul taking *Guns of Brixton* and Topper breezing through *Ivan Meets GI Joe*. Watanabe and his companions had also got to hear the "disturbing" rumours about Topper and drug problems, and the conflicts between Mick and Joe. On the night of the 27th show, Watanabe remembered that the set list was good, and he was sitting right in front of Paul Simonon, who was "cool, with sunken cheeks and athletic long legs" The band played *Know Your Rights* and *Should I Stay or Should I Go* from "The forthcoming album, still to be *Rat Patrol* at that point.

At the second Osaka show, the support band was a local band called Anarchy who had recorded *White Riot / Londons Burning* (as *Tokyo's Burning*") and *Safe European Home* with their own Japanese lyrics. The lead singer Nakano was "moved" by Joe and how powerful and strong he was as a singer but offstage was "sweet and gentle". Joe apparently had come up with some theories of CIA involvement in the deaths of Bruce Lee and Bob Marley. Some fans thought that The Clash had stolen one of Anarchy's songs, when they played *London's Burning*... as *Tokyo's Burning*".

In *Redemption Song* (Salewicz, 2006) Kosmo recounted that he caught Mick and Joe arguing over the new album while they were in Japan, and told them both to get out and see the city. Pennie Smith had travelled to Tokyo to take band photos for the *NME*. She visited Joe in his room as he tried to stuff a mountain of gifts from fans into plastic bags, not wishing to leave anything behind. This included his samurai sword picture in the incredible shot printed in the Christmas *NME* 1982.

In the Sounds article, Minakami had noted that Joe treated Kids "kindly and warmly", and that they gave the band presents all the time. Joe was as Minakami put it "Not ready for this", and had apparently started crying and turned to face a wall when a girl gave him a present at Tokyo station. Joe apparently also bought a new suitcase and filled it with letters and gifts from the fans and had it shipped back to London.

Looking at the tour pictures in *The Clash 1982 Japan* (Konno, 1982) you can see that the band are taken with the Japanese culture, visiting the Temples and gardens. There are some beautiful black and white shots of the band. I remember visiting the Joe Strummer / Julian Newal exhibition back in September 2004 and reading some of the letters from Japanese fans on display there. There was also a photograph of Mick and Joe at the window of a Bullet Train carriage. The picture was on show again at the Black Market Clash Pop Up Shop in London.

In The *Clash in Japan* article, Minakami wrote about how the band had visited the old city Kyoto (Complete with their "ghetto blasters"). Pearl and Paul apparently disappeared into a small shrine "for lovers who wanted to get married". Joe was stunned by some of the culture, and had stood for ten minutes on one of the stages that the Noh Plays (Musical Dramas) had been performed on. Perhaps he was contemplating the band's own musical dramas, past, present and future. A visit to a fortune teller presented Joe with a warning to keep away from "women who would bring him misfortune". The writer also mentioned that they stopped at a "sword shop" and that Kosmo bought "many knives" for his friends. At one of the gardens they visited, apparently one of the roadies had said "it's a long way from Ladbroke Grove". Minikami introduced Joe to the works of Yukio Moshima via a couple of paperback books . The author had killed himself, and had "right wing" views, and Minakami felt that maybe that had connected with Joe and his elder brother who had committed suicide and was a National Front member.

In between the Japan dates and travelling to New Zealand, on what was supposed to be a rest day, the band flew to Sydney for a Press conference to drum up business for the Australian dates. The Sydney press show was according to *Rolling Stone* (St John, 1982) a "real occasion" The band arrived forty five minutes late while they were en route from Tokyo to Auckland. And in usual Clash Style, it took place in the Mammals Department of Sydney Museum. They were due on a plane again in two hours time. Joe appeared with greased back hair, and according to Rolling Stone, "shirt opened to the waist" and saying "ullo ullo… sorry we're late, how are you all?" According to Elder and St John, they may not have sounded like the Rolling Stones, but they certainly looked like them! Joe was a young Mick Jagger, Mick was like Keith Richards. Topper and Paul fitting in the "mould" set by Bill Wyman and Charlie Watts.

Amusingly, Joe was asked about the state of English music at the time, and him commenting that "It's just posing, most of its coming from 500 years ago judging by the clothes" and that The Clash weren't "University Professors like The Gang Of Four, all plum in mouth preaching".

When talking about the forthcoming album, he stated that "We're going to deliver an album that those suckers at CBS won't even suss". And as we shall see later, to coin a phrase "Result!!"So they will serve it up with their Boston and Foreigner." Over the next half hour, Joe largely took over and talked about Tasmania, Linton Kwesi Johnson, RAR and the Brixton Riots.

In a newspaper article in the *Sydney Daily* "Four rude boys who like to Clash" (Molloy, 1982),the author had them down as a "Punk Band from Brixton" who once starred in a film called *Rude Boy*, and that they proved to be rude "one must also be loud, aggressive and hyperactive". Molloy also went on to add that "Australia certainly had nothing like these boys". Joe apparently spat on the floor of the museum, "then mopped it up with his "cravat""…I think they meant his bandana, unless Joe had secretly become Noel Coward on the flight over. A fairly scathing article which ended with "the band likes to think of itself as one of the last rock and roll outlaws, but yes they are in it for the money".

In The *Clash Shock* article in *Roadrunner* magazine (Unknown, 1982), the conference is presented in question and answer form. The band were asked if they want to make a lot of money, to which the reply is that they want to make money so they can keep going. Next they were asked if their albums make money, to which Joe replies, "The *Sandinista* thing, we'll never do that again." When asked why it had been called *Sandinista* and was there a reason, the reply was that, "We could have called it Furry Underpants; we wanted to draw attention to the fact." Joe also added that "Really I'd like to call the next one El Salvador, but I won't because we got left on the back of the shelf." He then went on to recount the story of trying to get a copy of *Sandinista* in New York for the studio Tape Op, and that he couldn't find a copy unless he went to a rare record shop and paid over the top for it. The band were questioned about the Central American theme (Sandinista), and despite the El Salvador comment, it was announced that the album would be called *Rat Patrol From Fort Bragg*.

His next comment had importance for later issues with the Record Company and the release of *Combat Rock*. He saw *Sandinista* as "Cassette Technology", and that if you didn't like a bit, you left it behind. You taped the bits you liked and "went dancing in the park all night", and that nobody got the idea. So fast forward to the mid 2000's, and we are in the iTunes / YouTube download age, same applies.

When asked about the new album, Joe replied with "It's R.O.C.K, it's not a load of bananas, like a red banana, a green banana, it's trying to be the same banana without being boring." He also added that they were trying to "boil it down", trying to "shuffle through the pack, we're trying to discover one card from the pack." The band were also asked when they would finish the new album, to which the reply came "I think we're going to finish it here, next week, a rush job… right!"

Mick was asked about "those romantic songs" he wrote for Ellen Foley's album, and why he never wrote "those sort of things" for your own album. Mick replied that they had tried songs like *Spanish Bombs* and *Lovers Rock*, and that they were pretty romantic. He added that he was willing to try, but that "everyone was putting us down in England for doing that".

Joe laid out a two part plan for the band. Part one was to produce a more AOR friendly album (which must have upset Mick somewhat), and to promote it hard and allow them to break as an International Act. At the same conference in the NME (Reines, 1982) it was reported that Joe was presenting a "business lecture", and that to make money in rock and roll, you have to play a large auditorium and have all your expenses in one night. The Clash however, play seven nights in small halls, because "We believe that to rock, it's got to be close like theatre, you've got to be able to see my face".

Also saying that if they wanted to make money, he'd go to the Budokan like Bob Dylan did, where you get 30,000 people coughing up thousands of yen, and all you have to do is stand there for an hour, then piss off to the airport, "Stuff the money in the plane, and bingo, there you have rock and roll!"

In the same *Tropic of Clash* article (Reines, 1982) more was revealed about the progress of the album. He talked about "punk" and how he liked the "aggro" that goes with that name. Reines also talked about how The Clash had been ensconced in Electric Lady Studios recording their fifth album provisionally entitled *Rat Patrol from Fort Bragg*.

In an Australian Newspaper article in the *Sydney Morning Daily* (Crosthwaite, 1982), Joe was reported as saying "I don't even know why we're here", and that they didn't "need our message", and famously, "you all just go down to Bondi Beach, look at the topless birds and drink beer in the sun" (based as the reporter noted, "after only two hours in the country". Crosthwaite also mentioned that it is pretty much a "one man show" from Strummer. "Dressed in army camouflage battle jacket, tight jeans and combat boots" and that "he raved like an electioneering politician". As the conference went on the other band members "looked on in jet lagged wonder". From a small article in the same newspaper the previous day, it seems that the choice of venue was a fairly last minute one, as they were to have held the conference in The Liberal Party Headquarters located in Anchor House. In an internal memo from the Head of Community Relations in the Museum, there was some concern that there was some doubt over the value of the "exercise", when the total time to arrange the event was taken into consideration. The objective for the museum it appeared was to "enhance their image as a lively place for the young". And that the "Intention all along was that they should be interviewed in a place which clashed with their image of rude, aggressive people". The author noted that the museum was a "quiet, refined place".

Again from *Rolling Stone*, the writers reported that with "Joe Strummers performance over" the band posed for photographers, and that the performance itself had been an "immensely amusing one", and a "holy rollin one man stand up political flag waving harangue" and that if Joe could deliver one tenth as good live on stage, it would be the performance to leave the others "flat footed".

On entering New Zealand, the band spent four hours at immigration and customs at Auckland Airport. This was a result, in all probability of the recent Topper drugs bust. In the *Rolling Stone* article *The Clash want to be Number One* (McSporran, 1982), Joe was quoted as saying "Obviously we were clean, man. We'd just come from Japan and there is no dope in Japan".

In the same Rolling Stone article, the writer talked about criticism by UK journalists because of their "apparent desire" to crack the American market, rather than continue to thrive in Britain and how their "fall from favour" was assured when the riots they had foreseen years earlier exploded in their absence".

Mc Sporran also talked about the intensified demand for The Clash to tour there since the release of *London Calling*, and that tickets for the initially only two shows had sold very quickly with minimal advertising. After talking to Joe about the audiences and how he was concerned about how he hated the fact that there were people with no money who want to get in to the show. Perhaps McSporran's statement summed up the criticism, that this concern "was hardly the portrait of a man who has sold his soul". Joe felt that the biggest criticism you could level at The Clash was that "we haven't sold eight million records yet, and we should have done that by now." He also made the point that "we want to be as big as any other group there has ever been. Our music is better than most of the crap that's being played and we're determined to raise the level". The writer asked Joe if the British music press who had turned on them were as politically committed as they were, or did he see them as a bunch of jealous writers who want to become pop stars? To which Joe replied "yeah to the second part".

As a final question, Joe was asked why they were going to Australia, and was there significance in the decision to mix the album there. The answer came back that it was just a place on their tour, and it was the only place they could book time early enough to get the album out in April. During the interview, Mick played six tracks from the new album, provisionally called *Rat Patrol From Fort Bragg*. So these would have been his original mixes, not the final Glyn Johns versions. The article also told of how despite jet lag and exhaustion, Joe was up early the next day in New Zealand, checking out the local area until 9am when the shops opened. He bought a four string guitar ukulele for $35 and started busking on the main street, chatting and questioning locals on the events and culture. This baffled McSporran somewhat, wondering why Joe didn't sleep until the afternoon, and if he must tour the city, why not in a "cocaine breathing limousine"? There were also reports of Joe hitchhiking to different locations in the city.

You can catch a TV Interview with band on YouTube, with a very relaxed looking Clash, apart from Topper, who seems distracted. Joe and Mick are singing while Joe plays his newly purchased ukulele with songbook. Significantly, or is it? They are filmed at a train station on a platform. Joe told the camera, "You can make life easy for yourself and not bother with it, but we're not very good at that, never have been". He also said "We keep going because we are the real McCoy, we're not going to fold up and in a few weeks you wonder what that was all about". Topper got up and announced "I've got to go sunbathing"

The dates are remembered by many people to this day. One of the audience at an Auckland show described it as "being like Beatlemania"

There was another press conference held in Wellington, where the issue of violence at Clash shows was brought up, and in the McSporran article in *Rolling Stone*, the tour promoter Stuart McPherson described an incident at one of the Auckland shows which impressed him on the ability of the band to diffuse "volatile situations" and that "The Clash is the most genuinely concerned of all bands I have seen".

Topper spoke about his production work with New York band Bush Tetras, and after investigating a little further, I found 4 tracks on a band compilation album for which he received a producer credit. Mick was questioned about the "failure" of the Ellen Foley album he had produced. Joe it appears then split off from the main questioning and chatted and gave journalists a performance on his recently purchased Ukulele.

A significant comment made by McSporran , was that he believed "one thing is for certain, Joe Strummer calls the shots". Up early each day, "Joe walked the streets making notes, pushing messages under peoples doors with instructions and observations about the shows that needed to be attended to". He went on to say, that "his overview is complete right down to the last detail and nobody challenging it".

In a review of one of the shows at the Logan Campbell Centre (reported as their sole NZ concert) for the book *The Greatest Rock Gigs of New Zealand* (Cartwright, 1982) reported that The Clash were touring *Sandinista*, a triple album that found them "playing everything but rock and roll." Cartwright also remarked that they played so quietly, you could have a chat, and that they were wearing colour coded sleeveless outfits resembling more a camp dance troupe than radical rockers. Less than complimentary about the whole affair, like other reports, it seems that the band were expected to be the same full on confrontation they were back in '76 / 77. Just for arguments sake, when I looked at the set list for the night, indeed, 6 tracks were from *Sandinista*, three from *The Clash*, two from *Give 'Em Enough Rope*, five non album singles and... eight tracks from *London Calling*, and an airing of *Radio Clash*.

It must have been frustrating for the band, who had new material to air, but having to not disappoint audiences by not playing "the old Stuff". Had *Combat Rock* been finished and released prior to the tour, perhaps the reaction would have been different.

In an interview with Mick entitled *Jones In Vain* (Campbell, 1982) writer Duncan Campbell wrote that nobody really knew what to expect from The Clash, the British music press had "recently branded them as boring" and that there were scathing reviews which talked of meandering relentless dub sessions". Were they going to see "a once great band in its death throes?". He added that "mature they may be, by their own standards, but you could never call them sophisticated".

When the conversation turned to *Sandinista*, Mick was keen to point out that "The Clash had discovered self-discipline since then, the next Clash album will be a single disc". Mick added that the new album would be more danceable, and the opening track would be entitled *Straight To Hell*. In the second part of the interview *Mick Jones part 2 - Politics* (Campbell, 1982). The writer talked about the press backlash led "naturally by the *NME*, who thought that The Clash had become pompous and had turned their backs on what was happening in their own country".

Again there is no real evidence of Topper presenting a problem for the band, as Campbell reported, "always present, and never losing his place, a backroom boy and therefore vital".

Two more dates were already booked, one in Auckland on 5th February, and Wellington on the 7th. The Australian dates were scheduled immediately after.

While in New Zealand, the band added an extra date to the tour. Reacting to a request and petition from Canterbury University students, via their Radio Station RADIO U. Largely inspired by a student, Michael Higgins, who was reported in *The Press*, Christchurch, (Unknown, 1982) "too many bands miss out the South Island, I am sure that a full house at the town hall would cover the cost of crossing Cook Straits". There were reports in *The Press* 6th February that the students had run up big bills in persuading the band to play. Phone calls to agents in the UK, New York and Japan. In the spirit of the benefit show, The Clash agreed via Kosmo to attend a party after the gig, and party goers would pay an entry fee, which would go towards the costs incurred.

In the *New Zealand Herald*, (Swift, 1982) David Swift wrote, "better leave town if you only want to knock us" and reported that the show was nearly stopped after the second song because of the "hail of gob" as Joe put it. Swift did mention the diversity of the crowd, and how they "rallied to the entertaining set from England's veterans of "new music". In the same review, it is Topper who stood out as the most impressive musician. This, despite the "Topper Situation", and how he seemed to have mastery of most styles.

After the New Zealand shows, the tour headed for Australia for a string of ten dates, including a seven night stint at the Capitol theatre in Sydney. In the press conference before hand, Joe was ranting "We're here because we are exciting. We jump about, wiggle our bums, and there's nothing wrong with that."

The Capitol Theatre was an art deco cinema which had a tin roof and was like being in an oven. Kosmo was quoted as saying (Salewicz, 2006), that they were "booked in to a posh hotel, The Kinks were also staying there and checking in at the same time. The Clash got kicked out, due to loud Charlie Parker music and Girls underwear?"

They shortly found a hotel in red light district. Joe had still stopped smoking weed and talked of getting himself fit for action. He began getting up at six, running and using the TV as weight lifting gear. Joe reportedly loved Australia, but was aware of a downside too.

Three "Aborigine guys" as Paul referred to them, asked him initially if they could come up on stage and talk about their situation. Joe agreed to this after he met them and it hit him The Clash had a certain power, because they could get these guys to talk to people who wouldn't normally pay attention to them.

Gary Foley was an aboriginal rights leader and at Sydney he came on stage to rap over a dubbed up version of *Armageddon Time*. After the show Gary went back to the hotel for drinks with Joe and Kosmo. The formally "chatty" bar staff served them but did not engage in conversation. Kosmo was later told that Aborigines "were like pigs mate".

At another show, an aboriginal dancer joined them on stage. He came back to the hotel for dinner, but upset the staff. He then got a phone call to say that his house had been smashed up during his on stage appearance.

The Australian shows were reportedly quite "heavy", over enthusiastic security guards and heavy police presence with mean looking dogs. In *Juke Magazine* (Manning, 1982), Joe had stated that "We play for about 2 hours, and we do everything", and as Manning reported, they were true to their word. He also added that "It might have been the 'peoples band' inside, but outside it was the same old story, security men hassling people about their dress". The shows were dubbed "The Magnificent Seven Evenings". Manning wrote how the band "strode"… not walked on stage… looking more "Rock and Roll" than The Stones! There were fights to be broken up, and the backdrop was mainly slides of scenes from New York Clubland, to the battles of South America and Cambodia. Manning wrapped up by adding "music still matters because we have people like this around".

Searching the internet, I came across this eyewitness account from "Greg", who also included a most impressive picture of Joe looking bloodied.

www.hikingfiasco.com/2014/02/kirin-j-callinan-st-jeromes-laneway.html

"If I think back to great concerts I've seen, then The Clash is tops", said Greg. "They played at the sweat-pit of Festival Hall in summer, they played full throttle, with barely anything on stage and certainly no freak wandering on to switch instruments. Hell, a brawl started in the crowd at the front, so what did Joe Strummer do? Well, he hopped into the crowd of course and broke it up. When he clambered back, his shirt was covered in blood. It was beyond epic."

One of the other Clash shows was at Cloudland in Brisbane, and immortalized in *Cloudland – Queen of The Dance Halls* (Lergessner, 2013) The author recalled that the show on 28th February was one of the last concerts at the venue. The band again took the opportunity to allow aborigine rights activists to take the stage, and Legessner wrote that "I was almost ashamed to be Australian on that night". The speaker was booed off stage, and Joe was angry and shouted at the audience in his defence. Lergessner also added that the band had exposed him to a whole new world of music, with bands being influenced by them in the inner city areas of Sydney.

In the local newspaper the *Courier Mail* (Walker, 1982), reviewing the same show, felt that The Clash "may have failed to win many converts to their explicit working class politics, but the four angry young men succeeded in staging a powerful rock show". And that the band kept the audience on its toes for a full two and a quarter hours. Describing the atmosphere as "electric" the moment the band walked out on stage. The writer also noticed that "unlike other bands who played in Brisbane, The Clash show was "devoid of gimmicks, no laser lights or special effects", and that "they carried the night on the strength of the music". Walker also felt that to appreciate the band fully, it was necessary to listen to the lyrics, and "that while the music was appreciated by the big crowd, the lyrics went unheard let alone understood by most".

Under pressure from the record company, the band had agreed to work on the album mix after the shows. But their ears were ringing from the shows and nothing sounded right. After a couple of nights of this, it was abandoned. In a "political move" The Clash had dinner with Paul Russell, MD of CBS Australia, who later replaced the then UK CBS MD Maurice Oberstein.

With the Australian dates over, it was time to move on to Hong Kong for a one night show at the AC Hall. In *Redemption Song* (Salewicz, 2006), it seemed that Pennie Smith rejoined The Clash posse to start working on photographs that could be used on the new album cover.

According to the author, the Hong Kong show on 25th February was marred by a "mass scrap" between Chinese and ex pat Britons, which caused Joe to stop the show twice. Joe allegedly threatened to do "Kung Fu" with some warring elements in the crowd. From the live recording, tastefully entitled *Hong Kong Dollar – Indian Cents*, the audience got a blasting of material from all of the released albums, plus *Know Your Rights*. The show was broadcast on the radio, and the track listing is likely to be incomplete. But certainly *Know Your Rights* is an interesting full on version with that fabulous Mick Rockabilly Echo Guitar. Topper took vocal duties on *Ivan Meets GI Joe*, solid as a rock.

According to The Big O website, accessed February 2014, www.bigozine2.com/archive/ARrarities06/ARclashhk.html The audience was about 1,200, and apparently, after the show a promoter commented "I think there was a stink about the concert afterwards and rock and roll was subsequently banned from that venue…"

In the Mojo article *Who Killed The Clash* (Snow, 2008), Kosmo remembered that even though a huge fan of Bruce Lee, Topper at this point could not be bothered to go and visit the place where "his idol had done his thing".

The final show of the Far East Tour was a short hop to Thailand, and show at Thammasat University in Thailand on the 27th. There seems to be some discrepancy over when the band arrived, the show was 27th February. In *Redemption Song*, the author wrote that they arrived in Bangkok on 23rd March, and were told by one of the promoters that *Radio Clash* was number one in the charts! The venue was an old cinema, according to *Redemption Song*, and rather than play the mighty Morricone theme before the start, the band were obliged to stand to attention while the National Anthem was played. The show was a "resounding success" in *Redemption Song*, with the crowd rushing the stage three songs in to the set.

In the sleeve notes included in *The Story Of The Clash* (written by "Albert Transom") Kosmo mentioned that "He" had spent the gig doubled up laughing behind a black curtain with his hand over his mouth because of the sight of all those blokes in turbans doing the pogo.

After a seemingly endless internet trawl, I managed to locate a person who was actually at the Thailand show. His name is Rusty Deluce, now a film cameraman and author based in Canada. www.rustydeluce.com/ Rusty very kindly answered my questions, for which I am most grateful, as little has been recorded of the show itself. Rusty was travelling after graduating from Queens

University in Canada, with his best friend. After travelling from India, they landed in Bangkok, pretty exhausted. Rusty picked up a copy of *Bangkok This Week* while waiting for his luggage. Skimming through the city listings, he found to his utter disbelief, "The Clash Appearing Live at Thammasat University Auditorium Feb 27th at 7:30. Tickets at Door".

Rusty ran back to his companion, pointing at the advert, and declaring that they had to get their tickets right now for the show, as he was convinced it would be sold out. Having no idea the band were touring, it was an opportunity not to be missed. He felt it was an unusual choice of venue for a band with a "more subversive appeal". Rusty had yet to see The Clash live, the band having pulled out of a festival in Toronto in 1980. A fan of the *London Calling* album and now intoxicated with *Sandinista*. It was as Rusty described it "A rich generous gift to music fans everywhere and at a bargain price".

He saw no other promotion for the show, and as he said "none needed". Like Joe and Kosmo, Rusty sampled the delights of a "Girlie Bar" in Patpong. The pair made a long trek to the Thammasat University Campus to get tickets for the show, then some days away, stopping people that they came across them, pleading for information about the location of the auditorium, and had the show sold out?. Finally they happened across an English speaking Professor who told them it was not necessary to buy tickets. Fearing the worst, Rusty was told that tickets could be bought on the night... the classic "Clash Walkup", even in Thailand!

As Rusty's travelling companion had already experienced a potentially life threatening incident at the "Girlie Bar", he decided against taking a camera with him to the show and look like a "Silly Tourist". The entry fee was about $5 US; I'm loving this... $5 and pay at the door!! Rusty only noticed a few "Westerners" in the audience, which he recalled were mainly "young, local and student". He recalled a somewhat shaky start as trouble broke out at the front of the stage. The music was stopped and Joe was particularly "pissed off". Unsure of the songs and some of the material being played, he recalled *Train In Vain* and *London Calling* and that both the band and audience settled down. Behind the band, a number of screens displayed pictures of the Vietnam War. And as others had noted, there were no "stage gimmicks", and no sign of any security staff or police. The highlight of the set for Rusty was *Armagideon Time*. As the show ended, they took the bus across town to the Hostel they were staying at. The journey was shared with another "Westerner" who proudly held up a backstage pass, and announced that he had been backstage with the band.

As Rusty pointed out, "It appears that Bangkok was a fork in the road for The Clash" as it seems that Rusty's own "Far East Tour" was also a turning point for him, as after further travels it led to a career in "Gold Smuggling" and later a career as a cameraman in the motion picture industry.

After the show, there was the opportunity for the band to take a "holiday" of sorts. There was still a photo shoot to do for the album with Pennie Smith. Topper was experiencing withdrawal symptoms. He had started using heroin again in Australia and wanted to get back to London as soon as possible. In *Redemption Song* (Salewicz, 2006) the author explained that they found a hotel complex to stay in outside the city. The photo session was scheduled for the morning after the Bangkok show. Topper had been booked on the next flight to London. Pennie Smith was widely quoted as seeing the band "dissolve in front of her eyes" and that she felt that she was taking pictures of a new band. There were some "snipes aimed at Topper".

The band went on a visit to The Bridge Over the River Kwai, and some of the pictures can be seen in the Mojo Magazine article *Who Killed The Clash* (Snow, 2008). Admiring The Clash sense of adventure, Pennie Smith mentioned the fact that wherever they went, they always liked to explore, and that while in Thailand they did go to some dodgy places.

It was here that another blow was dealt to the band, in the form of an unknown "lurg" as Pennie put it. Paul Simonon contracted an unknown sickness, possibly from dodgy street food, which he bought while out with Pearl Harbour, or from stepping into some pretty rank puddle filled with flies. The following day, whatever the cause, he was in the hospital in some agony. In *Redemption Song*, the author wrote that the diagnosis was a twisted colon, for which emergency surgery was prescribed. It did however prove to be some sort of food poisoning. Joe attended Paul's bedside with accompanying Buddhist monks who he asked to pray for Paul, but actually spent the time using the shower and facilities.

In *"The Future is Unwritten"* film (Temple, 2007), Kosmo explained that he and Joe went to a nightclub at Patapong Road in Bangkok, where they danced on tables and with the "girls" eventually being thrown out. Some evidence of this trip was captured in the lens of Pennie Smith in the NME Article *Tropic Of The Clash* (Reines, 1982)

As the band returned to the UK in March 1982, it was time to continue work on the still unfinished album… just as the Falklands war with Argentina kicked off.

Again from *Redemption Song*, it appears that after a meeting with Muff Winwood at CBS Records, it was decided that Glyn Johns would be brought in to remix the album. It seems that only Bernie and Joe attended the meeting.

As the month went by, a single from the forthcoming album was selected for release and penned in for 27th April 1982. Work was still going on to complete the album. A UK Tour had been announced to promote the single and forthcoming album, *The Know Your Rights Tour*.

The album should have been released to tie in, but was still unfinished. In the NME dated 17th April, there was an advertisement from Mead Gould Productions, who were offering an inclusive Coach Trip deal to Europe, where The Clash were scheduled to appear at the Lochem Festival on May 20th.

In NME News Pages April 3rd (Unknown, 1982) The UK tour was announced under a sub headline "Know Rights to miss The Clash Tour", where it was reported that the band had chosen the New Fair Deal Venue in Brixton for the culmination of the 19 date UK tour. The *Know Your Rights* single was to be released on 23rd April, and that the tour would be billed as *Know Your Rights*. Ticket prices were set at £3 and a maximum of £4.50 (Those were the days!!)

Support band would be Pearl Harbour, and that the album release date was to be announced the following week, provisionally entitled *Rat Patrol From Fort Bragg*.

The *Know Your Rights* single was reviewed in the NME 24th April (Du-Noyer, 1982), there were small adverts for the single, one ironically alongside a Levi's advert, the other listing the UK tour dates. In the same issue, the Nationwide Gig Guide listed the dates again, and mentioned that The Clash had a new single and Album to promote. As the tour dates loomed, the band were in rehearsals for the shows, and then, another calamity hit The Clash. Joe Strummer went missing!

Depending on which of the varying accounts you read, the AWOL episode may have been instigated initially by Bernie. Believed to be a "panic move" on the part of Bernie, who felt that the ticket sales for the forthcoming tour were not going particularly well. The reaction was that they had to do something to create some publicity. Joe would later go on to point out that the band had what was known as a "Walk up". People would just turn up on the night and pay to get in. Me personally, I'm all for this, no booking fees a year in advance, crazy prices?? (But I digress.)

In *The Clash – The Only Band That Mattered*, Egan took a darker view about the UK tour, and how interest in the band had declined in their home country, and Joe had staged his disappearance to drum up ticket sales.

The *Know Your Rights* tour was due to kick off in Aberdeen. In *"The Future is Unwritten"* (Temple, 2007), Kosmo recalled having a "very private meeting" with Joe, and that Joe was to disappear, and then he was to come back. It meant that Kosmo had to "deceive the group". Mick, Paul and Topper were not aware of either the Bernie Plan, or the revised Joe Plan! He added that Bernie felt that the audience were taking Joe for granted, so he was going to take him away from them, and then wouldn't have him, and they would know what it was like.

According to *Redemption Song* (Salewicz, 2006) Bernie had suggested that Joe go and stay with Joe Ely in the US, that he should go alone, and call him every day. It seems that Joe had an alternative plan.

Now in 1982, Joe was not alone in the "Front Man Disappears" headlines. In February 1982, Jaz Coleman from Killing Joke went AWOL just as the band were going to release their new album "Revelations". The motivation behind Jaz Coleman's disappearance was a little different, as he believed the world was heading for an apocalypse and that only Iceland would be spared. I can clearly remember Killing Joke appearing on TV on Riverside Studios playing *Chop Chop* and *Empire Song* with a dummy propped up at the keyboard. This would never have worked for The Clash!

In *Smash Hits* Bitz pages (Uncredited, 1982) it was also mentioned that Geordie the Killing Joke guitarist had upped and followed Jaz to Iceland a little while after. So what would the outcome have been if The Clash had lost both Joe and Mick in disappearing acts?

Mick had mentioned on Joe's return, that he wished perhaps he had done it too, but it had already been done by Joe, so there was no real point.

In *Post Punk Diary 1980-82* (Gimarc, 1997), the author remarked "Clash lead singer missing? Has he gone to Iceland to await the end of the world like Killing Joke singer Jaz Coleman?" and asked the question, "did he know something we 'mere mortals' didn't?"

Joe failed to turn up to rehearsals for the tour, and concerns were raised as to his whereabouts. According to press releases which appeared, he was reported missing on 21st April.

In *Passion is a Fashion* (Gilbert, 2004), the author reported that Joe had in effect double crossed Bernie and Kosmo. High on the list of issues were Topper and his worsening drug addiction, and the "fall out" with Mick over *Combat Rock*. Gilbert also wrote that a few days before he did vanish, he went to see Alex Michon (Clash Clothes designer) who said that Joe was really depressed and had talked about not going on.

In the Melody Maker News pages dated 1st May 1982 (Unknown, 1982), Joe was reported missing, "Just days before The Clash Tour officially started. The Band were due to play a 'secret' gig in Aberdeen on Sunday, and another at Inverness on Monday". The article then went on to issue an official appeal from the "Clash Office", asking for information about his whereabouts, and a phone number to ring.

In the same edition of the NME under the sub-line "Clash Mystery – Joe Goes Missing" (Unknown, 1982) The paper reported that the first two dates of the tour had been cancelled because Joe Strummer had gone missing, and that the remaining 18 dates of the tour were in jeopardy.

Bernie issued a statement along the lines that Joe had probably gone away for a serious rethink, and that "Joe's personal conflict is, where does the socially concerned rock artist stand in the bubblegum environment of today".

In *Joe Strummer and the Legend of The Clash* (Needs, 2005), the author remembered that Joe had "1 May…Take a Holiday!" written on one of his guitars, and "on the eve of the 19 date tour… he took it". There is I have to say some dispute here over whether it meant "The First of May… Take a Holiday" after the traditional International workers day, or "I may ….take a holiday". Whatever the meaning…Joe went!

Needs also quoted Bernie as saying "A lot of people want to destroy this band", but we won't let that happen, because we are an international group" Joe had last been seen the previous Wednesday when he had done a telephone interview with a Scottish Newspaper. There was even an appeal from a desperate Bernie, "Please can you help us?"

In the *NME* issue, Bernie was quoted as saying "We need the help of people to find Joe, we are all concerned about it, but I think he will be back once he gets wind of how important it is". Bernie added that he thought Joe had gone away to "examine what it is all about", and that he had "not gone religious or taken drugs or anything like that".

It seems that Bernie did seem to know more about the disappearance than you might expect, as he added that Joe felt resentment about the fact that he was slogging his guts out, just for people to "slag him off for wearing the wrong trousers".

And in true Bernie style, he added that "We've got to find the bloke. He'll get a bollocking when he comes back, but it's still better he comes back".

Interestingly, in the same issue of the *NME* was a "STOP PRESS" report from a journalist for The Face Style magazine, Steve Taylor, who revealed that he shared a compartment with Joe on a boat train to Paris, "Looking tired, wearing shades, travelling light, and consulting a cheap paperback guide to Paris".

In *Joe Strummer and the Legend of The Clash*, Kris Needs reported that Joe had "Seen a bloke reading the NME, but thought he took no notice".

In the *Melody Maker* the following week 8th May (Harrington, 1982) "The Clash…have you seen this tour?" It was reported that the band had been forced to cancel the first half of the tour, and that Strummer was still missing, and the band had no information on his whereabouts, apart from unverifiable sightings. Kris Needs wrote about some of the rumours, "Living in Amsterdam, found dead in a Scottish river, and going off to Darkest Africa".

The NME also dated 8th May has news headline "Clash Postpone Dates – Bring Me The Guitar of Joe Strummer" (Unknown, 1982c).

Here it reported that a "question mark' hung over the tour dates until Strummer puts in an appearance, and that there had been reported sightings of him in Paris, Scotland and even the Portobello Road in London. On this occasion, Paul Simonon was quoted. "Having known Joe for so long, I have faith that he'll return once he has reassessed the situation". Kosmo put in the final word, "Christ knows what will happen if he is still missing in July".

In *The Future is Unwritten* (Temple, 2007) Kosmo explained a little more saying that "This was really heavy, there was BIG money at stake with US promoters and a long forthcoming tour of the US", which became the *Casbah Club* US Tour. He also added that Bernie was agitated and that he had to tell the rest of the band that the situation was serious, "it could be the end… poverty to all". The issue was over the heavy cancellation penalty fees if the tours of the UK and US had to be abandoned.

The following week 15th May (Clerk, 1982) *Melody Maker* reported that with only three dates of The Clash tour left, Joe was still missing, and were unable to go any further with efforts to track him down. The tour was cancelled apart from three dates.

Topper was quoted "We've tried everything we can to find Joe. It looks like we'll have to wait for him to get in touch. We'll make it up to everyone when we do the shows in July".

In the same edition of *Melody Maker*, there was a full page advertisement for the *Combat Rock* album.

In the same week *NME* News Pages (Unknown, 1982) under the strap line "Still No Show Joe" it was reported that a further five dates had been cancelled, and that there had been no sightings of Joe in two weeks. The article also included the comments from Topper.

Also in this edition were full page adverts for the *Combat Rock* album, and an album review by X-Moore (more of this later).

Out the same week was the Mick Jones produced Theatre of Hate single *The Hop*.

When it got to 22nd May edition of *Melody Maker*, (Law, 1982) there was a rather piss taking article in their *Fat Lip* gossip column written by "Marshall Law", entitled *Not Just an Ordinary Joe* written in the style of a "wacky scientist", about a vision of the apocalypse leading Joe to disappear, and referring to Kosmo as "Kozmik Wino".

The *NME* in the same week, under the heading *Clash Blow Last Dates* (Unknown, 1982), it was reported that Joe was "on the point of return to the fold", but that the last three dates of the abandoned tour would be rescheduled. Kosmo reported that a private detective had been working on the case, and had located him. Kosmo was "last seen heading in the direction of Paris".

Joe's alternative plan had been to take the boat train to Paris, taking partner Gaby along too. He had apparently phoned his mother to tell her that he was fine, and was not to worry about him no matter what she heard. Joe was quoted in *Joe Strummer and the Legend of The Clash* as saying "I thought it would be a good joke if I didn't phone Bernie at all!"

In *Redemption Song*, Gaby related the story of how she had a friend who lived in Paris who had a flat they could stay in. Gaby was pick pocketed in Paris and lost her money and passport, at which point, Joe told her to go home, she had also talked to people in a restaurant and told them why she and Joe were there. Without her passport, she could not return.

In *Post Punk Diary* (Gimarc, 1997) The author mentioned a rumour that the disappearance allegedly started with the arrest in Paris of Gaby's mother, and that Joe had "bolted" out of the country to go and "lend aid in time of trouble". And that was the story "out on the Street". In the *Sten Guns in LA* article in Sounds (McCullough, 1982), Joe was asked about "The Runaway Attempt". Here Joe told McCullough that "I just got up and went", and that "My Girlfriends mother is in jail in France. So I had a personal reason to go there. It was a Bravado thing".

According to *Passion is a Fashion* (Gilbert, 2004) Joe even sent a postcard to Kit Butler who was working at CBS their record label.

As Salewicz again pointed out in *Redemption Song*, was Joe hiding from the pressure he was now under, probably angry about the worsening Topper drug situation and worried and fearful of the reception that the *Combat Rock* Album would receive on release?

Joe tried to disguise himself by growing a beard, and wearing an army jacket, as The Clash were well known in Paris, and as *Redemption Song* said, Joe and Gaby "immersed themselves in being Parisians for a few weeks" Getting some culture at the museums and art galleries, and in "up and at 'em style", Joe and Gaby both ran the Paris Marathon.

Interestingly, even the Paris Marathon story has been under the investigative spotlight. In August 2013, the Grantland.com website posted an article called "Did The Clash's Joe Strummer really run the Paris marathon?" In the article accessed October 14th 2014, the author, Michael Bertin cast some doubt about whether Joe and Gaby really did run in the marathon. The dispute is largely based on the "post marathon" picture that was taken by Richard Schroeder. The author does incorrectly state that Joe disappeared on the eve of the *Combat Rock* album release, he does recognize that neither Joe nor Gaby have competitor numbers on their t-shirts. Neither Joe nor Gaby appears on the finishing lists on the day. What name might Joe have used anyway? Richard Schroeder maintained that he was with Joe at the start of the marathon, and that Gaby dropped out after a few miles. They had decided to do the run after seeing some press on it a couple of days earlier and just did it.

grantland.com/the-triangle/did-the-clashs-joe-strummer-actually-run-the-paris-marathon/

And so, *Combat Rock* was released on the 14th May, but overshadowed by the fact that Joe was missing, and the UK dates to promote it were rapidly being cancelled. There was no tour, no Joe, and no news of his whereabouts… I can't imagine what was going on in the heads of the other band members, the record company, tour promoters and management. But it must have been a pretty uncomfortable time for all! In *The Rise and Fall of The Clash* (Garcia, 2012), Security Man Ray Jordan added "Joe went away a lot longer than anyone thought, it was a way of boosting tickets sales." He also rightly pointed out that "The Clash….It wasn't a church picnic!!"

As Kosmo was on his way to Paris, dressed by all accounts like an extra from a Rambo film, there were conflicting reports about how Joe was actually tracked down. According to Kris Needs, Kosmo was able to extract an address from Joe's Mum of his "Hideout!!"

Pat Gilbert had another version of events. The first lead to his whereabouts was in the first week of May. The band were booked to play at the Lochem Festival on 20th May. The promoter had been assured that Joe would play, but tickets sales were slow, because people didn't think the band would appear. A Dutch journalist and friend of the promoter mentioned that he had seen Joe in a bar in Paris. The promoter phoned Kosmo, and "The Game" as Sherlock would say…"was afoot". As Gilbert pointed out, Kosmo believed that Joe had to be found, otherwise "Everything The Clash had worked for would be gone".

There then followed the involvement of Gaby's brother Mark, who got a phone number of a girl who may know where Joe was, but she "freaked" when Kosmo rang her, and wouldn't tell him. Next a Private Detective was involved in getting an address for the girl (this may have only gone as far as him being able to get a trace on a phone number to a matching address).

Kosmo headed for Paris and the office where the girl worked, where he explained that he must see Joe. The girl gave in and told Kosmo to meet her at a Café later that day. He did, and in walked Joe beard and all.

In "*The Future is Unwritten*" (Temple, 2007) documentary, Kosmo gave his own version of events, explaining that he phoned a promoter he knew in Paris with the girls phone number, so that he could get an address. Kosmo got to Paris ala "*Full Metal Jacket*" met the Promoters assistant and headed for the office where the girl worked, bursting in, and saying he would be back with the police, and leaving his number.

Back at his hotel, the phone rang, it was Joe "Kos…it's Joe, how ya doing man", and arranged to meet at "so and so" at "like five o'clock". As Kosmo touchingly adds, "he walks in, and he has a huge beard, and I say "Fidel" and gave him a big hug".

As Joe returned to the fold, there was more trouble brewing. According to *Redemption Song*, Joe and Gaby were back in London in May 19th. When it was revealed to the rest of the band that Joe's disappearance had been a "Bernie scam", this certainly didn't help with the relationship particularly between Mick and Bernie.

One thing was very clear from the Joe disappearance, as Kris Needs pointed out in *Joe Strummer and the Legend of The Clash*. Joe showed how he could "shut down The Clash" and "he was able to force the issue". In *The Clash a Visual Documentary* (Miles/Tobler/Peachy, 1992) the authors pointed out that cynical record industry 'vets' saw Joes disappearance as a way to draw attention to the release of *Combat Rock*, but as the authors go on to say, this was unlikely, as with Joe unavailable, it meant no touring, or having to reschedule shows if he reappeared. Upon his return, there were calls for Joe to both explain and defend his actions.

The band were in a financial mess with unfulfilled UK dates and uncertainty about a forthcoming 23 date tour of the US which was due to start on May 29th.

There was also the issue of the booked festival appearance at Lochem in Holland. Despite the possible "no show" by the band, the date was to go ahead. The band still asked for their full fee even though the appearance had been "up in the air".

En route to the festival, the band stopped off in Amsterdam for an hour where they reportedly sampled the local coffee shops weed. In the *Q Classic Clash Magazine*, (Zanhorn, 1982) an article is reproduced by the Promoter of the festival.

Tickets had been on sales a month before the show, but word had gone around that Joe was missing. Ticket sales were very slow. By chance, Zanhorn was interviewed by a Dutch pop journalist who had seen Joe in a bar in Paris. The journalist was unaware that Joe was officially "missing". Zanhorn called Kosmo with the address of the bar, and Kosmo said that they would hire a Private Detective.

Zanhorn remembered the band arriving by bus, very late, and that they had picked up hitch hikers along the way, and were "absolutely out of their heads". There had only been 2-3 days notice publicly announced that The Clash would play. In true apocalyptic style, the weather was terrible; Zanhorn had been relying on the "walk up" to sell more tickets. After playing for half an hour, the show was stopped and the band demanded that Zanhorn stop the security people attacking The Clash fans. It was as he said a "Messy Situation".

The show restarted, and Joe invited the crowd on stage, fences were pushed down and according to Zanhorn, about 500 people got on stage, but even more dangerously, another 500 went under the stage to avoid the rain, thunder and lightning. The stage was in danger of collapsing, and the Dutch police wanted to intervene.

In a review in the *NME* 29th May (Sharr Murray, 1982) Charles Shaar Murray reported on the Lochem show, which included Bow Wow Wow, Tenpole Tudor and Saxon on the bill. He believed because of the appalling weather, and the skeptical crowd not believing The Clash would play, about half of the 16,000 crowd left after Saxon had played. He added that Strummer was "subdued", making no reference to his recent disappearance, but had "persuaded" the organisers to take down crowd barriers, which allowed fans to "swarm" into the press enclosure…

Zanhorne noticed a tension in the air between the band, adding that Topper looked pretty intoxicated before and after the show, but had been drumming pretty well. But he was "dead silent and stoned". Joe he remembered being "not stressed out…you know wired". He saw no interaction between the band and Topper when they walked off the stage.

Despite the problems, the promoter said that it was a great show, wild…but a financial disaster, as he believed he was "screwed" by the band for the full appearance fee.

The reality was that the band would need every penny, as they were potentially heading for financial ruin if more dates were cancelled, and commitments not met. In *Passion is a Fashion*, Gilbert backed this up by saying that the band needed the money to pay the cancellation fees on the aborted UK tour.

So, the actual show gave the festival goers a chance to hear three of the forthcoming *Combat Rock* tracks. From the Lochem Bootleg album, we got *Know Your Rights*, a quite different version from the album without the full on echo rockabilly guitar, and some interesting sound effects. Secondly, a version of *Ghetto Defendant*, without any guest vocals, and *Should I Stay or Should I Go*. Considering the chaos that was going on around them, the sound and performance is very good and no noticeable drumming problems. Ironically, one version of the Lochem Bootleg vinyl album has a certain "Tony Chimes" in the position of Drummer.

On returning from the Lochem festival, a meeting of the band plus Bernie was arranged at Paul Simonon's flat on the Saturday, the day after their return to London. In *Redemption Song*, Salewicz explained that Joe told Topper he was sacked, and that Mick was in tears, as was Topper. It appeared that Joe and Paul were in agreement. According to Topper in the same book, he was told that they had someone "waiting in the wings" to play on the upcoming US Tour. In the words of Salewicz, "It was beginning to feel like and extraordinary rock opera". In this account, it seems that Terry Chimes was already in waiting; as Topper went out for a walk, and came back with the suggestion that he go to the US with Terry as a backup. Topper was willing to go unpaid, and if anyone suspected him of taking drugs, he would go home. Nobody was willing to agree with this. An announcement was discussed, Topper suffering from nervous exhaustion, and Terry sitting in. It then seems again in this account that Topper was not being sacked, and if he got it together, he would be back in the band.

Topper claimed he tried to clean up, but read an interview where Joe had said categorically, that Topper had been sacked because he was a junkie. He then explained that he started injecting drugs, as he had nothing to live for.

It seems there was some contradictions from Toppers point of view, he maintained that everyone was pretty "fucked up", whether cocaine, drink or smoking huge amounts of dope. He also felt that Joe was anti-drugs, but did use them. Gaby recalled that Joe was anti cocaine, Topper maintained he did use it "principally for fuel to keep him going". In *Redemption song*, Topper was pretty honest about his state at the time, and that he felt Joe had no option other than to fire him. It could not have been dealt with in any other way. Topper felt that the stopover in Amsterdam was a "test", but he failed as he managed to get stoned there.

The decision did seem to come from Joe, possibly one of the many issues he had been mulling over while retreating to Paris. Later in *Redemption Song*, Salewicz added that the belief that Terry was waiting in the wings was incorrect, and that Terry only received "the call up" five days before the tour in the US was due to start.

In *Joe Strummer and the Legend of The Clash*, Kris Needs recounted a variation on the *Redemption Song* version. The band were present as were Bernie and Kosmo, and that Joe told Topper he was sacked, and when he laughed, Joe said it again. According to Pat Gilbert in *Passion is a Fashion* at the meeting, it was Toppers behavior that meant he was in no condition to do the tour of the US. There had been an incident in a dressing room where Joe was in front of a full length mirror, and Topper came in and asked if he minded… and proceeded to lie it on the floor and dump a load of cocaine on it.

At this point there was another twist in the balance of power within the group. Joe seemed to be calling the shots now, He had already shown that the group could not do without him, and he couldn't work with Topper anymore in the state he was in. Mick it seemed had lost an ally in Topper, and felt that he should have been given a second chance. But let's face it, there was an awful lot riding on the US Tour. If Topper had gone and blown the band out, cancelling the shows would have bankrupted them. They were already reeling from the costs incurred while Joe had done a runner.

In "*Westway To The World*" (Letts, 2001) Paul said that "they felt uneasy about singing anti drugs songs when Topper was of his head".

So there was an official announcement made about Topper. On the one side, Topper was leaving the group, but the band would not be splitting up, and would fulfill their US dates using "guest drummers" The band would then return to the UK to fulfill the dates that were to have been the *Know Your Rights* tour.

Kris Needs recounted that Topper blamed Bernie Rhodes for a large part of his "sacking", and that Mick had stood up for him. Needs also explained that Kosmo told the press that "There was a difference in opinion over the political direction the band would be taking". Needs believed that the door was never shut for Topper, and that if he could have got it together, he could have "walked back".

In "*Westway To The World*", Joe famously said that sacking Topper had been a BIG mistake and one that he regretted deeply, and that it was the "beginning of the end", an opinion shared by Robin Crocker.

In *Who Am I* (Townsend, 2013) the author revealed a "drummer loyalty" issue, but in this case, the record label had decided that the then Who / Detours drummer was too old, and they needed a younger drummer if they were to sign to the Fontana label. He like Joe, deeply regretted the action, but as with The Clash, it was for the benefit of their possible future success.

In "*The Rise and Fall of The Clash*" (Garcia, 2012) friend of the band, Jock Scott pointed out that "Topper was marginalized from the beginning, he was a Dover Boy, not a London Boy". He also pointed out that as a result, he spent more time with the crew, and that some were heavy drug users. In the same film, Pearl Harbour maintained that Joe "Couldn't stand junkiness", and that "Mick had expressed that he didn't want the sacking to happen".

Joe admitted much later that "ignorance ruled the day" and that he knew nothing about heroin, and it was only after Topper had been fired that his own friends "began to go down like flies".

With all this band activity, it was inevitable that the press would be looking for an explanation both for the disappearing act by Joe, and the shock sacking of Topper.

In the *NME* in May 1982, (Unknown, 1982) there was an interview with Joe, Mick and Kosmo. "OK here we go, Joe's back and Toppers gone, what else do you want to know" said Kosmo.

As the article said, "The Clash had reunited in Amsterdam to play their last ever show with Topper." And that "Strummer returned after weeks of rumours. An entire UK Tour was cancelled and re arranged, and *Combat Rock* reached number 2 in the album charts!" So amid all the chaos, came commercial success.

Joe was asked directly why Topper had gone, Joe replying that it had been Topper's decision and that "I think he felt it wasn't easy being in The Clash" and that he was striking out in a different direction, "because I don't think he wants to come with us" Joe added that they would continue as a trio, calling in guest drummers when they wanted to play a show or record.

As Topper left, long time drum roadie "The Baker" also left the fracturing Clash family. He had been a stable presence in the road crew since the early days of the band, and this must have also added to the "hurt" felt by both band members and other crew.

When asked why he vanished, Joe added that he wanted to prove himself, that he was alive. Mick explained their immediate plans to tour the US and the UK, and that after that they didn't have any plans. Mick also chipped in with "After that, we all disappear."

In *The Clash "Uncut Special"* (Martin, 2010) The author summed up this period a little bluntly. Basically when Joe returned from Paris, Topper was sacked and "old hand " Terry Chimes was brought back in, and that "That's when Joe knew The Clash were as good as finished". In the same article, Joe again explained that at no point did he leave the group and that he "fucked off to Paris" because Bernie told him to. Again he talked about "the walk up" and that the ticket sales for the Inverness show hadn't sold out, and that Bernie had panicked and said "someone's got to break an arm or something, you'll have to disappear".

Melody Maker (Harrigan, 1982) reported on the proceedings with the headline "Clash Latest! – Strummer back but Topper out" Adding that Joe was back with The Clash, but the bad news was that Topper had quit. The forthcoming US tour was going ahead, but that the band were not rushing into finding a permanent replacement. It also reported that the speculation was that "percussionist" Terry Chimes might be brought in was firmly denied by Kosmo Vinyl. The official statement being that Topper left because of a difference of opinion over the political direction of the group.

In the same week, Joe appeared as the front cover story on the *NME* in the Charles Shaar Murray special, *Why I ran out on The Clash*. In the news pages of the same edition, it was reported that Joe had been located in Paris after a month's disappearance, and that the band were back in action, but that there was a "further upset" with Topper Headon quitting last Friday. It was also reported that they were going ahead with the US tour starting the next Saturday, and that they hadn't at Press Time named the drummer who would be working with them. Joe told Shaar-Murray that he had disappeared because he had wanted to prove himself that he was alive.

He told *Sounds* magazine that he had done it to "shake The Clash up, to shake The Clash fans up, shake The Clash haters up, and shake myself up too".

Kris Needs interviewed Mick after Joe had returned, and Mick had said he wished he had done it, but that once it had been done, you can't do it. From Needs report, it seemed that Mick saw the funny side of the incident.

The following week in the same paper (Harrigan, 1982), the *Fast Forward* section reported that Topper had been accused of stealing a bus stop, and handling stolen electrical equipment, as well as being charged with girlfriend "Miss Donna Garner" with dishonestly receiving some hi-fi equipment.

With the band once again in turmoil, and a massive US tour planned, The *Combat Rock* album was released , *Rock The Casbah* was shortly being released in the UK as the second single from the album there was obviously no pressure!

The recruitment of Terry Chimes as drummer was equally shrouded in some controversy. As mentioned earlier, Kosmo had denied that rumours were correct. Topper believed that Terry was "waiting in the wings", on the day of his sacking, he was reported to have said that possibly Terry could have gone to the States as the backup for Topper if he went off the rails.

In his book *The Strange case of Doctor Terry and Mr. Chimes* (Chimes, 2013) Terry explained that he got a call from Bernie, and that he could tell he was having difficulty approaching the subject. Eventually, he asked Terry if he was available. Terry had to phone Mick to try and get some clarification, and was told by Mick "well we couldn't get Cozy Powell could we?"

It also became apparent that Terry was not familiar with the new material after the first Clash album, and didn't have them either. Terry also discovered that there was a rotation of songs, which stopped the band and audiences becoming bored with sets. This meant there was a repertoire of about 60 songs to be learned.

As if this wasn't enough of an issue, there were five days before The Clash were to start the US Tour, Paul was already back in New York, so the whole band were not available to rehearse.

In *Redemption Song* Salewicz confirmed that it was five days before the start of the US Tour that Terry received the phone call from Bernie. They arranged to meet at "Marine Ices" just a little way from The Roundhouse venue in Camden. Bernie appeared not to ask directly if Terry would rejoin and play drums, but asked how much he was earning, and would he like to earn three times as much? Salewicz reported that Terry asked directly what the meeting was about, as he was unaware of the Topper situation, and was told eventually that he was needed to do a tour with The Clash.

The pre tour rehearsals took the form of Terry on drums, Mick covering the bass parts and Joe on Guitar. Terry had to make "copious notes" on each song, and had a folder placed on his bass drum. As the time to leave to the US approached, there was yet another problem to contend with.

In the rush to get Terry in and up to speed, according to his autobiography, he had no work visa for the US, and had to take a chance on entering the country with a tourist visa. As Terry recalled, on the flight over, some of the road crew got involved in an incident with a passenger, and caused a disturbance. On arrival at the Airport in the US, there were security and immigration officials waiting.

Terry was identified as one of the trouble makers, and was given the third degree by security. With a passport identifying him as a musician, he could have been sent back to the UK, leaving the US tour in tatters as the UK one had been. From his own account, Terry believed it was better that he lied, and tried to say that he was a fan of the band and was travelling with them. Luckily this paid off, but officials who were short of time, admitted that they did not believe his story.

As I wind up this chapter, we leave Terry, Paul, Mick and Joe rehearsing in New York for the upcoming US tour, Terry still adding to his folder of notes, which when he reach for on his drum kit to turn over Pages, Bernie accused him of "looking like he was reaching for a Tomato sandwich".

We will pick up on the "Long Haul" of 1982 after some diversions

5. THE RECORDINGS

After the relative disappointment and lack of commercial success of *Sandinista*, and to some extent the Ellen Foley album. It seemed that there were two choices for the next album. One to carry on producing material which was eclectic remixed and extended or to try and deliver a commercial, more traditional album which would build world-wide sales. Joe it seemed wanted to release a single album, Mick wanted a double.

Certainly The Clash had four members with very different influences and interests. By the end of the 1981, Mick had according to *Redemption Song* declared himself the producer of the new record. Mick had become "entranced" by the Rap culture and this had led to some of the experimental mixes of *Radio Clash*. Mick even being nicknamed "Whack Attack". Joe (according to Salewicz) was "veering back towards his love of roots and contemporary music" and had told Bernie that he wanted to do real music, not punk stuff. Kris Needs wrote that Joe's love for Hip Hop and Dub was "cooling out" after *Sandinista*, and "Moving towards Americana and the Roots of Rock and Roll". I think it is quite important to remember that diversity is not a bad thing or a destructive thing. I already talked about Joe Ely, and how his first band had been made up of three members with very different musical leanings. In *Bit of A Blur* (Alex James, 2007) the Blur bass player backed this up when he referred to the period around the recording of *Modern Life Is Rubbish*. He actually felt that Musical differences were often cited as the reason for a bands disintegration, but they are "Actually what make a good group great"

Don Letts explained in *Redemption Song*, that Mick had the ability to "sweeten the pill", and that people didn't like the message to be too hard and direct. Mick he believed was able to contemporize Joe's messages, as he was the melody man, who would "keep it contemporary". Letts compared Joe to a "guy who rode horses while everyone else was riding around in cars", and it was Mick who "dragged it forward". Mick he believed was a crucial foil to Joe. I absolutely agree with this statement.

I guess this is another turning point in the story of the album. Mick having put himself in charge of the album and direction in terms of mixes. The disappearance of Joe and the subsequent shift in the power balance in the band on his return are very important.

Was Joe thinking about just the Topper situation while in Paris, or was there a more complex scenario where Joe felt he needed more control or certainly Mick having less control over the musical direction and new album format.

There is much talked about the recording of *Combat Rock*, and certainly the recording process and subsequent mixing have been one of the most controversial events in the stormy Clash story. Mick Jones recalled playing a couple of the new songs that would be for the new album at Bonds. But from the track listings of the many bootleg recordings, I see no live evidence of this. Never the less, it is possible…more probable that new tunes were being "cooked" up on a constant basis, and there were numerous sound checks for the Bonds Shows, which allowed time for experimentation.

In *Redemption Song*, Salewicz wrote that on "*The Radio Clash Tour*", Seven nights at Theater Mogador, the band debuted material from "the next album to be called "*Rat Patrol From Fort Bragg*", and that in April of that year they had "laid down versions of *Car Jamming, This is Radio Clash*, and *Sean Flynn* at Marcus Music Studios in Notting Hill." This was followed by *Know Your Rights, Inoculated City, Ghetto Defendant* and *Should I Stay or Should I Go* at Ear Studios in London"

In *The Last Gang in Town* (Gray, 1995), the author believed that Joe wasn't interested in a high quality sound. Musically, Paul was more interested in obscure rockabilly which he had listened to over the previous year, and that Mick had gone off in a completely different direction both musically and was embracing new technology. Gray also later remarked that the "material had moved away from the funky stuff that Mick liked, to more like the retro that Paul and Joe enjoyed"

In the *Mojo* article *Who killed The Clash* the writer said that "Joe feared that left to his own devices, Mick would drive the band down the *Sandinista* winding road to ruin" with "grooves rather than songs, self-indulgent musicianship." In the same article, it was said that Bernie and Joe's view was that they needed to keep the music "Tight and punchy" and "reclaim the public imagination"

Depending on which book you read, or press releases you see, the recording process is believed to have begun "proper" at the then Clash rehearsal space at a then part squatted building in Freston Road, Notting Hill. Although initially only a rehearsal room, the band were keen to record material there. Joe in particular was said to have been pleased with the sound.

The decision was taken to hire the Rolling Stones Mobile Recording for some demos of the new material. The Band started rehearsing for tour dates in September 1981, the idea being to try and combine rehearsals with song writing sessions as they had done for *London Calling*. Mick Jones recalled "We rehearsed in a kind of squat hall and hired the Rolling Stones Mobile Studio to park outside. We ran leads out to it and recorded demos there."

According to Kris Needs, "In August 1981, The Clash started recording and writing at Ear Studios, using the Rolling Stones Mobile. These songs included *Know Your Rights*, *Overpowered By Funk*, *Ghetto Defendant* and *Inoculated City*.

Both in *Redemption Song* (Salewicz, 2006) and *Last Gang In Town* (Gray, 1995) reference is also made to another Studio called Marcus Studios. Salewicz indicated that *This Is Radio Clash* was actually completed there after initial recording sessions in New York after the Bonds shows. Gray mentioned that some other material from the Marcus sessions was also in the running for the album.

In *The Clash- Punk Rock Band* (Bowe, 2011) the author simplified the recording period, "The Clash recorded the album in New York between April 1981 and January 1982". As time progressed, Mick wanted to move recording to Electric Lady in New York, partially motivated by the fact that girlfriend Ellen Foley lived there. This did see the beginning of a split over the album. Joe was now believed to have been interested in a "high quality" sound.

Although this seems a turnaround from Joe's initial preference for a less polished sound while recording at Ear Studios. Musically the band had always been diverse in their listening pleasures. Mick was very interested in technology, and was as I mentioned earlier "Off in another direction".

The decision to record in New York did present the band with a dilemma, particularly over the costs of recording. Equipment would need to be hired; expensive studio time would need to be paid for as well as accommodation and expenses. The band had to hire their equipment, as their own gear was not in the States, as no tour was scheduled there.

Again in *Redemption Song*, Mick it seemed was insistent that the recording be completed in New York Electric Lady in the week before Christmas. Reasons being that Mick wanted to be in "the midst of the cities sound of urban ghetto which inspired him". He was also involved still with girlfriend Ellen Foley, and wanted to be close by, so this seems to back up the earlier comment.

Salewicz mentioned that when questioned about this by the other band members, he threatened to leave. Joe and Paul were reportedly furious over this. In *The Clash* (Quantick, 2000) the author wrote that Strummer and Jones worked in separate studios while the recording was taking place.

Mickey Foote told Pat Gilbert in *Passion is a Fashion*, that "It seemed to me to be all enclaves", and that Joe had his "tepee" in the middle of the studio, and that "it was work, we had to do an album, that's why it was *Combat Rock*, it was like a battle".

In *Redemption Song*, Salewicz quoted Kosmo as saying "I don't remember the vibe at Electric Lady being overbearingly intense".

Jeremy Green was also required, but had recently become a parent, and as a result had to say he was unavailable to fly over. He was eventually persuaded to attend the sessions.

In *No More Heroes* (Ogg, 2006) The author talked about the recording in Electric Lady having Mick producing, "alongside Jeremy Green and a 'returning' Micky Foote. Tension began to develop as it was felt that Mick was not acknowledging budget issues".

Mick wanted to take charge of the production, and take control over the material that they had recorded in Ear studios. Mick it seemed also wanted to re-record the material that had been laid down there, as well as writing new material. Two camps began to develop, Paul and Joe, and Mick and Topper who were the more musical members of the band, and as a result, stronger arrangers.

The general philosophy was for the band to use all their influences and to try and make the sound their own.

At this stage, the band were still juggling their other commitments, there was constant touring, and during the Ear sessions, there was both rehearsing stage sets and recording of the new material.

In August 1981, Guy Stevens was reported dead from an overdose of drugs that were prescribed to him to get him off alcohol dependency. This had quite an effect on the band, as he had (depending upon your opinion) helped guide the band to produce the *London Calling* album. The outcome of these emotions was for the band to write and record the *Midnight To Stevens* track which only saw light of day on *The Clash On Broadway* box set. There is no reference to it ever being earmarked for the new as yet unrecorded album.

In late September, the band were off to Paris for the week of shows at Theater Mogador. From the bootleg recordings of the various nights, some of the new tracks were aired at these shows.

As well as album tracks, additional material was recorded during this time period. *This is Radio Clash* and the Futura 2000 collaboration *The Escapades of Futura 2000*, also known in a live context as *Graffiti Rap*. Both of these tunes were played at the Paris Shows. The Futura musical connection was made initially to provide a rap on track *Overpowered By Funk*. With a deadline rapidly approaching for the album to be recorded, progress was slow and the pressure was well and truly on. There were still issues over the number of tracks.

In *Clash Talking* (Johnstone, 2006) Joe was quoted as saying in 2001, that "The *Combat Rock* sessions were very difficult sessions. There was a bit of friction. When friction builds up, people stop communicating or maybe that's the cause of friction. But whatever it is, the result is that people don't tell each other what they think anymore. I think that kind of finished us off".

In *Rolling Stone The Year of The Clash* (Hall, 1982) The author wrote that The Clash spent a "Bleak Winter recording *Combat Rock* in New York" In a very poetic way he added that the band were "Eager to synthesize the disparate styles and sounds they had toyed with on *Sandinista*".

After the short Christmas break, and the Topper heroin incident, the band returned to Electric Lady Studios in January. As Kris Needs commented (Needs, 2005) "As with *Sandinista*, at Electric Lady, the album started ballooning, now up to 17 tracks, many of which were at 'Raga' length".

In *The Clash a Punk Rock Band* (Bowe, 2011) wrote that "Mick announced a 15 track double album, and that the rest of the band did not like it".

In *Last Gang In Town* (Gray, 1995) the author backed this up stating that "they were still recording backing tracks in between Christmas and New Year. The project seemed to be getting out of hand again". He also added that "The tracks were very long, like the extended 12" mixes of rap and funk that Mick was so fond of".

Salewicz, again quoted Kosmo as saying that "I really wanted a single record because I firmly believed that a great group had to be able to do that".

In an interview with Japanese magazine *Music Life* (Hayashi, 1981) Mick was asked why the new album was being recorded in New York. Mick replied that "We had decided to make a film documentary when we were doing a week long concert at Bonds. But it was extended to two weeks, and filming took longer than we thought. So, we decided to stay in New York until filming had finished, and we ended up recording the new album there."

Tracks were still being recorded between Christmas and New Year, and in *Redemption Song*, Salewicz also confirmed that "The Project seemed to be getting out of hand again", and that they seemed to have too many songs, around seventeen, which included material from the Marcus and Ear Studio sessions. The tracks were also long, and led to the widely quoted Bernie outburst "Does everything have to be a raga?".

At some point in the proceedings, the band managed to find time to record *The Escapades of Futura* with Futura 2000 taking the rap.

On December 30th, the band were working on *Straight To Hell* in New York which had according to Salewicz, evolved from a "Mick Guitar Doodle." Topper laid down a Bossa Nova beat, and there was the famous incident where Topper asked Joe to bang out a rhythm using an R Whites Lemonade bottle wrapped in a towel on his bass drum.

Another legendary story was the recording on *Rock The Casbah*. Joe later told Uncut Magazine (Martin, 1999) He had "seen Toppers talent with his own eyes." "I swear in 20 minutes he laid down the whole thing, bass, drums and piano." This does contradict Toppers own account of how he had turned up early at the studio one day, and put down the various components of the song before anybody else had arrived. In *The Big Cheese Clash special*, (Cheese 2008) the author reported that it was Joe who had disappeared to the toilet for 20 minutes and came back with a verse and chorus for the track.

As the sessions went on, Mick was looking at producing a double album; Joe seemed to be more in favour of a single album. As Salewicz reported, "65 Minutes…17 Tracks….led to conflict with the others." In *Vive Le Rock* magazine (Needs, 2013),the author reported that the band seemed fragmented, and that Mick was "Sculpting" another double album, while Joe "favoured taking the whole thing from the sessions at Ear Studios" and as Needs said "Amidst the car wrecking lots of Latimer Road"

In "*The Clash*"(Quantick, 2000),the author wrote that "It was decided to do a single album, not a double or triple, and that they would get an outside producer , not do it themselves, and to make it look modern and marketable"

In the same Kris Needs article in "*Vive Le Rock*", Topper had been quoted as saying that the band were hardly speaking, and that they would just bump into each other occasionally in the studio, and that Mick and Joe rowed about everything. He added that Mick was always late and turned up stoned.

In *The Last Gang in Town*(Gray, 1995), the author wrote that Joe and Mick were barely speaking, and as reported by Bowe, they were working separate shifts, "Mick laying down guitar tracks during the day, and Joe doing the night shift adding the vocals"

In *Joe Strummer and the Legend of The Clash* (Needs, 2005), Mick was working with a US engineer called Joe Blaney. In the same book, Needs quoted that Topper had felt that he was also contributing to the tracks, and that if he could have played more of his other instruments, he could have done more. But "When I did "Casbah", I was stoned out of my head".

Gray again wrote that as the work went on, Joe had begged Jerry Green to come over to engineer, as they were having problems communicating with the US engineers. Jerry Green eventually caved in, and left his new family for three weeks.

In *Passion is a Fashion* (Gilbert, 2004) band guitar roadie, Digby said that Mick and Topper were taking the music into a different direction, and that Mick was embracing new technology. One of Ellen Foleys friends was brought in to put synth keyboards on some of the tracks. This was Poly Mandell.

Marcus Gray quoted Paul as saying "I think at that stage, Mick's guitar had become a bassoon or something", and that it just wasn't a guitar anymore and was "sort of odd". He added that Possibly Mick had got bored playing guitar, and that he had equipment that would "make it sound almost like an orchestra"

In *What Makes Music Work* (Byrne, 2012) The author talked about the costs of recording, and posed the question "did we think about costs?", and how the costs did affect the way their music was recorded. He pointed out that if there was a limited budget, it acted as a "set of creative restrictions which for us (Talking Heads) and was generally a good thing" He also added that "Financial structures don't determine a melody, the lyrics or harmony, but they do affect how a record is recorded and therefore ultimately what it sounds like"

So what might have been the outcome of the "Mick Mix", if CBS had decided to pull the budget when the recording and mixing went badly over-time. As Byrne also pointed out, "The Recording studio became now a compositional tool"

The Studios

I thought it would be interesting to include some background on the three main studios where *Combat Rock* tracks were recorded. The general impression you get when reading about the album was that it was recorded and mixed in New York, as is also the impression about the *Sandinista* album.

Ear Studios

Freston Road, in Notting Hill was an interesting location. The area had been renamed "Frestonia" by the residents. In 1977, there had been an attempt to break free from the United Kingdom, and become an independent state. According to a *Q Magazine* article *The Real Mick Jones* (Perry, 2013) it was also close by to where Mick had recently bought a flat. In the early seventies, many of the houses in the street were empty, and squatters had become the majority. After an attempt to evict the squatters, they tried to declare independence. In 1982, the "State" celebrated its fifth anniversary. In 1995, Roddy Frame titled the last credited Aztec Camera album *Frestonia*, whether linked to his known Clash fixations or not is unknown. This is where Ear Studios was based.

Ear studios was at the time, a rehearsal facility rather than a modern, fully equipped recording studio. Again, a convenient location for The Clash members close to Notting Hill in London. It was also named "The Peoples Hall" .Today; this is one of the few remaining buildings from the "Frestonia" era, as much has been redeveloped. The studio was housed in "The People's Hall" and still stands today. I was keen to pay the hall a visit, but after investigating online, it appears that the building and the hall have been converted into luxury offices for companies such as Monsoon and Cath Kidson, the band Talk Talk, and Chrysalis Records. Wikipedia credits it as being the location for the recording of much of The Clash's album *Combat Rock*. It seems that this was a relaxed and convenient location for the band, harking back to the bands earlier days at Davis Road and Joe in particular at 101 Wallerton Road. Possibly Joe having the say here, trying to return to more earthy roots, and out of the grips of new technology and experimentation.

Whatever the reasons, it was decided that the Rolling Stones mobile should be hired to get down some of the new material

The Rolling Stones Mobile

It does what it says on the tin to coin a phrase. A mobile recording studio owned by the Rolling Stones. It has been rented out to a number of artists including Lou Reed, Bob Marley Led Zeppelin and Simple Minds to name a few.

According to Wikipedia (Accessed 09/09/2013), The Stones were looking for a new Environment in which to record. Mick Jagger had acquired a large country house, and tiring of the restrictions on (then) 9-5 recording studios, they thought they could use Mick's pad and put a control room in a van. The van idea was from Ian Stewart their then Road Manager.

Interestingly, among the top engineers and producers who were consulted, was a certain Glyn Johns. It was originally intended only for use by the Rolling Stones, but it started gaining popularity among other bands like The Who, The Faces and Led Zeppelin.

It was a multi track studio which could be adapted to individual job specifications. Interestingly, according to www.Philsbook.com (Burns), during filming on Frank Zappa's "*200 Motels*" film, the whole thing was painted in camouflage so that it would not show up so easily on the screen.... ready for Combat!

After being sold in 1996, it was used to record live performances by Patti Smith, The Ramones, and other bands at the New York Continental for a *Best Of NYC Hardcore* album. The mobile studio certainly was steeped in "Rock N Roll History", Deep Purple's *Smoke on the Water* and Bob Marley's *No Woman No Cry* singles were recorded with it, and in terms of albums, from the Rolling Stones, Led Zeppelin, through Fleetwood Mac, Simple Minds and the Live Level 42 album, *A Physical Presence*.

However, it was not to add its name to the *Combat Rock* album as the recording and production was shifted to New York.

Marcus Studios

Little seems to be documented about the use of Marcus Studios by The Clash for *Combat Rock* recordings. According to Phil's Classic Studios Series website accessed February 2014 www.philsbook.com/ it was opened in 1979 in a former Studio building in Kensington Gardens Square, London. The owners were Marcus Osterdahl and Leif Mases.

Marcus Osterdahl was a Swedish musician, composer, and arranger, pretty much everything, who opened the studio complex in 1979, and sold it finally in 1999. The most well-known album recorded there was the Gary Numan *Pleasure Principle* which launched the Gary Numan solo career with the *Cars* single in 1979.

Hard evidence of The Clash having recorded here surfaced in 2013 with the release of the Sound System Box Set where on the second CD, track 15. *Sean Flynn* is listed as (Extended 'Marcus Music' version.

Electric Lady Studios

Electric Lady Studios was established in 1970 "In the Heart of Greenwich Village", according to the official website www.electricladystudios.com

It has an incredible history, the building was a former night club called "The Generation", where Hendrix and others had performed. He and manager Michael Jeffrey bought it, perhaps with the intention of it continuing as a club venue. In the end it went through some major architectural work, and some state of the art recording equipment was installed.

In *Just Kids* (Smith, 2011) Patti Smith recalled a visit there, and how Hendrix had spent some time talking to her on the stairs, explaining what he wanted to do with his new studio. The Electric Lady website has undergone a face lift since I first accessed it in July 2013, and possibly for the better, as under the entry for *Combat Rock* album, there were some factual inaccuracies which upset my anorak type nature. It stated that "The Clash spent much of the early 1980s at Electric Lady Studios, recording some of their most popular work - including 1984's *Combat Rock*." In the next section, the site stated that "Recording for the album took place November 1981 to January 1982 with legendary producer, engineer and mixer Glyn Johns, and ELS engineer Joe Blaney in Studio C."

From my research, it appears that Glyn Johns didn't spend time with The Clash in Electric Lady, preferring his own and other UK studios.

The site also mentioned that they had recorded *Sandinista* in 1980 at the studio, in the same studio C with in house engineer J.P. Nicholson, "during March and April of 1980."

My knowledge of studios and recording is somewhat limited to my own bands dodgy demos of the late seventies and early eighties, but I can see that there might be strong reasons , particularly for Mick to work at a studio they have already spent a considerable amount of time, knowing the equipment, desks and the staff. In terms of a learning curve when the whole band were under considerable pressure

You can see Paul and Mick revisit the studio in a spoof interview from 2013 with Fred Armisen.

www.funnyordie.com/videos/b0dd8a3cef/the-clash-the-last-gang-in-town

The Album Mixing

As recording led on to mixing of the tracks, this is where the waters become muddied, filled with "confusion and delay" (Credit to The Fat Controller "Thomas The Tank Engine").

Mick was more or less in charge of the mixing of the tracks, but as time ticked by, there were arguments over the tracks lengths and experimental content. When Joe was asked about *The Magnificent Dance Mix* in Sounds in June 1981 (Lewis 1981), as in "Whose idea was it?" Joe replied "Mick really, Mick's the one who is into sound. He likes to keep up with everything, he always wants to remix!!"

Just prior to the Japanese leg of the tour, Gray wrote that Mick had presented the band with the "Final 15 track 65 minute mix. To be a double album, and did not include two tracks they had recorded, *Overpowered by Funk* and *Long Time Jerk*.

In a later interview in 1984, Joe referred to this as a "Home Movie Mix" album. In the NME article *Tropic of The Clash* (Reines, 1982), Joe had little to say when asked about the album mixing. "You won't get much out of me on that one" he said "Don't forget your talking to a man trying to deliberately forget about it over the last two weeks".

The interview took place just prior to the shows in Australia; where, studio time had been booked after the shows to enable the band to continue mixing the tracks.

Joe added that he hadn't thought about the tracks once, or listened to them, and that he hadn't looked at the sheet of seventeen titles. He would, he said be listening to them in the next few days in that studio in Sydney, and that he was "semi scared".

Prior to departing for the Far East tour, Mick and Joe had been mixing the album, and a last minute "dash" to the airport had been necessary. Joe was asked by Reines why it took so long for The Clash to do anything. (Referring I believe to the delays in the album release and mixing) Joe answered by saying that it was "Because of our disorganization, but in 1982, The Clash disorganization is Organisation, that's why we are mixing the album here (Australia), instead of waiting to get back to Blighty."

At this time, the album was still destined to be called *Rat Patrol From Fort Bragg*, and it is on this that Mick was also interviewed by Roz Reines. Mick told her that the relationships between the group were not great at the moment. "In fact" said Mick, "He hadn't spoken to Joe since they abandoned a mixing session at 4am the previous night."

In *Westway to the World* and others, Paul recounted the memorable argument over the bass level in the mix of *Know Your Rights*.

In *Passion is a Fashion*, Tymon Dogg recalled the sessions being intense, and remembered leaving Paul and Mick at 2:00am working on the mix for *Know Your Rights*, and finding them still arguing about it "looking like death warmed up" the next day at 10:00am. Paul had wanted it to be more of a "reggae thing." In *The Clash: Punk Rock Band*, Bowe reported that Joe said "we were working round the clock" and that he had a set of engineers to mix with, then he would collapse and Mick would come in with fresh engineers, and he would have a sleep on the floor. In *Last Gang*, Gray quoted Joe as saying "I don't believe that anyone is that great that they don't write crap sometimes" He felt that Mick had surrounded himself with "yes men" and went so far as to famously say that Mick "couldn't produce", to which Mick replied, "You bastard, I thought you were my friend."

In *Passion is a Fashion*, Gilbert wrote that when the band returned from the Far East, it was to work on the album, and that there were 16 or 17 tracks that were enough for a double album. But more importantly, CBS and Bernie didn't want another "VFM" release double album. As Egan picked up in *The Clash – The Only band That Mattered*, if there were any more VFM "gestures", it would probably have bankrupted the band. Some of the tracks noted Gilbert had percussion intros (which can be heard on the various outtake and bootleg album mixes). Joe apparently disliked the mixes Mick had done so much, that he compared it, said Gilbert "to telling Your friend his breath stinks."

Paul commented that Mick had done some mixing on the tapes, "but I don't think any of us were particularly pleased with it" Mick recalled that "well, the others said, you can mix it, and I'm like "oh shit", and it was a big sprawling mess at the time"

Gilbert quoted Kosmo that "No one in the camp (referring to the mixes) could please all parties", and that he thought it was an "Honest debate", "I didn't think it was a power play"

At some point, it was decided that Mick needed to be overridden, as it could not be decided on how to arrange a single album. It was felt that they needed an experienced producer/engineer.

Gray wrote that Bernie drew up a list of possibles; among them was Gus Dudgeon, but who Bernie mistakenly took for Glyn Johns. Johns had a reputation for "salvage operations" with the Rolling Stones, The Beatles and The Who.

Gilbert wrote that CBS Executive A and R man Muff Winwood had become involved in the search for a suitable mix, and sent tapes of the mixes Mick had done to Glyn Johns. He was reported to have found the tapes "enormously impressive", but agreed that the songs were long and drawn out, and "a little self-indulgent."

Johns himself in his *Sound Man* book and accompanying *Talks at Google* interview, told the story slightly differently. Muff Winwood had indeed contacted him, and explained that The Clash had delivered a double album which was not quite what they were looking for (The label that is). Johns was sent a Double Album Acetate to listen to. In his biography, Winwood he said had sounded quite desperate. Johns believed that Joe and Mick would "take it in turns" to produce each album. In the *Talks at Google* interview, he referred to this as "flip flopped." I'm not sure this is actually the case, but Johns was unsure who "had won", he believed that Mick and Joe both had attempted to mix it, each getting two weeks, Joe working in one studio with the tapes and Mick in another. The message from Muff was that that it did not "pass muster" in his opinion. Winwood wanted Glyn to "cast an unbiased ear" on the record, and by remixing it, make it "acceptable to all concerned."

Again from *Sound Man*, Johns had been skeptical about the music , fearing it might be just a racket. He was not a fan of any "punk" music, and had heard of, but not heard The Clash. Johns confessed that he had been pleasantly surprised, the music was self indulgent yes, but clever, and he thought he could get something out of it. What impressed him he wrote, was a "combination of Joe's energy and intellect" and Mick's musicianship which was "Quite remarkable." Topper's drumming also came in for strong praise. Johns was also attracted by "the abundant sense of humour."

In *Redemption Song*, Salewicz wrote that "After a meeting with Muff Winwood, it was decided that Glyn Johns would be asked to remix the album", and that the sessions would take place at the producers own studios in Warnford, (or is it Warnham?)West Sussex. Salewicz also noted that Johns did not drink or do drugs. He liked to work regular hours and did not do "all-nighters". In the Mojo magazine article *Who Killed The Clash* (Snow, 2008) Mick told Mat Snow that "The people at the record company had probably had enough of us by then and wanted something back on their investment". He also told Snow that it wasn't their decision to get Glyn Johns, it was Bernie's.

Johns accepted the "job", and as Gilbert wrote, understood this was to "chop the material down to a single album". Johns himself confessed in his book, that he was intrigued by the request from Winwood for help, and had a lot of respect for him.

Johns met with Bernie, Kosmo and Joe. Mick was not present at the discussions. In *Uncut* magazine (Martin, 2010) Joe told the writer that they had to "beg" Glyn Johns to do the mixing, because he didn't like producing stuff he hadn't recorded. "We gave it a go" said Joe, "and got it into listenable shape". In his own book, Johns confirmed that a meeting was arranged and that the band drove to Sussex to meet him. The "Band" however was Joe, no Mick, Paul or Topper, but Kosmo and Bernie were in attendance. "Despite appearances" said Johns, they were polite and respectful. Kosmo he recalled was quite "Charming". By the time the meeting had ended, Johns was apparently even more intrigued.

In *Sound Man* (Johns, 2014) and *Talks At Google - Glyn Johns in Conversation,* 2014, Glyn Johns revealed much more about the "Process" as he referred to it.

And so, to another clouded part of the story... There are `parties that believe that Wessex was used for the mixing, Gilbert maintains that Frestonia (Ear), then Greewich Village (presumably Electric Lady) and the "Final Edit" at Glyn Johns' own studio in West Sussex. Kris Needs wrote that Johns and Joe did go to Wessex Studios to mix.

Johns confirmed in his book, that the tapes were delivered to his house to be worked on in his studio, in Warnham, and that Joe went down from London the next day to start work.

Gilbert again wrote that Johns was a strict time keeper, who said that they would start at eleven. Johns seems confident that it was a 10 AM start. Joe arrived on time, but Mick arrived at 7:30PM, apparently "not a happy bunny." This was confirmed by Johns, Mick arriving after three tracks had already been reworked, but he recalled 7PM. Mick he remembered was pretty pissed off.

In Gilberts book, Johns found Joe "fantastic to work with" an "extraordinary bloke". Joe was open to ideas that were put to him, and he did not interfere with Johns. In his own book, Johns was fairly glowing about Joe. He felt that at the first meeting they had "Hit it off" immediately. In the *Combat Rock* Chapter of his book, Johns believed that Joe was one of the most "genuine" people he had ever met, "bright as a button, and unaffected by success".

Johns agreed that some of the material was too long and as he put it, "Started editing to make it more concise", and believing that it would make a stronger single album. Joe he found to be very enthusiastic, and encouraging Johns to be as "avant garde" as possible , and to change things substantially from the previously delivered album.

By the time Mick had turned up, the three tracks had been worked on, and Mick apparently didn't like any of it. Johns mentioned in his interview that after welcoming him, he played the mixes, Mick had sat "Unmoved". Mick had indicated that there were certain things he would like to change. According to Gilbert, Johns pointed out that they had started at eleven and that if he had only chosen to turn up hours late, it was "too bad". Johns himself told Mick in no uncertain terms that if he had been there at the start of the proceedings, he would have taken his requests on board. But he was not going to re do the tracks again, and in effect, it was tough shit!

Salewicz concurred that "Joe was there promptly at 11:00 AM for kick off" and that Mick arrived at 7:30pm…and "was confronted by a myriad of changes deletions and ideas" and that "Glyn Johns had rejected the tapes which hung around him like a tie".

Mick it seems disagreed but went along with the changes anyway, particularly re recording of the vocals and *Should I Stay or Should I Go*, and *Know Your Rights*. Gaby Salter told Salewicz that "Mick was very fixed, Joe could be charming but he wanted it the way he wanted".

Johns recalled that he realised that Mick was not happy about him mixing the album. The atmosphere then, was tense and unpleasant for Johns who next morning called Joe to say unless this improved he would not continue. From his own book, he remembered talking to Joe and saying how much he had enjoyed working with him, but that he did not think too much of his "mate", and maybe it was best that he did not continue. There were heated phone calls with Bernie Mick and Kosmo, and according to other authors, eventually Mick "got on with it". According to Johns in his book, a phone call came back a couple of hours later from Muff Winwood, explaining that Mick had apologized, and "Would not participate in the sessions from there on". It was only to be Joe. In the *Talks at Google* interview, Johns explained that Mick had agreed not to come again, and that he didn't see Mick again until the Shea Stadium shows with The Who.

A couple of Joe's vocals were re recorded, and the rest of the mixing was done in a couple of days. Johns does not mention the re recording of *Should I Stay or Should I Go* vocals, for which Mick must have been involved!.

It must have been hurtful for Mick, who really felt that he had done the work already. Johns was very aware of Mick's feelings, and believed that Mick "didn't know him from Adam". Kosmo believed that Mick actually had all the records that he had produced, The Rolling Stones and The Who!

Johns realised how difficult it would be for Mick to "let go" of the record, after he had invested such a lot of time and effort into it. As Johns added, "He was good enough to let me get on with it", and seemed happy enough with the end result, "after the dust had settled".

Again from the *Mojo* article *Who Killed The Clash*, Mick told the author that Johns had told him off for "tardiness", and had asked Mick if he wanted "things retained", to which Mick said "no", and apparently was not allowed in the studio. "All the things like the whale noises ended up on the cutting room floor" said Mick, and "By the time he realized what a fantastic record it was and we weren't a bunch of strops, and actually a really good group, I was too hurt. It wasn't him it was me; it was a major sulk, so unnecessary!" In *The Clash – The Only Band That Mattered*, Egan wrote that the album mix was done by Johns and Strummer, and that Mick was not present, and that Joe had announced that the album was "designed to sell".

Johns was pleased with the final results, and felt they had a great time working together. Again Gilbert wrote that after three days, the tracks had been sorted out. Some tracks were axed from the running order, and two for B-sides. *Walk Evil Talk* was dropped completely. The running time was cut from 77 minutes to 46. Vocals were re-recorded on *Should I Stay or Should I Go*, and *Know Your Rights* which were flagged as singles. As Egan wrote, the tracks were deemed commercial enough to be singles.

Kris Needs felt that despite John's "impressive CV", the album became "dry and punchy", and lacked the experimentation of the Mick Mixes. He also wrote that the album that came out of the mixes was a 12 Track 48 minute Single album. He also felt that The Clash music "entered a different dimension to previous work".

In *The Last Gang In Town*, Gray also wrote that Johns and Joe booked into Wessex for the mixing, and that the decision to use Glyn Johns was the "first acknowledgment by the band that they were prepared to compromise musically in order to achieve success" He added that the 12 final tracks were "overhauled", with guitars and drums pushed up higher in the mix in an attempt to give the album a "big sound which was more attractive to the American market". Tracks were trimmed down from "raga" length, songs losing verses and intros. Gray also pointed out that the more "rocky" songs were selected for singles and so were "re-worked", as Gilbert reported. Egan also concurred that the guitar and drums were boosted in the mix, and production was stripped of what he called "Bloops and squeals" which Mick loved.

Gray also believed that the "salvaged album" was "Joe's show", and that Paul and Topper were not really consulted. Contrary to other reports, "Mick rarely went to Wessex, apart from to record vocals again for *Should I Stay or Should I Go*. So again some confusion about whether Wessex Studios was used for the "Rescue Mission".

So at the end of the mixing sessions, the band had a single album with a more "polished" and less experimental mix. Rightly or wrongly, geared up for the American market, which after all was the biggest market in the world. According to Kris Needs upon returning from the Far East, the album was still not completed. Mick he said, "Continued to dominate the recording", but the other band members were unhappy with this. In Needs words "Joe got everyone to overrule Mick". The record company were panicking and "brought in Glyn Johns". Joe it seemed took over creative control with "the intention of turning the LP into an unashamedly commercial weapon in the war against Foreigner and Boston, with "atmosphere and experimentation".

Johns and Joe, said Needs "emerged with a 12 track 48 minute album on single disc" and that flexing his influence Joe had renamed the album *Combat Rock*. They had "trimmed of flab and got straight to the point". He felt that The Clash music had taken on a "sound painting technique".

In a *Rolling Stone* article *The Year of The Clash* (Hall, 1982) according to Hall, the plans by Mick to add a 12" EP with the album using four songs were "relegated to B-side Duties" and "numerous other cuts were made".

In the *Who Killed The Clash*, article in Mojo magazine (Snow, 2008a) Mick was pretty philosophical about the situation. Saying "The next thing I was told was that I couldn't mix. *Sean Flynn* was 15 minutes long before it was cut down". He also talked about how when on tour in Australia, for the seven nights in Sydney they had booked into a studio after shows to try and mix the record. "We sweated our guts out and our hearing was shot" said Mick, and that they couldn't do it. "We were pretty messed up by then, and when I was told I couldn't mix, I took that very badly. I went into a big huff".

Both Needs and Gray seemed to agree that the Mick produced album was not a disaster at all, Needs certainly prefers the unofficial *Rat Patrol* album to the Johns produced release.

The tapes for the album were "delivered" to CBS in April 1982, and the label wanted to rush ahead with the release, preceded by the *Know Your Rights* single.

Mick as Producer

So what was Mick like as a "producer", and what is the role of producer. Mick had always been very involved in the studio, and from research, this was particularly apparent during the recording of *Give 'Em Enough Rope* with Sandy Pearlman. Mick reportedly watched every move on the mixing desk.

By the time we got to *Combat Rock*, Mick had already mixed and produced (along with the band and Bill Price) the epic three disc *Sandinista* In the incredible outpouring of songs, the band had contributed a number of tracks to Mick's girlfriend Ellen Foley's second solo album *Spirit of St Louis*. Mick, also taking on the production duties too. The album was released in January 1981, and didn't perform particularly well in commercial terms. Egan in *The Clash – The Only Band That Mattered* pointed out that this album contained more of what we be classified as "Love Songs".

Kris Needs felt that Mick was "Besotted with the Sonic Revolution", as he put it "audacious master-mixes, editing and extending tracks into startling mutants". Mick had applied similar techniques when recording The Clash, as Needs pointed out, Mick was elated when the dubs of" Mag 7"and *Rock The Casbah* stormed the Clubs. Mick was truly inspired. The *"Dirty Harry mix"* of *The Magnificent 7* which was a bootleg mix, was as Mick told Needs "a kind of pointer" as they had done things like putting bits of movies on top, such as "Do you feel Lucky Punk" and "The Wabbit kicked the bucket"

In June 1981, Ian Hunter released his *Short Back and Sides* album, with Mick on production duties. Extraordinary when you think that Mick as a younger man, had followed Mott The Hoople around, and been heavily influenced by them in his own bands. The treatment that Mott The Hoople gave to their fans , in terms of getting them into gigs, crashing in hotels and lifts where and when they could providing the blueprint for The Clash and their incredible bond with their fans. Suddenly here was Mick, working with one of his heroes, producing an album.

In an article in *Vive Le Rock* magazine (Needs, 2013) Ian Hunter discussed the recording and production of *Short back and Sides*. Hunter said that Mick would "make demands", and on one occasion (possibly more!) Hunter said "stop right here or your going through that mirror. I had to tell him a couple of times". In the same article, Hunter felt that maybe Mick might not have been "mentally or physically equipped to handle the pressure". He also added that "he was a lovely bloke, but in those days he believed in miracles". Hunter later said that "he was pretty obnoxious, but he had energy and was working wonderfully in the studio. He opened up my eyes to a lot of stuff."

In an online interview with Mick by prismfilms.co.uk (available on YouTube 2015) www.youtube.com/watch?v=EH24nPESkWY

Mick looked back at this time, and how in some ways he should not have done it. It was a Co Production with Mick Ronson. Ian Hunter really liked what Mick had been doing musically, and encouraged him to contribute to his next album. Mick said that he played a few shows with Hunter and his band. Ian Hunter stood up for him, and really wanted him to do it. Mick believed that the problem was that Hunter was someone that he looked up to and respected so much. The result of this he felt, was that the Hunter album didn't turn out as well as it should have done.

The Ian Hunter album hit the American market, and got to number 62 in the Billboard charts.

In *Clash City Showdown* (Knowles, 2003) the author felt that Mick "may have been humbled by the failure of the Foley LP and the Ian Hunter album he had just produced"

I have already touched upon his production work with Theatre Of Hate, and this was in many ways groundbreaking and brave both on his part as well as the bands. Theatre of Hate were, in my opinion, an incredibly powerful live act, with aggression, attack, and tunes. The singles prior to the *Westworld* album were very experimental, heavily effected drums, like thunder, and dub influenced sound and fade ins and outs. *Rebel without a Brain* being the first produced by Mick, (released April 1981) followed by the "mega mixed" *Nero/Incinerator* 12" both on their Burning Rome label. As the band increased their following, they were also support act to The Clash during their residency at the Lyceum on the *Radio Clash* tour. The next single and album would be on the Burning Rome label but as an imprint of CBS. Mick again, taking the controls. The Clash connection probably came about through manager Terry Razor, who amongst other jobs, worked on the merchandising for The Clash, and had worked with the Stiff Records/Blackhill setup.

The album was quite a surprise to me in terms of the production, I had seen the band a few months before and they were full on, just pure energy, not unlike The Clash in this respect. The *Westworld* album was released in February 1982, and featured some of the trademarks of earlier productions, the echo and treated drums, dub style techniques, but at the same time considering the songs as a whole, not Mick just going wild on the desk.

In an *NME* review later in the year of a Theatre of Hate Gig (Rai, 1982)The writer seemed pretty negative about the sound of the album….when he was actually reporting on the gig. Harsh words "We all know The Clash production was a substantial influence on the ruin of the *Westworld* LP, even if he acted with the very best of intentions".

He added "Hate backfiring on Mick Jones guns with a tired but stubborn devotion" and "Jones insisted that rhythmic control and minimalistic guitar were the order of hate"

So was Mick out of control as he attempted to mix and produce the album that was to become *Combat Rock*. In *Passion is a Fashion*, band associate Digby remarked on how Mick had made use of Poly Mandell, a musician friend of Ellen Foley who came in to record keyboard and synthesizer parts on the album. He had "supervised him completely" and had gone through all the parts in one night, making very fast decisions. Mick he believed "had all the stuff planned in his head".

While researching this book, I read *How Music Works* (Byrne, 2012) and found some interesting views on the recording process he had observed. The recording process and the technology used said Byrne, "Put part of the creative process in the hands of the producer, the tape editor and the recording engineer". In the same book Glenn Gould (Musician) added that "it would be impossible for the listener to establish at which point the authority of the performer gave way to that of the producer and the tape editor". Byrne commented that it could be argued that these "technicians" were as responsible for how records came to sound and the composers or performers," where authorship of a recording was being spread around, or dispersed". Byrne also added that "recorded music often became the producers medium, in which they could sometimes out auteur the artists they were recording." In the case of *Combat Rock*, Mick wore "Two hats", both artist and producer, and maybe this was the problem, not having a more detached approach to the tracks.

When asked at the Sydney press conference, if he would do any more producing, Mick's reply was "I dunno, it rolls along by itself".

So, was it a bad idea to have Mick at the controls, as opposed to an outside party who might come in and put their mark on the finished product?

Glyn Johns Producer

Glyn Johns as I have mentioned had a reputation as a man who could "rescue" albums that were losing the plot during production.

In *Who Am I* (Townsend, 2013) Pete Townsend talked about how he had first met Glyn Johns in Putney, he was singing with a group called the Presidents. Johns introduced Townsend to Brian Jones and Mick Jagger in 1965 while the The Who (as the Detours) were supporting The Rolling Stones. Townsend was making the *Lifehouse* solo album and was having difficulties with it. "Glyn

Johns greatest strengths was to sequence an album to best serve the music". So possibly Glyn Johns was absolutely the right man for The Clash job!

As Townsend also added on the *Lifehouse* album, "by some miracle Glyn was putting together a single album from the rubble of *Lifehouse*". In the online interview with Bill Flanagan (*Talks At Google - Glyn Johns in Conversation*, 2014), Johns revealed more about this, explaining that it was originally a film project with a script that he just "didn't get", and told Townsend so. What he did see, was some great songs, and so an album came out of this *Who's Next*. As Johns pointed out, a Producer sometimes needs to tell people what they don't want to hear.

From the interview, it is clear that Johns was and is "old school" in his production values. He was very clear that the whole process should be simple!!! His memory of some of the songs he has produced is now hazy, largely as he pointed out, because he had after 50 years, done so much producing, that it was hard to remember it all.

In *No More Heroes* (Ogg, 2006) the author credited Johns as the man who "sorted out *Let It Be* for the Beatles, as well as working with The Who, The Stones and The Small Faces". Ogg also wrote that Joe "would later credit Johns with an 11th Hour rescue of the contents".

During the *Talks At Google* interview, Johns was questioned by a, let's be honest "young" and probably "happening" audience. He spoke quite frankly about he had to some degree received credit for songs and work, but largely it was down to the fact that he was there with some amazing people. He was asked if there was one particular artist that he felt was the "best" experience for him. He nominated Joan Armatrading as a great talent and someone that he learned a lot from. Few in the audience it seemed were aware of her and the material and albums that she had released. Johns was also questioned about the physical location, the questioner made reference to the great series that Dave Grohl had put together while creating *Sonic Highways* 2014, his most recent Foo Fighters album and the also fantastic film about *Sound City* (2013).

Johns told the audience that he would very often choose the studio to work in, as usually he found himself both the producer and the engineer. The priority was that everyone felt comfortable there so that the best possible performances could be achieved and recorded. This certainly seemed to back up Mick's if unpopular insistence on returning to Electric Lady in New York.

Also revealed in the interview, was the important point that, as a producer, he was actually there to provide a service for the Artist. A difficult role which could involved "wet nursing" people, piss them off or make them feel good, depending on the conditions at the time.

6. THE TRACKS

So...what do we have on the final *Combat Rock* Album, when all the tweaking, mixing, re-recording, tears and tantrums were done.

The problem for today's listener is that they probably aren't going to experience the album the way it was intended. Johns as we discovered earlier was renowned for his expertise in sequencing albums and aiding the "telling of a story".

Back in 1982, I went to the local record shop in Fishponds in Bristol, bought my copy, took it back to my shared student house and slapped the vinyl down on my music-centre. Side one, followed by side two, and in my opinion, a very definite "game of two halves".

With later formats, CD or Mini Disc, the listener had and still has the shuffle option, or sequential play option. What you don't get is the crackle of the run off on the vinyl, and that vital pause before you turn over the record and play side two, which just gives you a chance to absorb what you have just heard. In *Blank Generation* (Astor, 2014) the author discussed the great CD vs. vinyl album debate. Is the analogue sound of the vinyl release the only way to hear *Combat Rock*, or is the digitization for the CD and minidisc releases giving the listener a "superior sound". Aster wrote about a recording engineer called E. Brad Mayer, who looked at the sonic differences between analogue and digital sound. His conclusion was that there was no "inherent weakness" in the way CD's were put together or in the digital process. He found differences in what he called the "euphonic effects".

He identified that the vinyl had an intrinsic surface noise which added "warmth" to the sound, but there was a loss of treble at the "high end". Mayer felt that differences were mainly due to do with the cultural experience of the listeners. If they grew up with the "sound" of vinyl, they tended to prefer that sound. In the same book section, Astor wrote that producer Bob Clearmountain had been asked to "hear the record on vinyl, that is how it is supposed to sound". He dismissed this as a load of crap! So it seems that despite my own preference for vinyl, certainly on *Combat Rock* is it ultimately, a question of taste! In a BBC4 documentary *The Sound Of Song* (BBC 4, 2015), Steve Albini was asked to listen to his own band album on an iPod, he had never listened to an mp3 before, but told the interviewer that he barely recognized his own work, and that he felt there were whole layers of the bass end of the track that was missing.

In his *Talks at Google* interview, Glyn Johns was fairly adamant that he would never record anything he really liked in digital sound, and that what left him would be recorded in analogue, whether it turned up on a CD or not!

So what is lost for today's listener in the download/iPod/mp3 shuffle random world is the ability, unless you are particular, to hear the album as it was intended. Maybe the listener of today is only interested in the hits, and would ignore some pretty amazing music.

I wanted to take a look at the album tracks as album tracks, and look at the single releases and yet more controversy over these and their subsequent re-issues.

So to business…

SIDE ONE
• • • • • • • • • •

TRACK 1: KNOW YOUR RIGHTS 3:34

This was one of the earlier *Combat Rock* Tracks that was aired to the public live. Mick recalled that it was one of the earliest songs written for the album, and that it came together as they were touring the Far East (as did a few others) .The live bootlegs from the week long Paris residency (September 1981) seemed to indicate that the song was up and running before the Far East tour. This was confirmed in *The Complete Clash* (Blackmarket Clash/Topping, 2003) where the author wrote that it was "introduced" at the Paris shows, and written in Ear Studios.

Described by some as "The only outwardly political song on *Combat Rock*…rockabilly style" and by others as "A half return to their "shouty, punky glory days." Kris Needs described it as "a ranting strum guard rockabilly hump". Topping described it as the opening song on *Combat Rock*, "heavily metallic drumming, rockabilly guitar breaks".

In *The Clash The Music that Matters* (Fletcher, 2012) the author wrote that "Clash fans longing for a return to old ways, were no doubt encouraged by Strummers initial reassuring…with guitars" and that "it turned out to be a series of limited lyrical gestures set to a primary one chord jam".

I remember well, an earlier visit to Kays Records in Bristol to buy the track when released as a single, and was suitably impressed, particularly by the almost metallic rockabilly guitar which gave the whole track real pace and urgency.

In *Redemption Song*, Salewicz described it as a "Semi Rockabilly Beat", and how it indicated a growing rift between Mick and Joe. It was also the source of the previously mentioned "Stand-off" between Mick and Paul.

In *The Clash – The Only Band That Mattered* (Egan, 2015) the writer described it as "stripped back", and that it had the tone and pace of a Cossack dance, but as he also said it packed a powerful punch.

In *The Clash Music in Review* DVD Booklet (Meyers, 2007) the author wrote that the song was "pure Clash protest" and was a "tense, choppy song which translated brilliantly live".

As the lead off track on the album, it was also the first single. In *The Clash – The Ultimate Music Guide* (Mulholland, 2011) in *Uncut*, the author described it as "The latest in a badly chosen line of first singles off Clash albums" and that it was the worst song because it didn't seem to have "a sense of place". I suppose the track is starkly different from the rest of the material on the album.

In *Melody Maker Singles Review* (Humphries, 1982), The writer began the review with "Back with more of a whimper than a bang, but back at last". He went on to say that *Radio Clash* was the start; *Know Your Rights* takes it a step further". He commended the Glyn Johns production by getting "the crisp speedy surge of the Primal Clash".

The single received very little airplay, and didn't make the top 40 charts (in the UK).

Myself, I remember being shocked by the abrasiveness of the track when released as a single (a brave move indeed) and that so cool rockabilly guitar riff cranked all the way up.

In Rolling Stone (Fricke, 1982) the track was described as the track which "detonates the albums opening salvo", a fair description I would say, and "punctuated by Jones's rubbery Duane Eddy in Hell guitar break" I would agree wholeheartedly!

In truth, it is a standout track because the style and pace does not really match the other tracks, but I would make the point that (possibly Johns) made a good choice in track 2, as *Car Jamming* cleverly brings us down to a more steady level from a runaway start.

TRACK 2: CAR JAMMING 3:54

Car Jamming keeps the guitars to the fore, described as "part Funk, half sung, half rapped" Ellen Foley put in an appearance on backing vocals. "New York Street vibe" said another reviewer, another that the track "ultimately boils down to a fairly pointless song about listening to music in a traffic jam". Well the lyrics actually reveal more depth than this, certainly there are a number of references to the Vietnam vet situation, name checking "Agent Orange" and a mention of "a boy from Missouri getting his boots blown off in a sixties war".

Egan also picked up on the fact that it seemed like a series of observations while in a traffic jam, but allowing Joe to display what he called his "Streetwise poetry".

According to Topping in Complete Clash, the track was first recorded at Marcus Studios along with *This is Radio Clash* and *Sean Flynn*. He added that it was completed In New York, with "Motown style drums" and Joe half singing and half rapping. *In The Clash – The Music That Matters* (Fletcher 2012) wrote that the track was "clearly influenced by urban America" with a "Bo Diddley like beat, leaving room for Jones to offer funky guitar stabs". Fletcher picked up on the words. "riding aluminum crutches", refers to the Vietnam veterans who begged on the streets.

In *The Clash in Review* (Meyers, 2007) the author picked up the Vietnam theme again, the lyrics relating to a young conscript from Missouri who lost his legs. Myers felt that it was a "straight rock and roll song with a pop beat", which had Mick "squeezing in some interesting guitar lines".

In the *NME* album review (Moore, 1982) X-Moore described the track as "Malombo drumming, scratch Guitar, and talk of war".

On The Deviant Art website almightypineapple.deviantart.com/journal/The-Clash-Combat-Rock-Music-Review-295306488 in a *Combat Rock* album review, the track "follows a choppy guitar riff that makes for a mock dance beat". The reviewer felt that the song had an interesting melody, with background vocals from Ellen Foley".

The guitar is incredibly tight, Toppers drums distinctive, and there are a number of synthesizer parts and of course Ms. Foley backing up in the chorus.

TRACK 3: SHOULD I STAY OR SHOULD I GO 3:03

One of the two main "Hot Tracks" from the album. I had read that it was a cross between a track by The Sharks *Sophistication* and *Little Latin Lupe Lou* by Mitch Ryder. So off I went to investigate, and certainly the riff and bass lines are very close to The Sharks track. The same kind of "stop start" rhythm. The two songs are similar, but Mick took it to another place. Chris Spedding an early punk "collaborator" was a member of the Sharks. The Mitch Ryder track was a more 60's sounding record, with keyboards too, I can see where comparisons would arise. Egan also picked up on the Mitch Ryder and Sharks connection.

Joe had wanted to get Joe Ely to record backup vocals in Spanish, the studio tape operator Eddie Garcia phoned his mother for a translation. In 1988, Joe told the Melody Maker newspaper that the backup lyrics were "rubbish", not real Spanish, but "Ecuadorian Spanish". Egan felt that the Spanish vocals served no real purpose, other than to perhaps to allow Joe to "show off his Spanophilic tendencies".

Topping again wrote that it was rehearsed at Ear Studios, and called it a "retro Rock sounding mix" of the two tracks mentioned.

Much has been discussed about the meaning of the lyrics. Mick denied that it was about anybody special, nor was it a cryptic message about leaving The Clash. It certainly was quite ironic. Topping wrote that Joe seemed to have taken the view that it was a "leaving card". The author said that Mick had written it more about a personal situation. (Possibly Ellen Foley?) He had already written *Train In Vain* about his relationship with Viv Albertine from the Slits. That had also been a big hit in the USA when released as a single there. Egan called the track an "Anthem of Hesitation", which is a terrific expression!

The original version lyrics were changed for the Glyn Johns mix and release. The track was tagged as a potential single, and in the original lyrical form would not have passed the censors!

"On your front or on your back" became "So if you want me off your back". Topping had the track as being played live in September 1981. It has been noted that when Mick wrote the song he was in his "full on wack attack" stage, hip hop and New York dance music. The song was written and recorded as a "straight up, radio friendly rock and roll anthem". This may or may not be true, the seed of the idea could have been around for a number of years, but was pulled out of the bag at this time. It certainly had as one reviewer described "sing along qualities".

When released as a single it did extremely well both in the UK and USA, not once, but twice, but that is for later.

In *Redemption Song*, Salewicz wrote that it was "written almost entirely by Mick, assumed to be about his relationship with Ellen Foley". He also added that "It could be taken as a measure of pressure about Mick's future with the group", however, as he pointed out certainly the original lyrics were quite "racey". According to Paul Simonon, it was recorded when Mick and Joe were hardly speaking. In the archives of Joe, there are some satirical type written lyrics in the character of Mick. Lyrics included, "It's always whinge whinge whinge, when the crew go on the binge" This amused Mick said Salewicz when the lyrics were discovered and it was mentioned to him in 2004.

In *Crossbeat*, (Unknown, 2014) a Japanese magazine, the writer felt that it was "a combination of riff and danceable. The bass line reminds you of the Rolling Stones".

Ben Myers in *The Clash Music in Review* mentioned that although *London Calling* may have been their most recognized signature tune, it was "a great rock and roll song that remains their biggest hit". He called it "timeless and traditional rock and roll", and believed to be about his relationship with Ellen Foley. He also named it as "a song for which juke boxes were invented", and "quite simply one of the great modern rock songs".

In the *NME* album review mentioned earlier, X-Moore said that the track "sees Jones messing things up with Spanish, and hours of indecision".

In the *Melody Maker Singles Review* (Taylor, 1982), guest reviewer John Taylor of Duran Duran, mentioned that the track was the biggest FM hit at the time…"through no fault of their own". Taylor praised the production by Glyn Johns, and posed the question, what if Johns had produced their first album, "it would have been the masterpiece that the Sex Pistols made, and The Clash never did!"… Discuss???!!!

In *Combat Rock* (Mulholland, 2011), The writer posed three questions on the nature of the song. "Was it…?

1. The most contrived and successful attempt to make a hit song for US Radio?
2. A heartfelt question to Ellen Foley?
3. A plea to Joe to let him know whether he wanted the guy who started The Clash to be in The Clash anymore?

The writer believed that "it was all three depending on who you are with at the time".

In a *Trouser Press* feature, *Four Sides of The Clash* (Robbins, 1983) The author created a "listeners guide" and under *Should I Stay or Should I Go*, he branded it POP! Interestingly he described it as "amateur sounding guitar" and a "grunting bass introduction", and that it was a "wonderfully sloppy record" which had everything a hit single should have, "only it sounds more like a drunken outtake than your typical high gloss Foreigner concoction".

In 2003 in a retrospective of the greatest Clash Songs in *Uncut* magazine, The track took 23rd position in an all-star panel (Panel, 2003) Gary Crowley recalled hearing it for the first time and thinking "Jesus what's this?" and that it had a great riff, "really dirty, almost like The Kinks" (There was also reference made to playing air guitar!)

Author Steve Erickson took the view that people thought it was a "Mick throwaway", The Clash "trying to be T Rex" Erickson believed it was about what it seemed like, "a guy trying to figure out if the girl is going to sleep with him?"

So, is there a link here, was Mick actually making a parody of Meatloaf's *Paradise by The Dashboard Light* on which Ellen Foley sang on the *Bat Out of Hell* album… Stop right now… before we go any further…!

Steve Diggle (Buzzcocks guitarist) took the view that the band "made a conscious effort to 'fuck with the formula', and take themselves and their fans on a journey". He also added that "people go on about Radiohead, but they have never written a song as infectious as this" He also felt that the track "captured the very essence of The Clash and what they were about in three minutes".

In a 1981 Zig Zag article by Robin Banks, he commented on the live versions from the Paris shows, saying that it was "hauntingly dramatic, with Mick taking the vocals" and that it had a "persistent refrain that stays with you, making its presence felt – another *Train In Vain*".

TRACK 4: ROCK THE CASBAH 3:31

Rock The Casbah was without doubt a "Monster Track". The writing and recording of the song has gone down in Clash legend. But from my reading and research, all was not quite as it appeared. It seemed that Topper had the piano riff for some time, and tinkered with this now and again. This was confirmed by "The Baker" in *The Clash on Broadway* booklet, where he explained that Topper had been toying with the piano part for years. If they went to a studio and there was a piano in there, "he would always play it". Some authors wrote that Topper put down the piano, drums and bass for the track in Electric Lady, with no assistance after Topper found himself first one in to the studio. Other reports are that the engineer on duty that day added the bass. Whatever the real turn of events, the result was a rough demo. After the rest of the band heard the track, they wanted to keep the original recordings, but loop it to twice the length to make it song length. Mick later added guitar and Joe the lyrics. Topper recalled and implied that Joe came down and added the lyrics. Whether he meant right after, is not clear.

Pat Gilbert in *Passion is a Fashion* recounted a story that Tymon Dogg was messing around with Mick's brand new guitar synthesizer (the Daleks' handbag, as Paul later described it) Tymon it seems plugged in his violin and played some eastern scales. Joe began shouting "rock the casbah, rock the casbah". Tymon, said Gilbert, thought he was saying "stop The cadger".

The lyrics Joe wrote related back to the famous Bernie statement about why everything the band wrote had to be a raga. So the "the king told the boogie men, you have to let that raga drop" was the opener. It then became a comment on pop music and the reaction from extreme religious regimes. It was at no point meant as an anti-Arab statement.

In the John Deeth article *Turning Rebellion Into Money* (archive.today/k0Ob, saved from jdeeth. home.mchsi.com/clash.htm), the author wrote that the song "vaguely satirizes Iran's ban on western music". Deeth also noted that American radio would "normally avoid politics", but "poking fun at Iran" after embassy hostage releases the previous year was "non controversial and 'societally sanctioned'".

In a singles review (Bohn, 1982) in the *NME*, the reviewer didn't seem to get the point and wrote that "The Clash's faith in rock as a catalyst for social change is as unshakable as the Muslim faith they have inanely chosen to mock".

Back with Topper's version of events, he maintained that he had also written lyrics for the tune "soppy lyrics about how he missed his girlfriend". According to the Gilbert/Topper explanation, Joe "took one look and said 'how incredibly interesting'". He then screwed up the paper, and told Topper that he wrote the bloody words, and that he had a set of lyrics for this already.

In another interview, Topper said that when the others showed up, they were immediately impressed, and demanded to work with his demo. Two minutes long, it was spliced to double the length for the song. Topper received no extra compensation for the track, but got a share of the royalties from the other tracks.

In *The Complete Clash*, Topping remarked that the track was one of the most well known Clash songs to the general public, and that Topper was a great drummer (no doubt!!), also a "more than useful bassist, and could play a little jazz piano". The author quoted Joe as saying "he banged down the drum track, and then ran over to the piano and then the bass". Mick added what Topping called "Industrial sounding guitar".

The songs greatness said Topping, "lies in the ability to comment on serious ethical issues with humour".

When played live, there was no piano, and so came over quite differently, but became a key song in The Clash set. In *The Clash – Music in Review*, Myers called the track an "excellent disco funk floor filler, and that it was the creation of Topper, who built a drum loop in the studio. Myers also referred to the lyrics which Joe "discarded"! X Moore again in the album review in NME called it a "funk punching gem of a song", and how it gave you a "grinning rush, that only The Clash can spark".

In *Rolling Stone* (Fricke, 1982)the writer described the track as a "smart Alecky, funk inflected romp complete with snappy hook and party piano". Fricke clearly understood the message at the time, the banning of pop music by Muslim fundamentalists in Iran, and about having rights. Not about US troops bombing the crap out of the local inhabitants!

In *The Clash Ultimate Music Guide* (Mulholland, 2011) Mulholland looked back on the track. "The little drummer boy, who was apparently too drug addled to work with enters the studio before anyone else got there" and that "a few hours later, and The Clash have recorded their most commercially successful song of their career".

In an article *Rock The Kasbah…Later Rock*, the author believed that *Rock The Casbah* was "about as unlikely a hit record as will ever haunt the charts". Questioning if anybody understood the lyrics and that Joe had rarely sounded so "raunchy", and would the public not miss the "roaring heavy metal guitar" common to more typical pop.

In the Uncut All-Star panel of 30 greatest Clash songs, *Rock The Casbah* made number 16. In favour were a number of musicians. Clint Boon described it as "the all-time definitive punk pop record". Butch Vig commented that it was a big hit in the USA, but he didn't think many people had a clue what they were singing about. Norman Cook made it a personal favourite, "as it showed him that a white rock band could make dance music". Another DJ, Robert Elms remarked that it was "the sound of a band taking all these influences and making great fun music out of them".

Sir Bob Geldof remarked that *Combat Rock* was crap, but that *Rock The Casbah* was "a classic".

One of the more interesting opinions came from musician/stand up Ed Hammil (possibly Ed Hamell) who commented that "good lord, it's a weird ass radio hit isn't it" and that "the lyrics were 19 years ahead of their time, and with all that Buena Vista Social Club, so was the music".

My favourite, from Mickey Bradly of the Undertones, who said "couldn't make out the words, but it doesn't matter", and that "The Undertones had a song called *Casbah Rock*… it wasn't as good".

TRACK 5: RED ANGEL DRAGNET 3:41

Lyrically, the song was based around the shooting of one of the Red Angel Guardians who patrolled the streets and subways as vigilantes in New York.

Wikipedia (Accessed 10/3/2013) described the Red Angels as a non-profit international volunteer organisation of unarmed citizen crime patrollers. It was founded in 1979, in New York, created to combat widespread violence and crime on the New York Subway. Their only powers were those of citizens' arrest.

Around the time of writing, the story was in the newspapers, the shooting of Frankie Melvin. In The *Clash on Broadway* booklet, the incident took place on New Year's Day 1981, Melvin having been shot by a policeman in New Jersey. It was a misunderstanding, as Melvin was seen as the aggressor in a street situation. The date seems a little adrift from the album date, from other sources, the event happened on New Year's day 1982.

Joe famously wrote the lyrics in a spiral on a Hotel envelope as that was the only paper available to Joe at the time.

Topping wrote that the track was sung by Paul in what Mick called a "Jamaican Marlene Dietrich" style. The author also wrote that many of the *Combat Rock* songs created images inspired by Scorsese and the *"Taxi Driver"* film from 1976. So much so, that Joe used some lines with permission from the movie script in the song. Kosmo took the part of Robert DeNiro.

Fletcher Noted that Paul performed with less of a reggae influence than in the past, and that he mostly chanted his way through the song. He also noted that the song acknowledged its "cinematic influence". Salewicz backed up the story in *Redemption Song*, and that the song referenced Travis Bickle in *"Taxi Driver"*, and that Kosmo delivered the "Travis Rap".

Ben Myers Clash Music in Review wrote that the track saw the band "Soaking up everything New York had to offer", and that the track was "stripped down atmospheric funk rock". X-Moore in the NME wrote "tuff as a bass bin, as Simonon lays down his dream".

Adam Sweeting in *Melody Maker* (Sweeting, 1982) wrote that he felt that the song was not really about people fighting against street violence, but that it was "about a Scorcese movie".

The tune itself features some keyboards in the mix, but it's the pumping bass line and the guitar stabs and almost 50's affected guitar riff that really sets this track off. What is clever for me, is that although there is obviously the New York/US influence, Joe seems to bring it back to London too with the aid of Jack (The Ripper) "feeding on the birds of night" and not even the "bobbies bicycling, could stop the blood and feathers flying".

On the Consequence of Sound website (accessed 17/04/14) consequenceofsound.net/2009/04/rock-history-101-the-clashs-red-angel-dragnet/ Tim Nordberg produced an article on 25th April 2009, on the *Red Angel Dragnet* track. He included some "atmospheric" background story about the Guardian Angels on the El train, and the inspiration for the tracks lyrics, which are credited in this piece to Paul. "Probably thinking about Vigilante Justice in America, he might even have been watching *Taxi Driver*". The article speculated how the lyrics were inspired by the newspaper article about the shooting of Frank Melvin. *Red Angel Dragnet,* said the article, "is a misguided paean to a vigilante anti-crime organization that didn't turn out quite as it appeared" The writer noted that it had a rock solid bass-line, a couple of lyrical gems (if a bizarre delivery from Simonon) and the priceless Kosmo taxi driver DeNiro impression.

In the *Sten Guns in LA* article (McCullough, 1982), Joe talked about the "*Taxi Driver* bit" and how Kosmo had given the "Travis speech" one day, and Joe couldn't get it out of his head. "It's so true of this place" said Joe.

But it wasn't only The Clash with an obsession for the Scorsese movie. The failed assassination attempt on Ronald Reagan had been carried out by one John Hinckley. The trial was on going in 1982. Hinckley had developed an obsession with actress Jodie Foster in the film, and wanted to impress her through various plots including a planned hijacking and the assassination attempt on an important person's life. There was an attempt to organize a petition to have Martin Scorsese stand trial over the content of "*Taxi Driver*", as McCullough pointed out "the movie that so influenced *Combat Rock* and what he called "current Strummer thinking".

In *The Clash – The Only Band That Mattered* (Egan, 2015) the author felt that it was a bizarre track, and gave him the impression that there were an assortment of instruments playing at the same time instead of what he referred to as a "sound painting". Egan believed this to be the weakest track on the album, but personally, I like this a lot. It has a great bass line, Simmo on vocals, some great twangy guitar, and of course the Kosmo/De Niro speech. The original mix (more about this later) also has keyboards much more at the fore. Perhaps unfairly, Egan mentioned that Paul got vocal duties in the same way that perhaps Ringo from the Beatles would be given a track to sing by Lennon and Mc Cartney, "to keep the fans happy". He also believed that possibly Joe stepped back from certain songs to avoid flak about content, or giving Mick the more "sensitive" songs to perform.

TRACK 6: STRAIGHT TO HELL 5:22

Described casually by Topper as a "doodle with a bossa nova beat". In the same way that the London connection is made with the New York subways in *Red Angel Dragnet*, in *Straight to Hell*, Joe managed to merge (if you interpret as such) the Northern English industrial towns, with the Vietnam conflict and in particular the GI "offspring" from the relationships between local Vietnamese women. Reading the lyrics about the "railhead towns and Steel Mill Rust", I am also drawn to the film "*The Deerhunter*", where the three main characters are steelworkers from Pennsylvania, go off to Vietnam. The backdrop to the US scenes is pretty bleak, as Northern Britain could be. Once again, Robert DeNiro is in the spotlight.

Kris Needs wrote that the lyrics dealt with the way that society "consigns outcasts to the Dumper", and that Joe referred to unemployed steel workers, offspring of American GI's and immigrants in general.

In *The Complete Clash*, Topping wrote that *Straight To Hell* contained some of Joes' finest lyrics, and that the song was a "harrowing series of snapshots of debased humanity". The "Speaking in English in quotations", he believed may be referring to those who spoke the "Kings English", (the Upper class) and those who lived in decaying rusted steel towns. As he put it, "In the blink of an eye, the listener is transported to Vietnam for the "Bamboo Kid" and "Coca Cola not Rice". The final verse heads off to The USA with its problems with "crack culture" and misery. Stirring stuff indeed, and as one author wrote, "An emotional Cornerstone" to *Combat Rock*.

In *Passion is a Fashion*, Gilbert found Digby, a Clash Roadie from the time, who remembered that it was recorded in one day. The day before New Year's Eve, in 1981. According to Digby, there was "lots of percussion and innovation going on". Joe he remembered had stayed up all night working on the lyrics; the vocals were put down and finished at 11:40PM. Joe and others went to Times Square and got there just before midnight and was quoted as saying that "I knew we had done something really great"

Topping confirmed that the backing track was recorded at Electric Lady on 30th December 1981, and Topper asked Joe just prior to the Take, to play his secret weapon, an R Whites lemonade bottle covered with a towel. Joe hit the bass drum front with it.

In 2003, in *Riot of Their Own* (Simonon, 2003), Mick and Paul looked back at The Clash songs. Simonon remembered that the song was all different bits that came together, in the same way that "Broadway" had, "Me and Topper doing something at a sound check which would suddenly work out". Mick remembered that "part of it was what was going on in Equador at the time, it was going to become like Vietnam", and that the Latin feel to the tune was probably an unconscious thing because of what was going on in Central America.

Kris Needs wrote that *Straight To Hell* was created, "starting with Mick's guitar riff, over which Topper put an unusual drum pattern based around a bossa nova rhythm". Topper remembered that Mick's guitar line would not work with a rock beat to it, which is why it ended up as bossa nova. As with other tracks, *Straight To Hell* was edited down during the Glyn Johns sessions, some observers felt that the dropped verse that shaved off one minute should have been left in. The original was approaching seven minute "raga" status, cut down to a little over five.

Ben Myers in *Clash Music in Review* felt that *Straight To Hell* was possibly "the last great recorded moment of the bands career". He also pointed out that it was a "truly International sounding song". He added also that it was one of the bands most "downbeat moments, but also one of their best". From the *NME* album review, X-Moore related the track to the then current conflict on the Falklands. Writing that it wouldn't be played on HMS Invincible (part of the UK "Task Force" of ships), and how "British workers might start wondering what they are doing 8000 miles away from home killing Argentinian workers"

In *Rolling Stone* (Hall, 1982) Hall described the track as "the sweetest and most powerful and most relevant song to Americans" about the plight of Vietnam's post war American orphans. I watched a BBC TV news piece in April 2014, which followed an ex Vietnam Vet who returned to the country to try and find his son who he had left behind when he was evacuated from Saigon. He walked the streets with a guide to try and trace his son and partner. After several weeks, it appeared that his partner may be in the US already, and possibly his son. The "Coca Cola and

Rice" children had found themselves victimized by the incoming regime, some forced to live in the jungle away from the other children. The US introduced a "repatriation" scheme for a limited period, and many left for the US to seek a better life. Happily in this case after months and a Facebook campaign, the Father and son were reunited. So, even today (as I write) the song has a deep relevance.

In *The Clash - The Only Band That Mattered* (Egan, 2015) the writer described it as a "moving meditation" on the dispossessed people of the world, and how the lyrics take you almost flitting across the world, the US, Vietnam and the UK.

Looking at the comments, again from the *Uncut* 30 greatest Clash Songs, it certainly seems to have had a big effect on the panel. Terry Chimes held it up as his favourite Clash song, even though he didn't play on the recorded version. He enjoyed playing it live as it was slower and he could listen to the song as they were playing. Roddy Frame of Aztec Camera labeled it a "beautiful, beautiful record". He also noted that the The Clash were always a bit "ahead of the game", and recalled playing the album with headphones over and again and "hearing all those lovely things that were happening in the music". He felt that it showed that "the whole punk thing could go somewhere".

Don Letts put forward that the track showed how "Strummer moved the lyrical goalposts of what rock music could deal with".

Radio presenter Gideon Coe felt that it was the sound of a band falling apart, but a beautiful record. Alex Cox was in agreement of its beauty. Perhaps a fitting round up to the panel comments was from Adam Sweeting, who described it as "the audio version of *Apocalypse Now*".

On *The Rave Reviews* website constructivist.wordpress.com/2008/06/08/the-clash-combat-rock/ the writer pointed out that the use of the word "san" is restricted to Japanese, and would not be used in any other Asian culture. They felt that as they admitted, it was nitpicking, but "the error detracts from Strummers otherwise sophisticated rendering of immigrant hopes and dilemmas".

In the *Sounds* article *Sten Guns in LA* (McCullough, 1982), the writer questioned Joe about the meaning and that it seemed to be about heroin. Joe responded by saying "not really, it's about having no place in the world to live" and that kids who were growing up with Thatcher were being denied "their actual piece of this world they are entitled to". Verse one said Joe which dealt with the "Amerasian" off spring of American GI's, and how they were looked down upon and not allowed to go to the USA.

The third verse did deal with heroin "all the junk they sell people to kill them off with". McCullough asked if it was about heroin from personal experience, to which Joe replied that he had never taken heroin, and if anyone came around with it, "I just tell them to get out! I think junk's evil – no doubt about that".

As side one draws to a close, for me, it's like a very definite shift from the more straight ahead songs, and into something a little darker in places and certainly more cinematic. Was this deliberate? Was it the work of the master "sequencer" Glyn Johns, I'm not certain, but it works.

SIDE TWO
....

TRACK 1: OVERPOWERED BY FUNK 4:48

Whatever I was expecting, I don't think this was it...

Side two opens with a full on synth attack and funk workout. It certainly got the critics hot and bothered, one said that the track should have been called "Overpowered by Dullness", another that it was a "train collision between the JB's and Prince, with Joe Ranting a stream of abstract phrases". The track features a rap from Futura, who as Mikey Dread had contributed to *Sandinista* and acted as a musical collaborator, acted not so much as a musical collaborator but a cultural one. "If you ain't reggae for it? Funk out".

The lyrics do just seem to be a series of statements, with no real common trail.

Topping wrote that the track was originally recorded at the Ear Studio sessions, but the recording was finished at Electric Lady in December 1981. Lyrically, he believed that the word "funk" was a metaphor for the word "greed". In *The Clash – The Only Band That Mattered* (Egan, 2015) the author believed that prior to a musical genre, funk was a word used for "objectionable".

The Futura rap towards the end of the track is I guess what gives the track its street edge. Without this, the track would meander on, and not really go anywhere. Futura gives the listener an education in how he operated as a graffiti artist on New York, and how as fast as the Transit Authority tried to clean off the graffiti on trains and buildings, the art was back the next morning...Funk Power...Over and Out!

Egan made a remark that The Clash were "comically susceptible" to people with a certain "outlaw aura", and believed that Futura was probably less eloquent with his words than with his spray cans.

The keyboards come courtesy of Poly Mandell and certainly take the lead, interlacing with the "shakalaka guitar" from Mick (Topping's words!!) He also believed that the track might be a genre pastiche, and that the band might have been in danger of "overdosing on dance music pretensions". Topping also thought it was a bold attempt at "something alien to them. The synth and bass follow the same riff, while Mick's guitar chops over the rhythm, and Topper is in "full high hat disco mode". To my ears, Ellen Foley also helps out on backing vocals on the "don't you love our western ways".

It was aired to the public during the Paris Residency, but dropped thereafter, perhaps it needed the synth keyboards to carry it over, but on listening to this on the Paris Bootleg albums, it stands up very well as a live piece, particularly helped along by Toppers incredible drumming

Tony Fletcher called it a "self-evident slice of hard hitting Clash funk", but felt it lacked the ideas of *Radio Clash* and the *The Magnificent 7*. "White Funk" he noted was the latest Hip sound on the London streets. Ben Myers called it a "forceful and muscular funk song" and X-Moore called it a "song that rattles and argues over a funk battering"

From the review on Deviant Art website mentioned earlier, the writer was not clear if the track was "the band embracing this cheesy new 80's sound, or ridiculing it"

TRACK 2: ATOM TAN 2:23

An interesting "call and response" track between Joe and Mick who share next lines. Kris Needs summed up the track as "phantom style superhero figure in a rain battered motel".

Topping described the track as "a slow soul groove". Recorded he said at Electric Lady, and never performed live. He felt it addressed the pressures affecting people in modern life. In *The Clash a Visual Documentary*, it was described as being about life after a nuclear holocaust.

X-Moore in the NME also read it as the two vocalists "swapping vocals on the sadness, blood and madness of life after a nuclear war".

The nuclear theme was taken up by Myers, as he wrote that it was another song "written beneath the mushroom cloud of nuclear age paranoia". He also pointed out that it does sound "too hastily constructed to leave a lasting impression". In *The Clash – The Only Band That Mattered* (Egan, 2015) the author made a comparison between the track and the "similar themed" *London Calling*, but that the track lacked the tunefulness or vitality.

Tony Fletcher remarked that it was the albums shortest track, had double tracked vocals and might possibly have been a "blueprint for the future Big Audio Dynamite".

The synthesizer again is used, but a little more subtlety employed, and the Mick response lines do have a pretty loose/sloppy quality to them. The bass is prominent, so perhaps Paul won the fight over this one! Egan also felt that it was the music or "instrumental chops" that stopped the track from being "completely pointless".

TRACK 3: SEAN FLYNN 4:21

Pat Gilbert wrote that this song was named after Errol Flynn's son who was in Vietnam at the time author and writer Michael Herr was. If you want to get an idea of where The Clash's heads might be at with regards to Vietnam, I would recommend reading the Herr book Dispatches. You can pick up cheap second hand copies (see reading list).

Sean Flynn used to head off to the front line in his role as war photographer, on a Honda motorcycle, one day he never returned and was reported missing in action. He had left Pnom Penn with fellow photo journalist Dana Stone; they were stopped at a checkpoint, never to be seen again. He was a very highly respected Time Magazine Photo journalist. It is believed he was executed in 1971.

As well as the information from the Herr book, a character possibly loosely based on Flynn appeared in the "*Apocalypse Now*" movie. Dennis Hopper played the part of the unnamed "photo journalist". In *Melody Maker* (Sweeting, 1982).The writer said that he felt The Clash had "nicked the idea from Michael Herr's book *Dispatches*…or "*Apocalypse Now*".

Not too many lyrics to really get to grips with here, the whole track is very atmospheric and as Fletcher said "deliberately Cinematic". Recorded he noted at the same time as *Radio Clash*

But what lyrics there are seem to fit the general atmosphere, "the drums beat into the jungle floor", "rain on the leaves" and "they filled the sky with a tropical storm"…

But possibly a world away the rap and funkiness of *Radio Clash*!

Topping gave some insight into the track, reported that it was written during the "Vanilla Sessions" for the 1981 Tour, and recorded at Marcus Studios in April 1981. It is not clear if the "Vanilla" reference is correct.

The saxophone which floats across the track was played by Gary Barnacle, who remembered Topper creating and oriental style backing with percussion, and then Joe and Mick collaborating with him to produce the backing track. Jeremy Green engineered on the track, and felt that it was more like an Irish reel in construction. By the time the track got to *Combat Rock*, it was cut in half by Glyn Johns.

In *The Clash – The Only Band That Mattered* (Egan, 2015) the author felt that the track was the "strangest thing in The Clash corpus", and that if you were not aware it was about the photographer, you might not get it at all. Egan called it an "exotic sultry mood piece" which is a pretty fair summary, and picked up on the soundtrack like qualities of the music.

Ben Myers noted that the track was a "near instrumental", which used flutes (as well as the saxophone) to create an Eastern Sounding atmosphere. He added "As a musical experiment…it just about succeeds!!"

TRACK 4: GHETTO DEFENDANT 4:26

Described as reggae influenced rock…well yes. Another track with a guest vocalist, not a rapper this time, but famed beat poet Allen Ginsberg. It appeared that at one of Joe's vocal sessions, Ginsberg just turned up. Joe asked him if he would contribute "the voice of God" to the *Ghetto Defendant* track. Apparently, Joe had told Ginsberg that he was the greatest poet in America, and "what could he do with this?" Ginsberg asked for some names of "punk dances". One was currently popular in San Francisco at the time, and that was The Worm, and Ginsberg improvised a poem around the lyric.

In *Redemption Song*, Salewicz reported that Ginsberg wrote the lyrics on the spot to recite on the track. Despite a number of late night sessions working on three or four lyrics, not all made the Glyn Johns final cut, and the verse he helped on most was also cut. Pat Gilbert had a variation on this, writing that Joe had requested that Ginsberg "drop by", which he did with Peter Orlofsky (poet and Ginsberg's life partner), and added spoken word to the track.

Topping provided a different variation on the Ginsberg story, saying that Ginsberg had gone to the studio to ask The Clash to back him on a record of his own. But that he ended up being on theirs! In *The Clash – The Only Band That Mattered* (Egan, 2015) the author noted that Ginsberg got no "composing credits" on the track.

In *The Clash on Broadway* booklet, Kosmo explained how the connection was made firstly at one of the Bonds shows, when Ginsberg got up on stage and recited something to an impromptu Clash musical backing. This was a piece called *Capitol Air*. (Available on some bootlegs, and recently, I discovered this on YouTube.)

So what is interesting about the inclusion of Ginsberg on *Combat Rock*, is that it means the album spans generations of what could be called "protest poets". Ginsberg was big in the 50's and 60's particularly, and was involved in the anti-Vietnam protests, in the middle we have Joe, and on the album the at the time newest form of protest poetry, Futura representing the rap scene. In *Redemption Song* again, Kosmo played down the importance and influence of Ginsberg on Joe as a "lyric coach". Ginsberg did spend time working on other lyrics with Joe. Ginsberg however told Kris Needs that "some of Strummers stuff was on a par with some of the great writers he had come up with".

Ben Myers also recognized the significance of the collaboration by adding that "it signaled a great meeting of alternative culture minds… the reigning punks, and the king of poets".

Gilbert took the lyrics to be about heroin, particularly in the ghetto, and how it was sapping the will and ability for its inhabitants to organize politically. This theme was taken up by Salewicz in *Redemption Song*, a protest ballad he agreed, about a conspiracy theory that the government actually encouraged heroin in the Ghettos to act as an anesthetic. In an article *Don't Call Me Woody*, (Shannon, 2014), the author was in agreement, when he wrote that the track "asserts that drug abuse, far from being subversive, is a powerful tool for stifling youthful rebellion".

Kris Needs believed that the track started life as a dub tune at Ear Studios, with Joes lyrics about "inner city addiction to Afghanistan medication". He also felt that the lyric may have also been inspired by Toppers own heroin addiction. Topping backed up this saying that the track was written and rehearsed at Ear Studios in 1981. It was said Topping, a mid-paced reggae tune with Mick playing harmonica".

As with many of the tracks, the final *Combat Rock* version was edited down with Ginsberg's verse left off, only to appear on The *Clash On Broadway* album set. The track was played at the Paris Residency in September 1981.

Tony Fletcher called the track "a lone diversion into proper reggae" and that it indicated with the input from Ginsberg, "that The Clash had moved on from their dub infatuation". He also felt that Ginsberg brought a "quietly authoritative secondary voice that traversed the world war torn hotspots past and present". In the *NME* album review, X-Moore wrote that the track "Bumps along the middle of the road, but the message is still hard, never conciliatory".

TRACK 5: INOCULATED CITY 2:38

Kris Needs had this track as another song from the Ear studio sessions, which carried a very strong antiwar theme, and as Topping said the futility of conflict, "no one knows what we're fighting for". He also confirmed it was a song from Ear Studios. It was another song aired at the Paris residency shows.

Ben Myers wrote that the track "sees war from the viewpoint of fallen soldiers, regardless of which side they are". In summary he felt that it was "more like a freeform jam with lyrics shoehorned in as an afterthought" and "decent but not memorable".

When questioned about his "interest in war" by Dave McCullough in a *Sounds* article, Joe had responded by saying "true, I am interested in war, but it's an anti war interest". He went on to point out that we hadn't experienced war that our fathers had.

Mick takes the lead voice on the track, which makes this stand out a little, a mid paced verse chorus arrangement, until you hit the later part of the song. Enter the infamous "2000 Flushes" sample. This was later to spark controversy and legal proceedings!

The inclusion of a small section of a Flushco Inc. advertisement for a toilet cleaner in the track was an innovative move on the part of Mick. It was certainly a pointer to the developments he made in Big Audio Dynamite. But he had already pulled off a similar stunt with the Theatre of Hate *Do you Believe in the Westworld* single. If you can track down the 12" single, where a sample has been used from the John Wayne movie The Comancheros, the line "pretty soon your'e gonna catch on I ain't your friend". Another sample of dialogue and soundtrack music from the same film, "you're gonna live a lot longer if you follow after me".

In *The Clash – The Only Band That Mattered* (Egan, 2015), the author picked up on the use of the "sample", but felt that Mick had only really included it as that was what other rap records were doing at the time on the Radio, and that the sample gave the song it's title. He also felt that the song had a kind of marching beat. Interestingly, he also felt that the content was very similar to *The Call Up* and that possibly the band were victims of what he called "subject repetition", or "theme exhaustion".

The inclusion of the advert actually predated the sampling and copyright issues which flooded in during the mid 1980's… so "get three coffins ready…"

The result of its inclusion was that the Flushco company lawyers swung into action, and tried to sue, eventually agreeing that the sample section be removed from the subsequent repressings of *Combat Rock* through the use of an injunction. Flushco maintained that the inclusion of the jingle in a "Punk Rock" song hurt their image!

Innovative though it was, and it seems to blend so well with the track itself, you have to ask what was the relevance of the toilet cleaner with an anti-war song?

Tony Fletcher wrote that "the track could easily have appeared on a Big Audio Dynamite album" and "that the inclusion of the advert showed a growing infatuation with sampling".

Fletcher raised the point that Mick was always accused of "stretching out Clash albums beyond all common sense, yet this BAD imprint is the shortest track on Combat Rock" (In fact the second shortest behind *Atom Tan*).

TRACK 6: DEATH IS A STAR 3:04

The final closing track on Combat Rock is the second of what might be called more movie soundtrack orientated. In Joes' interview with Roz Reines in the *NME*, Joe explained that the song was about the way "we all queue up at the cinema to see someone get killed". He added that "these days, the public execution is the celluloid execution", and that he was examining why he wanted to go and see these movies.

Described on the *Deviant Art* website as a "good closer", with a "distant, almost Syd Barret-era Pink Floyd aura".

Tony Fletcher wrote that the lyrics take you "on the last journey to the jungles heart of darkness". Gary Mulholland also considered the song to be about the death of relationships, industries and communities, as well as the death of popular entertainment "and the death of The Clash". Later he added that it was about our "abhorrence of real violence, while we sit in darkened rooms getting off on armies of killers and slaughter of Hollywood".

The song itself is as Topping points out, "half spoken, mainly acoustic, with crickets chirping in the distance". The piano is played in what he called a 1920's jazzy style, a Spanish guitar and Topper using the brushes on the drums. Depending on the version of events, it may have been Mick playing the piano, or Tymon Dogg. But certainly Tymon is credited on the album sleeve notes. This is another track that came out of the Electric Lady Sessions.

It is a melancholy song for sure. Ben Myers wrote that it was a "Jones sung tune" and was laid back and jazzy, "four punks turning their hand to lounge music….unremarkable!" Mulholland again described it as a "mournfully quiet and diseased ragtime ballad". With Joe's spoken lyrics and Mick singing, it is almost a duet, and as Fletcher pointed out, it had an arrangement similar to a "show tune farewell".

Adam Sweeting summed it up as a "dark little vignette of love and death, sung breathlessly by Mick and Joe" and "cocktail Piano tinkles a tango over an acoustic guitar strum". Indeed as he pointed out, it was the last time they were heard on record together as The Clash.

Topping looked at it as a "striking if rather solemn and downbeat end to an often bombastic and radio friendly world of *Combat Rock*. A damned strange way to end *Combat Rocks'* tour of The Clash vision of the American gothic experience".

In *The Clash – The Only Band That Mattered* (Egan, 2015), the author called the track "a weird closer to a weird album".

And as Mulholland added in his summary "The perfect sonic epitaph, perhaps to a band who made their name into a way of life".

7. ALBUM SLEEVE AND TITLE

Much has been made of the significance of the *Combat Rock* album sleeve. I wanted to look at this and the inner sleeve because I consider it to be all part of the album package. I know that many writers concentrate on the music, and rightly so, but The Clash were about the music and the image, so I feel justified. I'm looking initially at the first pressing of the UK vinyl release.

The front cover is a colour photo taken by Pennie Smith while the band was in Thailand after the final date of the Far East Tour. It was perhaps a strange end to such a high profile tour, and it seemed that the band wanted to move on and get the album cover shot done. Pennie Smith had a brief from the record label to produce a shot that could be used on the front cover. A band shot on a railway track which leads off into a vanishing point.

Some rock historians might see a similarity with the layout/composition with that of an album released by The Animals called *Complete Animals*. Although released in 1990 on CD format, the photograph on the cover was taken at an unspecified date and featured the band dressed in military gear (armed) sitting on a railway track which in this case turns off to the right of the shot. Whether there was any conscious or unconscious decision about the composition is debatable. Somewhere along the line, there was an idea to produce a cover that would have "futuristic Asian cities, vivid colours and Chinese calligraphy as a back drop".

When I spoke to Jules Balme, the album sleeve designer, he was not aware of this proposal, only a brief which involved using the group picture taken by Pennie. In another twist, in his autobiography *Sound Man* (Johns, 2014), the author presented a hand drawn cartoon of an album sleeve which was drawn in thick felt pen on one of the acetates of the original "Micks mix" double album . The picture showed one hand holding the artwork, the other finishing off the title.... *Rat Patrol From Fort Bragg*. Johns believed that Joe had done the sketch, but a look at the hand holding the paper points squarely at Paul...Rings on fingers and ID Bracelet and watch.

In the Mojo Magazine Article *Who killed The Clash*, (Snow, 2008) Pennie Smith said that she shot mostly in black and white, the band, she reported wanted the photo this way.

Other pictures from the photo shoot went on to grace the cover of re issued singles and promotional posters and postcards. It appeared that at some point Pennie was told that the pictures were "The Big One", and would be the cover of the *Combat Rock* album, and so needed to be in colour. Pennie in her words "shot off a roll of colour film and sent it off". As she was taking the pictures, she believed that she saw The Clash "falling apart before her very eyes". She had always noticed that previously the band had been quite tactile with each other, leaning on another's shoulders, but that this didn't seem to be there anymore.

In terms of the personal interaction going on in the shot, again much has been debated about the body language going on. It seems that only Topper is looking directly at the camera. Mick looks down, Paul looking somewhere off and Joe looking at the camera with one hand over his right eye. His left eye is squinting at the camera. Not exactly a "boy band" promo shoot and certainly no airbrushing in this one. Paul looking cool as fuck with cigarette in one hand (another prepped ready behind his ear) and the only band member to make physical contact with anyone else, and that is Topper. So does this really reveal another story behind the state of band relationships at the time? Does the fact that they are almost all looking off in different directions reveal their state of mind at the time? Joe told Chris Salewicz that he was trying to focus his near sighted eye, but was it, as Salewicz wrote, that he couldn't see clearly anymore? Mulholland sees the shot with Joe "Looming "over the others, saying that he was probably squinting in the sun, "but it could be a coded message to the fans, wondering if he can sack the drummer without destroying the most important thing he would ever do".

In *The Clash – The Only Band That Mattered* (Egan, 2015) the author commented on the picture which saw the band "astride Thailand Railway Tracks". He found it a peculiar picture, with Joe covering his face (although not completely!!) and that the others were distracted, "but not by the same thing".

Again, rock historians have looked for hidden messages in album sleeves, for example Abbey Road by the Beatles, where Paul McCartney is the only band member bare footed, the group cross the road in a specific order. John Lennon in white (was he the angel) Ringo in black for the undertaker, Paul in his suit but no shoes (as shoes were not required in heaven), so maybe he was dead? George dressed in his denims, so perhaps he was the "grave digger"?

This is of course open to interpretation!

In the *Uncut Ultimate Music Guide* (Mulholland, 2011) The writer talked about the cover, and how "most people were just so happy to be holding the new Clash album, that they didn't notice what it was telling them, or didn't want to". Personally, I was happy holding the new Clash album.

During my interview with Jules Balme, he explained how the he had attended a meeting which was to decide on the photo to be used on the cover, and that it was pretty much a unanimous decision that the best one was the one which ultimately was used. Pennie Smith he confirmed only took a couple of rolls of colour pictures. The meeting was at Kosmo's flat, and that they had hired a projector to show them. Despite some of the earlier comments, it was felt that the ultimate cover shot had a "good vibe" to it. The choice of a colour shot rather than a black and white photo preferred by both Pennie and the band, was a concession Jules believed to please the US Record Label, largely insisted upon by Bernie.

So if we look at the clothes the band are wearing, there has been much said about the "combat threads" and their appearance on the *Combat Rock* cover. But from my observations and "Clash clobber" fixations, I only see Topper in an Alex Michon/Simonon cut off jacket. Mick looking splendid in what is probably a Michon made tan shirt and red braces. Paul is wearing military tiger stripe shirt (and from other shot similar trousers). Joe in his cut off Clash tour t-short and again probably Michon made piped military styled trousers. It doesn't seem like a very staged photo shoot when compared to more latter-day group sleeve shots.

Akito Watanabe from The Strummers in Japan, was aware of the cover photograph being taken in Thailand by Pennie Smith. "Shot in good taste, and not posed".

The final shot is framed by the grey/green camouflage background which continues on to the back sleeve. The front cover is finished off with the band name and titles in bold red combat style stencil font captured by two red stars.

Mulholland called it the "ugliest Clash sleeve, but no big deal". He had a problem with the front picture. "Beneath the rockabilly meets GI Joe hair and clothes…the band look as disconnected as they feel" "Mick and Paul" he said "are posing like rock stars" (well this is their job surely, Mick was…and Paul couldn't stop himself…he just has the "look") looking in opposite directions, feet apart, but miles from each other". He also rather bitchily said that "Mick didn't get the message about wearing black. In the picture, Paul is wearing camouflage shirt and trousers, Joe Combat green trousers.

So…on to the back cover which has the camouflage background. Jules Balme explained that this background used for the back cover was created with an airbrush on some board. He remarked that in hindsight, he felt spray paints might have made a better job of it.

The track listing up until recently with some of the later CD Format reissues retained a very bold Side One and Side Two split. Set at a jaunty angle in yellow in a more traditional serif style typeface. Jules explained that originally on the first proof, the titles were created to look like the credits on a film, but were then amended to use yellow type and set at an angle. It was interesting talking to him about this, today, all this could be achieved using Photoshop and creative software. Back in 1982, it was all lovingly crafted, and type created with Letraset.

In red bold caps is "MIXED BY GLYN JOHNS" and "MADE BY THE CLASH"…just so that you know. The album catalogue number appears within a red flag in the top right FMLN2 and a CBS logo alongside. Bottom left in White stencil style is the Band and title in a red box. These were what Jules referred to as "devices" to hold some of the required information, company logos and codes. The catalogue number was pretty crucial. "Back in the day" if I can use that expression, the catalogue number was the means by which albums were ordered from suppliers, sales recorded in shops for stock control and gathering chart information. Having worked in record stores, later in the charts department at Gallup, I can remember issues with artwork not making the catalogue number easy to find read and record, either by writing down in sales diaries or later inputting using a data collection machine and keyboard. Later, as music product was bar-coded like a can of beans, I remember talking to upset designers and album buyers alike, as to some it seemed that the value of the music and artwork was devalued in some way, making it more like something you would buy in the supermarket as a more throwaway item.

Sandinista had the catalogue number FMLN1, and to keep the continuity going, *Combat Rock* took FMLN2. At the time the Farabundo Martí National Liberation Front was still a collection of left wing Guerilla organizations who were fighting in the Salvadoran Civil War, possibly encouraged to band together by Fidel Castro. Ten years after *Combat Rock*, the FMLN became an official political party in El Salvador. In *The Clash – The Only Band That Mattered*, Egan pointed out that the catalogue number is "implicitly anti-American", yet the album is very American in other ways.

Another interesting addition to the sleeve is the *Know Your Rights* graphic, which also appeared as a free sticker in the KYR single release, and variations of the cassette version. In discussion with Jules, he remembered that Kosmo had come in with the idea of the open book and gun (probably on the back of an envelope!) The "Future is Unwritten" had been originated by Joe. Eddie King who had laboured over the Mag 7 stickers began work on the logo and between him and Jules the final graphic emerged, with the red star and lightning bolts. Jules credited the concept really to Kosmo, but as with things creative, it was a "group" collaboration.

No official credit is listed for the artwork on the outer sleeve, Pennie Smith confirmed that she only took the group shot, and after some research, I was able to track down Jules Balme as the designer of the sleeve. Contrary to my belief that the band and record label must have wanted a "rush job", to meet the increasingly delayed release date of the album, Jules did not remember being under any more pressure to complete the sleeve than usual. Typically record labels always wanted everything "last minute".

In the US, the album release was delayed slightly because the US label had added the "Home Taping Is Killing Music" warning graphic. This was a bone of contention for The Clash, and they demanded its removal. The disapproval came from the fact that they were aware that some US Colleges had individuals offering to record an hour's worth of tracks the buyer chose from the *Sandinista* album for $3. It was one way of getting their music heard. Kosmo was quoted as saying "we don't care how many people tape our records". In *How Music Works* (Byrne, 2012) The Talking Heads front man/solo performer had an interesting view on cassettes and taping. He talked about the record labels trying to discourage "home taping", as they were concerned that people would stop buying 45's, preferring to record them off the radio. He felt that the large campaign that was run was "fairly ineffectual propaganda" and that all it did was alienate the music fan/consumer from the companies selling the music.

So early on, the companies missed the point about sharing music with others, I used to make tapes of records and swap with my mates, it was a way of being able to listen to new records and artists. At this time (late 70's and early 80's) we were never going to hear a lot of these records on the radio, except perhaps on John Peel late night. The tapes acted like samplers. In comparison to today's download bonanza, "home taping" was really small fry! David Byrne concurred, saying that he found out a lot about other artists and even styles of music from cassettes given by friends. He ended up buying a lot of LP's as a result.

Inside the album is a printed inner sleeve with the lyrics reproduced, created by Futura in I guess, a graffiti style font. It's pretty hard to read on the 12" album. In the later CD pressings....you don't stand a chance. Jules said that this was largely at the insistence of Joe. The originals were in a notebook from Futura, and the pages had to be separated out and each page photographed, and then added to the layout. Some of the other content was handwritten by Jules in the style of the Futura lyric sheets. Printed in army green with white type, clearly there is a side 1 and a side 2. At the top of the inner bag is the track listing for each side, again lovingly created with Letraset.

On to the record labels themselves, there is the camouflage style background and red box with "*The Clash Combat Rock*" and our loveable little stars. Track listing again, in yellow type, along with the credits. When discussing the album artwork, Jules commented that during the "baking" process of the labels being pressed on to the vinyl, the camouflage effect had become less apparent and changed colour a little.

As a bonus, the first pressings came with a free poster, or in my case two free posters. Jules Balme designed a round sticker for the sleeves containing these. This was a black circle with a red star and "Free Poster Inside" in white lettering, and the catalogue number at the bottom.

The first poster, a replica of the album sleeve folded which opened out to 24" x 24" poster, the second a large 22"x 33" colour tinted Pennie Smith Photo of the band relaxing around a table in a bar in Thailand drinking bottles of "Tan" aka Coca Cola. This photo in places almost looks like it was taken in another time. It has a cinematic still shot feel, certainly less tense than the album cover shot, and this time two people look into the camera (Topper and Paul), Joe and Mick seem distracted by something off to their left. The Photo was tinted by the artistic hands of Paul Simonon, with the catalogue number "device" added by Jules Balme. The poster was also available in the Japanese version of the album.

There have been a number of versions of the cassette release. The design has varied from territory to territory, and left largely in the hands of the local record company art departments, as they add their own specific requirements to the artwork.

So there we have it, the *Combat Rock* cover, perhaps as it was intended to be received. Other formats and later re-issues and represses would make cuts and concessions to design and cost restrictions.

So what about the album title itself? For the run up to release, the title was penciled in as *Rat Patrol from Fort Bragg*. In numerous interviews with the band this seemed to be the case.

So, what happened or caused the change of title. *Combat Rock* appeared to come from Joe between the aborted band mixing and the final Glyn Johns mixes. Perhaps Joe felt that the title needed to be snappier, and as it turned out topical with events in the world, (did he see the Falklands war coming?) as well as the lyrical, musical and thematic content. It may be that the title was considered too long by the record label who were on the hit album trail; perhaps they exerted some pressure to make the change. In *33 Revolutions Per Minute* (Lynskey, 2010) the author wrote that the sinking of the Argentinian Warship The Belgrano, was what inspired Joe to change the album title, and that he also wrote an unreleased track called *Falklands Rock*, and referred to the lines "exocet exocet – two elections to win".

Perhaps it was some sort of power move made by Joe, to wipe the slate clean of the original album mixes and double album planned by Mick. More than likely the pressure was coming from the US label and Bernie who wanted to maximize sales of the album in the United States. It may be that the title would not be easily understood by the different territories the album would be sold in. Perhaps it was considered "too American", the meaning lost on even the UK album buyers, but the use of *Sandinista* had already inspired a lot of album buyers to go off and find out what it meant, and become aware of the political situation in Central America. In *The Clash – The Only Band That Mattered*, Egan believed that the *Rat Patrol* title would have been greeted by "Groans of contempt" all over the band's "homeland", and that it was "military-esque yankophilia".

Jules Balme was not aware of the *Rat Patrol* title being brought up. His brief from day one had been to produce an album sleeve with *Combat Rock* as the title; there had been no deviation from that. In the "*Uncut Special*", Mulholland wrote that he felt the title was "unimaginative, but fitting" and the slogan "the future is unwritten" was to "lend the title to the Julian Temples film about Joe". When questioned about the *Combat Rock* title by Dave McCullough in a Sounds article in 1982, post release, Joe revealed that there was a "conscious pun" in the title as suggested by McCullough. "It's a sort of drunken in-joke of the bands." Joe went on to say "We know we are a rock band now, and we know that rock's unfashionable, but I meant it seriously at the time." He also believed that the album was re-titled by Joe "to allude to lyrical themes, the bands infighting, and the band trying to win back British fans from the increasingly hostile music press".

It might be worth looking at the original title a little more, as there is much more to this than first appears. According to Wikipedia en.wikipedia.org/wiki/Fort_Bragg Fort Bragg is the largest US Army base in the United States, the "fort" itself named after a confederate officer from the 1800's. During the Vietnam years, the "population" of the base increased dramatically. It is the base of the airborne and special forces divisions. Some of these troops were involved in the situations in Central America which had got the band so hot under the collar. In the 80's here were a number of troop deployments to Grenada, Honduras and Panama.

So this would have been much on the bands minds, particularly Joe and Mick, who seemed to be absorbing the military/political goings on in Central America at the time.

It is the *Rat Patrol* which after some research (well TV Watching) proved so interesting.

The *Rat Patrol* was a TV Series from the 1960's set in World War 2 which followed the fortunes of a small band of Special Operations troops (loosely based around the Long range Desert Group). Using only jeeps and light armaments, these crack troops would attack the German Afrika Korps led by Field Marshal Rommel, with lightning hit and run raids against convoys, facilities and fuel and ammunition dumps to hinder their progress. The series was shown in the UK around about 1967, but was removed from the TV schedule after the British Second World War veterans complained about it. It seemed to present the case that America won the war in North Africa where the series was set.

In fairness, the characters in the TV series were not all American, three Americans and one British. The rat part of the name came from the Desert Rats as the troops were nicknamed.

The shows were about half an hour long episodes, and followed a pretty set action packed formula. All wrapped up in half hour scripts. You could say the progammes were almost like a moving picture version of some of the Commando series graphic comics which were around, certainly when I was a kid in the late sixties and seventies. Prime comic fodder I'm sure for the likes of Mick, and a peep into his lock up in West London would probably back this up. Paul had always had a bit of a "thing" for guns (and ammunition). Being a little younger than The Clash, I can still remember the standard film fodder on TV was cowboys and Indians and lots of war films. What is interesting about this in terms of The Clash Connection, is that the series had four main "hero" characters, (that's two in each jeep if you're counting). There are two sergeants, Sam Troy and our token "English chap" Jack Moffit. The other two men hold the rank of private, "Hitch" Hitchcock and Tully Pettigrew. The leader of the group is Troy, and Moffitt is the very intellectual "thinker". The two privates just get their heads down and do the job. Now, if any of this is sounding familiar, stick with me.

Substitute Joe for Troy, Moffitt for Mick, "Hitch" (the Ladies man, complete with "cool hat") for Paul and Tully (the "driver" for Topper, and what do we have….a Rat Patrol for the 1980's. The similarities are amazing, although you could debate that Mick might be or had been the equivalent of Troy, as Joe is more regularly known as being the real thinker, multi lingual (to a degree) that the Moffitt character was. Four men, with different backgrounds and skills, against impossible odds. There is a strong bond between, and no one got "left behind", no matter what the risks.

There is even an episode where Tully gets wounded, and the group takes him to a field hospital behind enemy lines to get treated. Does this storyline ring any bells with the Topper heroin issues?

So what do we have, four soldiers on a series of daredevil missions behind enemy lines to disrupt the progress of an encroaching enemy. Sound familiar? Were The Clash using the traditional record business or the establishment in general as the "enemy"? Taking off on commando raids around the world and spreading the word of reason, equality, enlightening the audiences about the political shenanigans and manipulation by the US. There is even a regular bad guy, German Commander Hauptmann Hans Dietrich, (surely not Bernie).

I watched the full two series of *Rat Patrol*, for research purposes of course, and you can still get these on DVD. I would recommend it if you still hanker after your youth and like some light entertainment. You can also catch episodes on YouTube if you don't want to make a heavy investment.

As Steveacoustic said in his Amazon product review. www.amazon.co.uk/The-Rat-Patrol-Season-DVD/dp/B000JU9OJO "So, The Rat Patrol - historically accurate it ain't, but cracking good fun it is".

To round up this little section, it is worth noting for The Clash fanatic, that parts of the first series were actually filmed in Almeria in Spain, in the same area as Sergio Leone used to film the *Dollars Trilogy* Spaghetti Westerns, and where Alex Cox and Joe et al were to film *Straight To Hell*. (And yes, I did go there to have a look, and soak up some of the atmosphere!)

MORE INFO

There are some good sources of reference material about this at Wikipedia en.wikipedia.org/wiki/The_Rat_Patrol and the ever present IMDB www.imdb.com/title/tt0060018/

8. ALBUM REVIEWS

Combat Rock certainly got what you would call "mixed" reviews, not just from the music press and the critics, but The Clash fans as well. The well-polished commercial sounding album (Side one at least) was probably enough to anger the fans of old, who may be dreaming of the band producing another "The Clash/*The Clash*" album. But this could never happen, not only for the band and their development, but even technologically. Witness a "return to basics" with the *Cut The Crap* album. Now I know hardly any of the then band even played on it, but like it or not, there had been huge steps in sound recording, sampling and digital technology.

What *Combat Rock* did for the band was introduce them to a much wider audience than ever before, certainly in The US; they picked up a lot of new listeners and album buyers. Not the same kind of die-hard fans perhaps The Clash would normally attract, but they parted with their dollars (and Eskimo pence) to hear more. In The *Who Killed The Clash* article, Terry Chimes made a comment that "In '82, normal people who did a day job and went to the office would come and see us, so we were breaking into the mainstream".

In *Let Fury Have The Hour* (Schalit, 2012), in a chapter called "Clash of The Titan" the "*Punk Planet*" writer said "*Combat Rock* succeeded beyond anyone's wildest dreams, making the band a household word in the United States". For some people, there was quite a "violent" reaction to the music and songs, so I hope to show some of these in the following chapter. It was not the first time The Clash had been accused of a "sellout", an accusation that repeatedly reared its head every album they had released after the first. *Give 'Em Enough Rope*? – Sellout to the US, over produced etc. etc. *London Calling*, although revered by many, and as with *Combat Rock*, brought a much wider audience to the group, "selling out to US "(again, not punk rock enough) *Sandinista* - selling out to the US (is this sounding familiar), too much dub, over indulgent? *Combat Rock*...let me guess… selling out to the US?

Joel Schalit also had a word or two about this theory. He believed that *Combat Rock* was one of the "most explicitly political records to top the American charts since the late 60's" and that "any record that combined spoken word rants with funk and sneaks Allen Ginsberg into a Top ten album, is pretty subversive in my book".

What is interesting about some of the opinions and reviews that I have found, is that some were taken from the time of release, and some twenty or thirty years later. The later ones looking back now at an album that is now you could say "out of time". The opinions are made after a lot of music and technology have broken through to our internet, download, mobile obsessed listeners of today.

Trying to play devil's advocate here, let me ask the question, "What did you expect?" The Clash had released the "epic" *Sandinista* album with its multicultural cross genre mash ups, and even a little bit of tape played backwards. What could their next move be? I'm sure they would not have wanted to revert back to previous sounds and formulas. Boundaries were there to be pushed, and The Clash were not afraid to push them. The experimentation was there, Mick in particular emerging from the studios as "The Mad Professor", even if the other band members and presumably the record label were not keen on his final results.

It is an often quoted point that one of the reasons for the final demise of the (let us say the established lineup) was that they had had no significant break either from each other or from their work, probably since 1977-78. From my research and reading, it really hit home that they were just an incredibly hard working bunch of creative people. The late 1981 to 1982 schedule is quite extraordinary. So the band had been slogging around Europe and the US, and had not made a really significant commercial impression. The record labels (both in the UK and the US) had put up a considerable amount of money promoting recording and releasing their music. Was it time for the band to make that hit album? Was there heavy pressure from the top for them to produce a huge selling album? Certainly they were in quite heavy debt to CBS after the release of *Sandinista*, and it was the return of Bernie which saw them back on a more steady planned recovery. Did the band feel enormous pressure to get themselves out of debt, and to start reaping the rewards that the music business could provide if they "played the game"? Creatively and Artistically, did the band, particularly Joe and Mick, feel "appreciated" as great song writers?

They had been given a pretty rough ride by the press, particularly in the UK, who had begun to ridicule their every move. Quick to criticize, but at no point did anyone really explain what they thought The Clash should be doing and why! With all this being aimed at them, perhaps it was a way for the band to get back at the critics, who could say what they thought, but the public were voting with their wallets, and their albums were selling huge quantities.

Or was it, as it now appears, that the band made a pretty clever what seemed like a compromise, but was actually a way to fend off the debt collectors, get their music played, and still get their important message across?

In *The Clash - A Punk Rock Band* (Bowe, 2011) Topper was quoted from May 1982 about the album, he said that it was "A more international style of music , that features funk influences, reggae influences and jazz influences, put into our own form or the first time". So a review from *Downbeat Magazine* (Goldberg, 1982) a US jazz magazine should have been no surprise, when the writer said "If you listen to one rock and roll album in the next year, make it The Clash. More than the up-tempo elevator music one mostly hears by bands like Journey on the radio"

I would say there was a split in the reviews not only related to general impressions about how "good" or "bad" it was, but also the "seriousness" which the album is looked at. It is a strange situation I guess, a UK band heavily influenced in writing material about the state of US culture and commenting on that.

With the rise of the internet, one of the very positive aspects is that here, anyone can write, do a critical review, and "publish" it on some form. They are not reliant on an editor chopping sections out, or waiting for a hard copy of a paper or magazine to "hit the streets". The reviews I mention come from both sources, hard copy and on-line.

The UK Reviews 1982

So how did The Clash fair at the hands of the UK Press and commentators at the time?

In the NME under the heading "Blows Against The Empire" (Moore, 1982)The author X Moore saw the album as a comment "about the farce that is the Falklands war". He also added that "Five years ago, everybody loved The Clash (At least they say they did)" X-Moore presented his case in point form, all three of them. One - He felt that *Know Your Rights* was the best Clash single since *White Man in Hammersmith Palais*, He called it a "Furious Chant with the same anger". Number two - he believed this to be their best album since *Give 'Em Enough Rope*, a "Sharp statement, powerful propaganda". Number three – "the album is an album of war".

He also went on to add that The Clash were "still not afraid to experiment" and that the album was mixed by Johns and Strummer for "the voice", because "anger isn't squealing feedback" but "anger is a rough voice". He recognized that it was on the second side that the "arguments really start to burn". "The future is unwritten" wrote X-Moore, "yeah…then start writing it".

Melody Maker reviewed the album on release (Sweeting, 1982) "Like the record, hate the title" said the writer. He felt that he had doubts about the way The Clash "milked death and repression until it became meaningless", but said that he would be listening to album "for a while yet". Sweeting added that *Combat Rock* was a "fairly logical successor to *Sandinista*, "But its leaner and more concentrated, still eclectic, not very eclectic". In quite a lengthy review Sweeting went on to say that the music itself was varied and "generally worked", often delivering "attractive imagery", but "leaving doubts about its motivation".

Unlike X-Moore, Sweeting was not impressed with the opening track, and even called it a "non single" if ever he heard one. He took the approach that The Clash commenting on Vietnam was both romantic and dark, but was voyeuristic, or as he put it "a zoom shot from a low flying helicopter".

In *NME* (McCullough, 1982) The writer claimed that "it is closer to Fleetwood Mac *Rumours* than The Clash". Mark Cooper in *Record Mirror* wrote that "the Clash couldn't punch their way out of a paper bag".

In an uncredited *NME* Clash interview(Uncredited 1982), the writer said that "*Combat Rock* was the most extreme and direct Clash album since the first". Another quote from the same interview which is worth a mention "*Combat Rock* says playtime is over" and "there's an edge to the album, and an edge to The Clash again".

Smash Hits published an article *Strummertime and the living is easy* (Silverton, 1982) which included an album review. Silverton wrote that "after the commercial suicide" of *Sandinista*. They had slimmed down the latest set of recordings to "the more easily digested and marketed *Combat Rock*". Silverton went on to talk about the *Rock The Casbah* single release, and how they still would not appear on Top of The Pops in the UK. There was a also a reference to that fact that for the first time since the band began , they were actually starting to make money as Silverton added "not in the Rod Stewart bracket".

The following week in *Smash Hits* in an album review (Silverton, 1982)the author put in a more detailed album analysis. Starting with "never a bunch for the easy life, The Clash have made another LP as puzzlingly bitter as *Sandinista*. He also noted that, where as other bands would have made a "more straight forward record after the previous one failed to sell," The Clash had taken some of that album's elements such as "touches of funk, winding songs and guest appearances" and added, said Silverton "a new range of influences" He felt that the album was very much "Joe's album", and that his singing was better than ever and "the lyrics as sharp as ever". He ended with "If you like the sound of someone searching their heart, you should like *Combat Rock*".

In the *Sounds* article *Sten Guns in LA*, Dave McCullough remarked that at the time, "As Bob Dylan was heading back to The Clash rock and roll style, The Clash seemed ironically to be heading towards the narrative style of the likes of Dylan, Morrison and Joni Mitchell". He ended by saying that "there's that kind of richness on *Combat Rock*, that's what I'm saying".

The US and World Reviews 1982

In a reprinted Japanese article from 1982, (Konno, 1982) The writer felt that "in spite of the poetry pieces" it was "substantial" and with quite a few songs worth listening to. They also picked up on the fact that the "combination of folk (*Straight To Hell*) Funky (*Overpowered By Funk*) and a "healing kind" (*Sean Flynn*) made them wonder whose album it was they had been listening to, but that these songs were more interesting than the "hit songs".

One of the most staggering reviews appeared in the US magazine *CREEM* (Metzer, 1982) Published in September, about four months after release. The writer spent some time discussing the merits of PIL and Throbbing Gristle and The Fall, eventually getting down to The Clash! "Like *Sandinista*" He said "it had to be the most arch subversion yet of a major labels time and money".

He believed that the band had "finally officially tried to work from within the beast", he also questioned their motives, "in spite of ever droning refusal to play ball with the company", they are "titillated by the ever growing lure of total rockout rockhood" saying very little about the album until about halfway through the article, he began to compare "fifth albums" with the Beatles, Stones, Dylan, The Doors and The Grateful Dead. He talked about the lyrical imagery, compared the album to post-Beatle George Harrison, and then rounded it off with his own bold statement "This mere word jockey rates *Combat Rock* (by the standards The Clash have brought on themselves) a relative pile of shit!"

In the *Rolling Stone* article *Year of The Clash* (Hall 1982)the author wrote that "the albums funk is so subtle, and the politics so finely tuned, that Americans who enjoyed *Mag 7* and *London Calling* might quibble at first". He mentioned the two guest "poets", Ginsberg and Futura, but that the biggest surprise guest was "Britain's war with Argentina", which started "shortly before the band packed off the tapes to CBS".

In a US fanzine called *Communist Atrocity* they were none to impressed in their article *Fuck The Casbah*. Although very little discussed about *Combat Rock* itself, the writer felt that the band were "now just boring, jaded elitist rock stars bullshitting the public (like Jefferson Airplane/Starship) with commie propaganda" and that "they seem to be content to snort coke with Andy Warhol and Brit Eckland".

In *Rolling Stone* (Australian Edition) (McSporran, 1982) . The writer felt that with *Combat Rock*, "they're spanning a whole movement, Ginsberg the old poet, acknowledging Strummer the young poet" and added that Mick now had "one of the most distinctive and innovative electric guitar styles in Rock Music".

Rolling Stone magazine (Fricke, 1982) reviewed *Combat Rock* on June 24th , a little more constructive and coherent compared to the *Creem* review. Fricke talked about The Clash falling out of favour in the UK, and how the "cynical press were drunk on funk and futurism" Fricke said that the message of *Combat Rock* is "Pop hits and press accolades be damned".

Calling it a "declaration of real life emergency" and a "demanding document of classic punk anger", maybe I would question the classic punk anger. Much of the album, particularly side two is a little more than three chord bash which you might associate with punk.

Fricke also pointed out that the album is "short on practical solutions and long on the horror of the problems". At the same time said the writer, the album was "stirring, inspirational rock and roll, arranged with a good pop sense" and an album of "fight songs" and that "although the album may not have any answers, it could be our last warning: sign up or shut up".

The review in *Downbeat Jazz* magazine (Goldberg, 1982) didn't focus specifically on *Combat Rock*, but more on the band themselves and their development. But Goldberg referred to *Know Your Rights*, and the "this is a public service announcement" opening line. He went on to say that "that single line does a good job of summing up The Clash", and that "this is a band that makes rock and roll with a message". He also wrote that to The Clash the message is just as important as the rock and roll, and how they often used sarcasm to make their point ("all three of them"). After reading this article several times, it is possibly one of the most eloquent. Goldberg said that "The Clash's embracing of numerous kinds of International music, and commitment to keep music alive in the minds of their fans, is a very important part of what they have accomplished". He went on to add that they had continued to demonstrate on every album since *London Calling*, that "music, like people, should not be segregated".

Post 1982 UK Reviews

In *"The Ultimate Clash Review"* (Mulholland, 2011) Mulholland wrote that *Combat Rock* "may not have been the greatest Clash album ever", but that it was "an enduring testament to their talent". In another statement, which I would agree with, well certainly Side 2 and *Straight To Hell* from Side 1, he said that "the music felt and smelt like the steamy jungle of Vietnam".

He also rightly I believe, made the point that although everyone in the world is "largely appalled by American economic and military violence, while remaining helplessly seduced by the culture and imagery that this produced". Of the finished album after remixing by Glyn Johns, Mulholland called the result "Fiendishly Clever and Kind of magical".

He also made the point that in 1982, the album sounded like it was about Reganism, New York, Vietnam hangover and Scorcese movies". At the time he wrote the article in 2011, it was "more like a record drenched in dark irony".

In the *Q Classic* Article *What's my NAM* (Hutcheon, 2010) The writer also picked up on the Vietnam angle, but also that The Clash had been in danger of "becoming the kind of dinosaurs that punk rock was supposed to have made extinct"

He also added that "little had gestated in the westway", and that what informed the bands "new world view" was "Vietnam chic".

In *The Music That Matters* (Fletcher, 2012) the writer felt that *Combat Rock* was "the musical counterpoint to *Taxi Driver*". It was not a classic album said Fletcher, it lacked the violent revolt of *The Clash* and the "guitar grandeur" of *Give 'Em Enough Rope*.

In another *Mojo* review of *Combat Rock* (Harris, 2003)The album was seen as "the classic lineup's last hurrah!" and that *Know Your Rights*, *Car Jamming* and *Straight To Hell* "proved that their talents remained intact" but the writer felt that "a good two thirds of the album rang hollow".

In *The Clash* (Quantick, 2000) David Quantick called the album "messy, but also a polite record" with "immense sales". He also believed that it was their most "professional piece of work" and that "diligence had paid off, aided by constant touring". It had made them he said "proper stars for the first time".

He also commented that there was nothing like the album in the charts at that time, "punk sat next to Rolling Stones rock and roll and rock disco". He wrongly I feel pointed out that there was no reggae present. It was always there in some capacity, *Ghetto Defendant* anybody? And the techniques and elements were still in there. Quantick was obviously not a fan, "musically a couple of superb tracks" he said "resting in a thick grimy gravy of dullness". He also felt that maybe Glyn Johns production had "numbed the sound with record store friendly wall of wool".

In the *Kerrang Essential Guides*, www.kerrang.com The Clash albums are reviewed with a paragraph each. I think unwisely, it suggested that by 1982, the band were megastars, "no longer could they claim to be punks" (did they claim to be punks?) and "nor did they, said the review". The album it said was "built on touring the arena and mega domes of America". I'm not so sure, the big US tour venues kicked in more after the album release I would say. "Gone was the anger, replaced by stadium rock anthems". Again, I would have to pull them up on this one; much of the material played on tour covered a career spanning then five albums. With the policy of "mixing up the set" and having a huge repertoire to choose from, I don't think they focused on the "stadium rock" songs. *Career opportunities*???

In *How Music Works* (Byrne, 2012) Byrne talked about how "gathered Masses in sports arenas and stadiums" made demands on the music to perform a different function "not only sonically, but socially". He also mentioned that bands tended to write "arena rock" in response to this… "Rousing stately anthems". I think it would have been hard for The Clash to have imagined at the time of writing the *Combat Rock* material that they would be playing huge stadiums with The Who by the end of the next year.

In my attempt at getting some opinions from "the people that count", not just critics, I got an email from Paul in Whalley, Lancashire. Paul explained that as a big Clash fan, he "lost it with the *Combat Rock* album". He felt that *Should I Stay* and *Rock The Casbah* were "wishy washy pop tunes at best". He felt that they had become a bloated stadium rock band, looking for fame and fortune. He went on to express some pretty strong opinions about *Cut The Crap* album too, but maybe this is for another book.

Another email contributor, Jeremy Vanes, felt that *Combat Rock* was a "dying great band shooting to the end". He also added that "it has many great word pictures - *Know Your Rights* and *Ghetto Defendant*." Some of the music he found exciting, but he didn't really feel that "most of it hangs together". "Most" he added "were never played live, and were thus studio confections".

From Tokyo, Akito Watanabe from The Strummers remembered that *Know Your Rights* came first, and that his expectations were "fuelled" by this. He did however remember being "puzzled" by *Combat Rock*. It was not the same was the first album, which he held in particular high regard. He felt there was no feeling of energy, no "strong stance" and not the same "brute force". He regarded *Ghetto Defendant* with Allen Ginsberg as a "classic" but, like many, confused by the flow of the side 2, which was "boring and chaotic".

Watanabe flagged up *Straight To Hell* as his favourite album track, "The sound was very dramatic, and the talent of Mick Jones as an arranger is shining", and you had to "digest the words of Joe Strummer".

Looking back now, Watanabe enjoys the album that was such a huge success for the band, and it is pleasant to listen to frivolous songs like *Overpowered By Funk*. *Should I Stay or Should I Go* and *Rock The Casbah*, are very good pop songs.

Pete Winkleman the CBS Product manager who worked on the album release told me in an interview, that he felt that The Clash were always important, and that *Combat Rock* really delivered what they were capable of. I mentioned that there were mixed feelings from the fans of the band and he was perhaps a little taken aback. "Clash fans should be proud of and love this album, because it was bringing together the US Influences and took a "world view"

In *The Clash - The Only Band That Mattered*, Egan wrote that he found the melodies to be "skeletal", and that the tunes were lengthy "mood pieces" in origin. He added that they seemed to be unresolved and were almost like abstract paintings.

Kris Needs made the point, that you could contrast the first album recorded over three weekends, with the months of wrangling and remixing with *Combat Rock*. As Mick Helford (part of the management team) said on a *Sky Arts TV* documentary "the thing with The Clash was…they could never agree on anything!"

Post 1982 US and The World Reviews

Trouser Press magazine published an article in April 1983 *Four Sides of The Clash - A Listeners Guide* (Robbins, 1983). In this, a comment was made that "somehow, The Clash's most obtuse album, has proven to be by far their most commercially successful". Robbins added that it had some great moments, but was a "flimsy" album. He noted also, that it had sold over a million copies and made The Clash genuine "rock superstars" in America.

In an uncredited review in the *Crossbeat* magazine (Unknown, 2014), from Japan. Some meaning may be lost in translation, but I think you get the drift. The writer reviewed it as being "chaotic" and a little "over ripe". They could detect a "new core of exoticism and hip hop, which improved in the solo work by Joe and Mick's later years" They added that "the songs show the variety and delicate sense about rhythm they have had since they started", and that they still had good sense and ideas as musicians. The writer also felt that the album had a worse reputation than *London Calling* and *Sandinista* because "You cannot feel the power which you can in previous albums"

After *Sean Flynn*, the writer felt that the album became "slipshod" and it felt like the songs were predicting the end of the band. In summary, they wrote that The Clash were not punk any more, and that Joe had admitted it and that now the "concept of mixture" was well known, and that you could now feel the "Coolness" of the album.

On the Ultimate Guitar website www.ultimtate-guitar.com Member "RANT" posted in 2008 that "after two albums of musical tourism, *Combat Rock* finally sees The Clash develop a sound that is truly theirs". Describing them also as having an "adventurous sound", RANT identified certain parts that "clearly show a band falling apart", focusing on *Car Jamming* and *Red Angel Dragnet*. In summary he said "think of it perhaps as a soundtrack to the late 70's early 80's Vietnam that never was".

So, not for the first time was someone of the opinion that particularly after *Sandinista*, The Clash had refined their multi influences into a more distinctive sound. I agree in part, but would say this is more true of the more "left field tracks" on side two and part of side one. I think you have to take the more straight ahead songs like *Should I Stay/Rock The Casbah* and *Know Your Rights* out of that description. *Straight To Hell* is singled out as the "timeless" track, and that the album proved that "great break up albums are far more interesting than those from stable bands"

On the same website came a review from contributor KBASS9267, who posed the question "what the hell were The Clash trying to prove on this album?" "I wouldn't call it punk though". Well now, I don't think The Clash made a "punk" album since their debut. "The guitar sounds so bad", they added "it wasn't even funny". This contributor seemed confused as to why there were additional instruments on the tracks like trumpets, saxophones and flutes. Their firm advice "download *Should I Stay or Should I Go* and *Rock The Casbah*... don't buy the album!"

On another website www.punknews.org accessed 5/2/2013, is another posting by Joe Mornia from 2002. Quite interesting that people are still buying the album, not just sad old men like me who buy the reissues! But people who have not heard he album before. Joe "saved up his $7.30" to buy the album, as he had every other Clash album. He certainly wasn't sure about it. *Know Your Rights* got a positive response, "lyrics nothing short of brilliant". On *Car Jamming*, he hated at first, but slowly came to like it, "but you have to be into reggae to like it"

Should I Stay or Should I Go was compared to *Train In Vain*, and probably rightly so, another Mick penned song about uncertain relationships. (Was it Ellen Foley and Viv Albertine?)

Joe made an amusing remark about *Rock The Casbah*, "it disgusts me" and "the kind of stuff they play on soft rock radio, and I think they do… you know that station your mum listens to". Well he was right on the money there. *Overpowered by Funk* also got a rough ride "an embarrassment, but kind of fun to listen to".

In *Clash City Showdown* (Knowles, 2003) a book I would highly recommend, the author has a chapter called "Combat Rock Conundrums". In this he said that *Combat Rock* was "traumatic" for him, and that amongst his friends, it was looked on with great scorn. *Death is a Star*, was a pretty shitty way for a band that entered the world with *White Riot* to end. As with Joe Mornia, Knowles was confused by it, not knowing what they were trying to accomplish. He had some pretty forthright views, and was critical of some of the tracks as being incomplete half written songs, he included the material that ended up as B Sides (*First Night Back In London/Long Time Jerk/Cool Confusion*) as well as album tracks like *Red Angel Dragnet* and *Sean Flynn*.

He felt that they were "the product of a band trying to write songs on the spot, with little inspiration".

In *Christgau's Record Guide to The 80's* (Christgau, 1994) Robert Christgau talked about how many saw *Combat Rock* as the point at which The Clash went "bozo once and for all". He felt that they were actually "well ahead of a lot of their respectable competition" and that he guaranteed "they were not sinking into pop slime". He felt that they were evolving, and hoped that some day they would write songs "as terse and clear as *Janie Jones* at this higher level of verbal and musical density".

On the eMusic website www.emusic.com accessed in 2013, Ira Robbins Of Trouser Press Magazine had reviewed *Combat Rock* 30/6/2009. Here Robbins wrote that "Cutting away from *Sandinista's* relaxed sprawl for a single disc of arty urban grit on *Combat Rock* was a smart move". He also felt that it enabled them to "break free of the New Wave marketing ghetto," and "making The Clash chart stars". He also picked up that it was a "blueprint for Mick Jones's subsequent adventures in Big Audio Dynamite".

On the Ultimate Classic Rock website ultimateclassicrock.com/the-clashs-combat-rock-turns-30/ (Accessed 19/1/2014) looked at the album 30 years on. Annie Zaleski wrote that at the time of release the "punk band were at a crossroads" She pointed out that although *Sandinista* was considered something of a disappointment in the UK, in the US it had actually charted higher than *London Calling*. Zaleski added that *Combat Rock* "continued in the "genre clashing" vein of *Sandinista*, but there was laser precise focus and concise song lengths", and that it was "remarkably cohesive", despite being "somewhat unorthodox". Well observed, she analysed the various side one songs and their multiple genres, and like myself identified the "game of two halves" theory. The second side she noted "is even stranger", picking out the almost spoken word "psych-folk " feel of *Death is a Star*, the "mournful saxophone" of *Sean Flynn* and cameo from Allen Ginsberg in *Ghetto Defendant*. Zaleski identified the album as a "remarkable lyrical achievement", the band acquiring the knack of writing ugly truths about the US, which as she said "white American songwriters didn't dare "and wouldn't until Bruce Springsteen's *Born in The USA*.

So, to the website *Cool Album of the Day*, coolalbumreview.com/?p=19935 where the author Paul McBride from Brisbane placed emphasis on the Topper story of how *Rock The Casbah* was written. Possibly a little misinformed, Topper was a "talented prog and jazz drummer", and that the song was recorded in Wessex Studios in London. The band had also apparently "left behind their band of the people persona, and were filling stadiums". The author commented on the album track by track, *Know Your Rights* was in "fairly typical Clash fashion", but I would disagree! *Car Jamming* is considered to be "heavily influenced by reggae", but I would challenge this comment also. *Should I Stay or Should I Go*, they had as a song destined to be "spewed out by every cover band, sung badly at every karaoke bar and used in Jeans adverts until the very end". In a bizarre twist, in the film *Code 46* (Winterbottom, 2003), who would pop up in a karaoke bar singing it, but Mick Jones. The song was "covered" by many, and indeed parodied by The Stash as *Should I Suck Or Should I Blow*. *Overpowered by Funk* "was likened to the first two Red Hot Chili Peppers albums". *Death Is A Star* it said sounded "like a children's story" or "something the Beatles might have done in their more psychedelic moments".

"The fact that they managed to make it half listenable is a testament to the power of The Clash" he said in closing.

On the *Treble* website Accessed 16/04/2014 is a review posted in 2006 by Paul Haney who noted that The Clash were bigger commercially in the 80's, but the critics "turned the other cheek", largely because of "the punk ethos of selling out". It is amazing to think that five albums into their career, people were still holding up that "Clash credibility rule". The band hadn't produced a punk album since their debut, not in the clichéd, formula style that perhaps was expected. They had already defended themselves over *Give 'Em Enough Rope*, *London Calling* and *Sandinista*. Haney said that *Sandinista* was "messy near brilliance". On the "hit singles" *Should I Stay or Should I Go* and *Rock The Casbah*, he called them brilliant pop songs, and "two of the 80's most endearing hits". www.treblezine.com/reviews/the-clash-combat-rock/

In the online *Rave Reviews*, dated 8th June 2008 by The Clash Constructivist, constructivist. wordpress.com/2008/06/08/the-clash-combat-rock/ the writer didn't rate the album as "up to the same standards as the first three records", and although they felt that the twelve tracks was "more manageable" (than *Sandinista*). It "packed too much of the unremarkable". The author praised *Should I Stay Or Should I Go* and *Rock The Casbah* and "at least half the rest is pretty decent".

Another US website www.939bobfm.com/Music/Album.aspx?id=4099 accessed 4/5/2014, Stephen Thomas Erlewine reviewed *Combat Rock*. The writer believed that "on the surface, *Combat Rock* appeared to be a "retreat from the sprawling stylistic explorations of *London Calling* and *Sandinista*." Like Paul from Lancashire, he had the two singles down as "stadium rock" sounding. He put the "muscular heavy sound" down to Glyn Johns production. He did also point out that the album contained "heavy flirtations" with rap, funk and reggae. On the issue of "selling out", he felt that if it was an attempt of a sell-out, it was a strange way to sell out. Where I have an issue with this review, it is where Erlewine believed that the band were being torn in two directions. "Mick Jones wanted The Clash to inherit The Who's righteous arena rock stance" while "Joe wanted to forge ahead into black music".

I just don't think this rings true, Mick's interests were with what might be called "dance music" at the time, certainly he enjoyed the "rock star" lifestyle, probably more so than the other band members, but I feel musically, the band were a very different animal from The Who. Joe's interests were possibly more focused on more earthy "roots" music, not black music in particular.

On the *Deviant Art* website almightypineapple.deviantart.com/journal/The-Clash-Combat-Rock-Music-Review-295306388 a review was posted 10/04/2012. The review made *Combat Rock* the last "significant" album by the band. It talked about how originally the album was going to be called *Rat Patrol From Fort Bragg*, but that the idea was scrapped after "internal wrangling" over "Mick's mix". The review discussed how the band "dove into social and political issues with both feet". The writer found it fascinating that rebellious figures (such as Joe) "embraced parties and systems which would either neuter them or completely destroy them if they found themselves fully entrenched in that system". The review also pointed to the offbeat nature of some of the songs and the "sound collage" that was produced, and that it was a far from conventional, commercial rock album, which had unique themes, asymmetrical arrangements and "inner stress".

Rightly, the author identified side two as containing some less accessible songs more "niche" like. In the *Anger can be Power* collection of writings, D'Ambrosio wrote that the album was "loosely based around Strummers concept of what he called urban Vietnam". The author also felt that although "highly over produced", it was still "never the less a jarring record". In *Clash City Showdown* (Knowles, 2003) the author commented that the main weakness with the *Combat Rock* album was its "disunity", "too scattershot for a single album, and seemed like *Sandinista* sides 6 and 7". He also felt that side 1 "held together" but side 2 was "where it all fell apart".

In a review on www.musicko.com dated 16th October 2010. The reviewer "Emilio" wrote that with *Combat Rock*, Strummer "clearly wanted to move the band into other styles (with black music topping the list)" and that "Mick wanted to stick to Rock and Roll". He went on to add that the differences could not be reconciled, and that Mick left after touring *Combat Rock*. I would say this statement is a little wide of the mark. I would have Joe more rock and roll, Mick was off in the distillery, refining various brews. Mick was clearly heading off in a different direction, but the classifications are wrong here. Emillio also went on to say that "everybody hated *Combat Rock*, including the punks and the press". The charge being that they had "sold out". Not really true, the album sold very well in the US and UK reaching high chart positions and going Platinum. www.musicko.com/the-clash/combat-rock-the-clash-%E2%80%93-album-review

In the *Sounds* article *Sten Guns in LA* (McCullough, 1982) Joe had explained to the author "we want to be free…if possible. I'd rather be free than go down as a has-been just to regurgitate". He also said "it's very difficult for us, because the first album just keeps on getting more and more relevant".

"Don't spin *Combat Rock*, said Emillio, if you are looking for variations of *Should I Stay or Should I Go*, because you are not getting that".

In another set of on-line reviews from rateyourmusic.com/release/album/the_clash/combat_rock/ Contributor "Digital" wrote in 2013 "While most of the album is dull as dishwater, it still produced two hit singles which I never tire of hearing, so this is not such a failure".

Contributor "Smelsch" felt that "side 2 is a total write off – the snake on The Clash snakes and ladders game that takes us directly to *Cut The Crap*". "No sign of life or intelligence, save for *Rock The Casbah* wrote "InseuFighter" and finally "If you like the sound of someone scratching their head, you should like *Combat Rock*" wrote contributor "Nudespoons" in 2012.

In a 2009 review of *Combat Rock* on the sputnik music website www.sputnikmusic.com/review/33969/The-Clash-Combat-Rock/ the reviewer Matthijs Van Der Lee took a long hard look the album, writing that "it maintains the habit of incorporating a variety of genres into the band's sound, but is much more straightforward".

Although "thankfully" said the writer, "the album was cut down to a single album, it did still share Sandinistas inconsistency issue". Van Der Lee, felt that the second side was a "let down", and that the material never really "got off the ground". *Overpowered by Funk* he felt had "no decent groove" and just didn't fit as well as it should. In summary, it is the hit singles that "save" the album.

The Opinion of The Band members

In *Uncut Bringing back the Glory Days* (Martin, 2010) Martin wrote that Joe had told him that the making of the album "amid simmering tensions" and "the usual organisational chaos", had been an exhausting and dispiriting experience for him. "We were stupid" he said, "the company needed another album so we ended up recording it on tour".

When interviewed for the *Sounds* article *Sten Guns in LA* (McCullough, 1982) Joe admitted that America "is our big influence", the album was recorded there and that it had a huge American influence all through it… but as he said "I'm not sure if it's good".

Joe was quoted as saying "I think we made *Combat Rock* really quickly, I don't remember being in the studio too long". He also remembered that "maybe because they weren't joyful sessions, and we couldn't see a way forward" and "maybe we had run out of operational juices at the time".

He also added that "*Combat Rock* had some of the best tunes we ever made on it. *Straight To Hell* was one of our masterpieces, but the band had to shatter after that record".

Mick believed that the album was not focused or as well put together as it could have been, but "in the end, who cares, we have got a better life now because of it".

In *The Clash - A Visual Documentary*, upon finding out that the album had gone to number 2 in the UK album chart, they were "supposedly… astounded".

Again from the Dave McCullough article in *Sounds*, Joe had said that "It was great to be accepted in our homeland. For that we'd give up everything, everything we had meant in any other country all over the world".

The Conclusion

Gary Mulholland summed up I think very well. "Something conceived in such personal, fiscal and pharmaceutical chaos had no business ending up as it is, making the most coherent musical and thematic statements". He added that it "takes the globally informed influences that made up *Sandinista* into a unified sound".

The Only Music That Matters (Fletcher, 2012) said that the album was recorded in a "confused Clash landscape" and this is a fair assessment of the situation I think. He also felt it was a "memorable swansong because it was home to a couple of anthems that cannot be contained by the album itself". In *The Clash - The Only Band That Mattered* (Egan, 2015) the author felt that the album had allowed the band to claw back some respectability, but that dissention within the band, and egotistical behavior had caused a rupture in their ranks.

Again from *The Clash - The Only Band That Mattered,* Egan made an interesting point in that although the album was very successful, it did seem a little strange that what might be considered "left field music" at that time was not generally appreciated by the masses in the US. Egan did acknowledge the band's "enthusiastic and business minded" touring of the US was helpful in generating sales.

In *33 Revolutions Per Minute* (Lynskey, 2010), the author discussed the "international perspective" which featured in The Clash albums, possibly as far back as *Give Em Enough Rope*. The free poster with the album identifying "political hotspots" around the world, certainly would have opened a few minds. Lynskey felt that the International Perspective was really developed with *Sandinista* and *Combat Rock*. He also quoted U2's Bono as saying "the lyrics of Joe Strummer were like an atlas". I would have to agree, certainly *Combat Rock* takes you around the world, The US, UK, The Far East and the Middle East and Europe.

9. ALBUM FORMATS

I thought it would be interesting to look at the various formats the album was produced in. The changes in technology and media over the last 30 years or so have been extraordinary. Looking at the available formats in the year of release, the record label would have the options of Vinyl album, cassette and in the US, the "legendary" 8 Track. A format which never caught on in the UK, and was in many ways, was the predecessor to the cassette tape. It has an interesting history and worth looking at if you are a fan of music en.wikipedia.org/wiki/8-track_tape

For the UK then, I have already talked about the vinyl album, and the limited edition posters

The cassette version seems to have appeared in a number of variations of the main album picture, and to some degree each territory seemed to do their own thing with this.

The Discogs website www.discogs.com/Clash-Combat-Rock/master/14918 currently lists 67 versions 10/05/2014, covering about 17 countries, although I have found another version from Mexico since my research on this book began. Another absentee from the Discogs list is a version of the album that was released in South Africa (Catalogue Number ASF2747). I can find little documented about this release which is listed here theclash.ch/music/dbabfragen/detailed/lp_regular_select_out.php?itemregular=Combat+Rock and author of *The History of Joe Strummer & The Mescaleros* Ant Davie has a copy of this rare item. Rightly, in email conversation, he raised this as a political hot potato. The early eighties saw a strong campaign to wipe out apartheid in South Africa. The cricket fiasco I mentioned in the earlier chapter about 1982 was big news, with some cricketers not agreeing with restrictions being applied to them earning money from playing overseas. In 1985, there was a strong campaign set up by a number of high profile musicians as Artists Against Apartheid founded by E Street Band guitarist and "Soprano" Steven Van Zandt. The *Combat Rock* release predated the movement, but it raises the issue of the record label releasing the album in a somewhat "controversial" territory.

There have been an incredible number of re-releases of the album since release year, and as new formats and technologies have come along, the record label has re released it. With the birth of CD, *Combat Rock* along with the other Clash catalogue were released on this format in The USA before UK and Europe. The mini disc format came (and went) and *Combat Rock* made an appearance with The Clash catalogue yet again. If you go to the colour section of the book, you will find more on the many formats of the official album.

Title (Format)	Label	Cat#	Country	Year
Combat Rock (LP, Album)	Discos CBS	47265	Argentina	1982
Combat Rock (LP, Album)	Epic	ELPS 4287	Australia	1982
Combat Rock (LP, Album)	Epic	144761	Brazil	1982
Combat Rock (Cass, Album)	Epic	WPET-37689	Canada	1982
Combat Rock (LP, Album)	Epic, Epic	FE 37689, FMLN 2	Canada	1982
Combat Rock (LP, Album)	Epic, Epic	FE 37689, FMLN 2	Canada	1982
Combat Rock (LP, Album)	Epic, Epic	FE 37689, FMLN 2	Canada	1982
Combat Rock (LP, Album)	CBS, CBS	CBS 85570, FMLN 2	Europe	1982
Combat Rock (LP, Album)	CBS, CBS	CBS 32787, FMLN-2	Greece	1982

Title (Format)	Label	Cat#	Country	Year
Combat Rock (LP, Album)	CBS, CBS	CBS 85570, FMLN-2	Greece	1982
Combat Rock (LP, Album)	CBS	85570	Israel	1982
Combat Rock (LP, Album)	CBS	85570	Italy	1982
Combat Rock (LP, Album)	Epic	25-3P-353	Japan	1982
Combat Rock (LP, Album)	Epic	LNS17416	Mexico	1982
Combat Rock (Cass, Album)	CBS	41-85570	Netherlands	1982
Combat Rock (Cass, Album)	Columbia	COL 40-32787	Netherlands	1982
Combat Rock (LP, Album)	CBS	CBS32787	Netherlands	1982
Combat Rock (LP, Album)	CBS	85570	Netherlands	1982
Combat Rock (LP, Album)	CBS	85570	Portugal	1982
Combat Rock (LP, Album, Unofficial)	High stereo light	593	South Korea	1982
Combat Rock (LP, Album)	CBS	CBS32787	Spain	1982
Combat Rock (LP, Album)	CBS	S 85570	Spain	1982
Combat Rock (Cass, Album)	CBS	40-32787	UK	1982
Combat Rock (Cass, Album)	CBS	FMLN 40-2	UK	1982
Combat Rock (LP, Album)	CBS	FMLN 2	UK	1982
Combat Rock (LP, Album)	CBS	FMLN 2	UK & Ireland	1982
Combat Rock (8-Trk, Album)	Epic	FEA 37689	US	1982
Combat Rock (Cass, Album)	Epic, Epic	PET 37689, PET37689	US	1982
Combat Rock (Cass, Album)	Epic	FET 37689	US	1982
Combat Rock (LP, Album, 1st)	Epic, Epic	FE 37689, FMLN 2	US	1982
Combat Rock (LP, Album, 2nd)	Epic, Epic	FE 37689, FMLN 2	US	1982
Combat Rock (LP, Album, RP)	Epic, Epic, Epic	E 37689, PE 37689, FMLN 2	US	1982
Combat Rock (LP, Album)	Epic	EPIC-245	Venezuela	1982
Combat Rock (LP, Album)	CBS, Suzy	85570, CBS 85570	Yugoslavia	1982
Combat Rock (LP, Pic Disc, Album, Promo, Ltd)	Epic	AS 99-1592	US	1983
Combat Rock (LP, Pic Disc, Album, Promo, Ltd)	Epic	FE 37689	US	1983

Source: Edited from www.discogs.com and own sources.

10. MARKETING AND PROMOTION

Looking at the marketing and promotion for the album, back in 1982, there were very limited channels available in the media to promote artists and their music. At the time of the album release, there was no YouTube, no MySpace, no downloading, no internet radio stations, and very few regular dedicated Music programs on TV.

According to Douglas Kean who worked at CBS in 1982, and worked on The Clash promo for *Combat Rock*, it was Joe who did the promo work for the band. Douglas commented that the other band members were either in no fit state, or unwilling to participate. This did put an awful lot of pressure on Joe.

In an interview with Pete Winkelman, the Product Manager at CBS UK for the *Combat Rock* album, I was able to get some information from the point of view of the record label themselves.

I asked Pete what if any was "the brief" for the album release and campaign. He made it clear that he just wanted to achieve the highest chart position possible. At this time and certainly from my experiences at Gallup in the Music Charts Department, everything was about the Chart position, that is what generated kudos for those involved, and added to the value of a person in terms of promotion both inside a company and elsewhere. It might even increase sales of an album!! A strong chart position in the UK would also rapidly increase the chances of an act being picked up for release in other territories, particularly the US market. Pete explained that he was a "driven" man who loved his job and was always thinking about ways he could promote the acts he was looking after. He was committed to getting the album to chart, and was willing to go "all the way" with it. In terms of money to spend on *Combat Rock*, there seemed to be no budget restrictions he could detect. He felt that there were "powerful figures" in the US side of the label who were really pushing the band and album. He wanted the album to chart high. He believed that there was a lot of interest in the band (despite some pretty negative vibes in the music press), and there was a certain amount of anticipation about the next album. Would it be a four album set, or had they learned from the experiences with the *Sandinista* release?

Pete wanted to get the record shops involved in the release, getting them talking about it, getting them interested and motivated. Often overlooked I feel, are the record shops. Behind all the glamour of the "bizz" were the people who actually got the records to the fans. They were the source, and they had the specialist knowledge and enthusiasm for music. I don't think many record shop owners were there for "the money", I don't think music retail was a business that attracted a "quick buck". Important to remember that in this period, supermarkets weren't selling CD's at a loss to get you in to buy your fruit and tins of beans, there were no online stores selling at rock bottom prices, and in the main, if you wanted to hear anything that didn't make the radio playlists, or find out about other interesting stuff, the local record shop was as good a place as any to get help and guidance. To get the high chart position in the first week, Pete needed the pre orders to be high, so the maximum number of albums would be shipped off to the stores. I can remember putting down deposits on forthcoming albums well in advance to make sure I had it on day one of release. I remember the mighty long wait for the Siouxsie and the Banshees album of *The Scream*. The longest wait ever..! Nowadays, we have people prepared to queue outside the Apple store for an overpriced piece of technology, just to have it on the first day it is available. On recent performance (2014 post iPhone 6), it might be a sensible move to wait a couple of months for the problems to be identified and dealt with! Same principle I guess, just on a different scale. To incentivize the "record dealers" (as they were amusingly called), Pete introduced a sense of competition by awarding some of his Bernie and Clash approved *Combat Rock* jackets as prizes for the best pre sales orders from the shops. The whole concept it seems was met with some shock by some at the label, "why would they give anything like that away to the stores? Perhaps these were usually reserved for the label staff, and "influential people".

The *Combat Rock* notebook/paperback book mentioned in my introduction originated in the US, and Pete believed some were shipped over to use as promo "tools" or as Pete referred to them "toys".

I was interested in how Pete had come to work on the *Combat Rock* album release, and even this has a "story". He had been working in the product management team, his line manager being Kate Mundell. She had worked on the *Know Your Rights* single, and had it seems "fallen out" big time with Bernie. Pete was given the job of mending fences with Bernie and The Clash, as well as seeing through the album release. Another part of "the brief" which I mentioned earlier was "not to fall out with anyone!!" I can only imagine what Kate Mundell might have been going through, bearing in mind that *Know Your Rights* was released and Joe had disappeared and the UK tour was seeing dates cancelled one after another as there was a "Joe no show". Bernie must have been under enormous pressure from a situation partly of his making.

Pete remembered the band being unhappy about the marketing, not really interested in the hype; they just wanted to sell records. He found the band and Bernie quite intimidating. In his one meeting with the band prior to release, he remembered a lot of sarcastic comments, evil glares and dirty looks. By comparison to the world weary band, he must have seemed like a "young kid".

What is interesting is that Pete was totally unaware of any of the drama that was unfolding around and within the band. The use of the FMLN2 went completely over his head. He was totally unaware that Joe had been missing, and that Topper had been sacked. His position was not that close to the band as perhaps the A&R department would have been.

The same stresses and strains within the band were matched at the label by the "scoring of points" within the departments and different labels within the CBS umbrella organization. Competition was strong between the company and the other record labels they were competing against in the market.

Most of the contact with the band prior to the album release was through Bernie, on the phone and a few meetings. Pete recalled a very intensive period of about three weeks of daily phone calls and heavy pressure. In true Commando/Special Forces style, Bernie "went in did the job, and left". After release and the intense pressure, suddenly there was nothing, no contact and it would seem no appreciation for his efforts. "Bernie", said Pete, "was there when he needed to be and then was off". It certainly seemed to be that Bernie had got his wish for "complete control". With other artists, Pete might have had the flexibility to come up with ideas and run with them to promote an album. But anything at all had to be run by the band first for approval. Instead of Bernie making suggestions, it felt to Pete like he was being reigned in and not get carried away with anything that could be seen as "uncool" or "un-Clash" like. There was, felt Pete, a very definite vision of what was "Clash-cool" and what was not. In the UK, no promotional materials, or artwork or "toys" were allowed to be created in-house at CBS, everything went through Bernie and in the main it seems to Jules and Eddie. The *Combat Rock* army jacket needed a lot of convincing by Pete that is was a good idea, cool enough and of good quality. It was finally agreed. The inclusion of the poster with initial copies was again a Bernie and the band decision; they had after all done a similar operation with *Give 'Em Enough Rope*, and the double sided poster of political hotspots throughout the world.

Pete was not, as mentioned, involved in The Clash "notebook", and also the two picture disc versions of the album which appeared in the US as "radio promo". He did mention that it was very unusual for the US Company to spend "Big Money" on a UK act, but The Clash seemed to be the exception. This does seem to back up Pete's belief that there were greater forces at work in the US label.

So after all the hard work and ideas, what was the outcome for the label? As a result of the excitement drummed up, the Presales were actually triple what was expected. All the presales counted for the first weeks sales, and gave it an impressive chart placing. The Number two spot took a lot of people at the label by surprise; Pete believed a Top Ten album was expected. *Combat Rock* pipped a Sister label (Epic) release that week, and the following week the Epic label held a "post mortem" to look at what had gone wrong. Looking back now, working on the album was, said Pete "part of my education".

TV

A recently introduced 4th UK Channel, called… Channel 4 had started in November 1982, with the intention of broadcasting more niche and not necessarily commercial output. *The Tube* was one such program. *The Tube* began broadcasting in November 1982, The Clash never made an appearance of this more "left field" pop program from the North East. By this time, they were touring the US pretty comprehensively. In the UK, a big series that had just started on the BBC was *The Young Ones*. This starred Rik Mayall (recently deceased 2014), Adrian Edmondson and Nigel Planer. Each programme featured a live band playing in the run down student house which was the setting for the show. At the time, according to Douglas Kean, all the bands wanted to get on there, it was a very important show. Rik Mayall and Ade Edmondson were big Clash fans, and wanted them to play. Sadly, this never happened, much to the disappointment of the CBS Promo team.

In Japan, there was much made of The Clash visit, there was coverage of their arrival and a great deal of excitement. One of the shows was recorded for Japanese TV and has appeared both as a bootleg and "official release" *The Clash Live Sun Plaza in Tokyo* in January 1982.

News of the forthcoming arrival of The Clash was also on the News channel in Tokyo. According to Akito Watanabe of The Strummers, the February 1st show was recorded for Channel NHK on a programme called *The Young Music Show*. The credits on the live DVD credit it as the *Young Music Show* (Possibly they mean *New Music Show*).

www.thestrummers.com/akito/records/bn2004_07.html

In New Zealand they also hit the TV screens, as mentioned earlier, being interviewed for an unnamed pop program with Joe strumming his recently acquired ukulele.

The Clash had appeared on US TV *Saturday Night Live* again after the release, but just prior to the Shea Stadium shows on the 9th October 1982. This was great for the bands national coverage. The band wanted to mingle with any fans that might be waiting to see them, and arrived through the main entrance of the station, not the stage door. While waiting to go on set, a plan was drawn up to stop playing in the middle of the scheduled performance of *Should I Stay or Should I Go*, hold up a ghetto blaster to the microphone, and blast the audience with *Rock The Casbah*. Watching this back (catch it on YouTube or more "unofficial Clash Collections" on DVD) the big moment arrived, only for the ghetto blaster to fail to play. Joe flung the ghetto blaster in the air, which was caught by a roadie (off screen), narrowly avoiding some audience casualties. They also played *Straight To Hell*.

Video/MTV

The Clash were fortunate indeed to be in at the early stages of the MTV channel in the US, and conveniently have a video director/producer as a good friend

In *Rock History 5* (Press 2005), the author included a chapter on "Hip Hop Rock and MTV". *Rock The Casbah* was discussed and assessed as "a good example of early MTV at its best" as they went on to say, "jam-packed with conflicting audacious rapid fire images that may or may not have anything to do with the melody or lyrics.

The shoot for the video then, took place after the album release. Don Letts was travelling with the band who were still on their *Combat Rock* tour of the US. While in Texas, the video was shot. Don Letts revealed that the mood on "set" was not happy. Mick, famously wearing a camouflage hat with a veil, which Joe pulls from his face towards the end of the song. (Mick was having a "moody").

The video was shot in front of an oil well, with two actors, (one may have been Bernie) "running around dressed as an Arab and an orthodox Jew".

Apparently, Mick had wanted to perform in red all in one long johns and his Doc Martin boots, much to the hilarity of the others. Don sensibly advised him against that move, and he stormed off to get back in his fatigues! The star of the video may or may not have been the armadillo… what reference the little creature had to song, band, video is unknown. In an *NME* Article *Stations of The Clash* (Tickel, 1982) the writer discussed the video with Don Letts, acknowledging that the armadillo may well have upstaged the band. Tickell admitted that after seeing the video, it had made him want to listen to the album again. "Quite an achievement" he said "as I couldn't abide it". A result, I would say!

Clash fatigues were the order of the day and Joe sported his Travis Bickle/Kosmo inspired Mohican cut. Upon which Mick was quoted in *Flexipop Magazine* as saying "I woke up one morning and we were in Discharge" (UK Hardcore Punk band of that era). (Needs, 1982). In Vietnam, US troops would get a Mohican haircut, when they believed they were going to die.

This from Bob MacDonald, a colleague of mine from the Charts Department at Gallup during the late 80's, "mainstream radio in the US was very conservative in 1980-82, but MTV (launched in August 1981) shook the tree by being quicker to spot British acts, and *Rock The Casbah* in particular caught this wave - but paradoxically, the band supported The Who on their farewell US stadium dates at about this time and drew criticism from fans and the music press".

It was the UK Acts that had recognized video as an important promotional tool, the New Romantic acts and more colourful acts such as Culture Club were producing exciting and "good looking" videos which impressed the MTV programmers. The US acts were still relying on radio and touring to sell records. With videos receiving regular plays on MTV, the radio stations started getting requests for songs that were being shown, fueling the greater success of UK acts, The Clash included. In *Mad World* (Majewski & Bernstein, 2014) John Taylor from Duran Duran recounted how the MTV management had arranged a meeting with the Duran Management, and had said "we need more content". As Taylor went on to say, "if there had been more videos for *More Than A Feeling* (Boston) and Journey, for all the music that was played on the radio at that point, that's what they would have played".

In Japan, from my research with Akito Watanabe from The Strummers, he remembered a TV Show called *Best Hit USA* which played music videos. *Rock The Casbah* was featured extensively. He felt that this exposure further enhanced the awareness of The Clash in Japan, but did not significantly affect sales of the album. He went on to add that the album was easily available in Tokyo where he lived.

There had been an ongoing film project going on with Don Letts at the helm. "*On Broadway*" this had started around the Bonds Shows in 1981, and was still technically on the go through to 1982. This could have been another valuable promotional tool for the band, but money dried up, and the project was eventually abandoned. It might have been saved with some of the money from the Stadium shows, but sadly was not.

Radio

I am indebted once again to the knowledge and wisdom of Bob MacDonald as guidance for this section. In 1982, Radio play was still quite limited, in the UK, Radio One was the still the dominant power, daytime play lists were hard to crack, but John Peel remained as the savior of anything out of the standard chart fodder. In 1982, the station was celebrating 15 years and the lineup of DJ's was a mixture of "old and new " Looking at the "team photo", still standing were Tony Blackburn, Jimmy Saville, Dave Lee Travis, Noel Edmunds and Simon Bates. Of the "newer blood", Peter Powell, Kid Jensen and Mike Reid" The newer, younger DJ's did make a difference, and evening shows began to "champion" other music apart from the playlist staples. Douglas Kean a member of the CBS promo team in 1982 remembered driving Joe to the BBC to do an interview with Kid Jensen. He remembered that there were a few fans waiting outside and Joe spent considerable time talking to them. After the interview, he continued talking, and eventually, Douglas, Joe and fans hit Camden for a gig. Joe paid for a taxi for some of the fans to get there. As well as Radio One, there were independent, commercial local radio stations. These were funded by advertising and sponsorship and generally played a mixture of "oldies" and current hits. These included LBC and Capital Radio in London. There were also some BBC funded local radio stations which were targeting an older listener with talk base programmes, phone-ins and occasional music. None of these were really going to take a risk with bands like The Clash.

In the US, Radio was on a much wider and greater scale. There were local stations, and networks of local stations. These were commercially run with no licence payers to offend, but sponsors to please. Some stations were specialist, whether that be country and western, Soul or R&B. College Radio stations were free to choose their own playlists with no pressure from sponsors or shareholders, and these stations were much more aware of "counter-culture", and were less commercially orientated with regards to playlists.

The US operated completely differently to the UK. Not restricted by one National Station, it offered an enormous choice, potentially. As stations were commercially backed by advertisers and sponsors, it was necessary for the stations to play what might be called the "safe bets", during this time, largely AOR, the likes of Boston and Styx and Foreigner. From the mid 1970's, there had been a shift from stations acting as "tastemakers" trying to be first to play new hits. The emphasis was now keeping listeners tuned to the station and not "touching that dial". The more "Adult Orientated Rock" attracted older listeners, who had grown up with rock, and despite their added years, still wanted to hear the genre. Radio stations became much more aware of marketing and "testing" songs before airing them. Bob MacDonald identified the Fleetwood Mac Album *Rumours* as being the major sign post for the AOR genre.

Bob MacDonald again, "the US radio breakthrough for The Clash came in early 1980, shortly after the release of the *London Calling* double album, when *Train In Vain* created a buzz on college rock stations and became their first US chart single as *Train In Vain (Stand By Me)*. The single entered the Billboard Hot 100 (which unlike the UK charts, was based on airplay and sales) in March 1980 and peaked at No.23 in May.

The story of The Clash and their relationship with US radio is dealt with in some detail in the book *Stealing All Transmissions* (Doane, 2012)

Music Press

There was a heavy reliance on the printed word, mainly in the music press and magazines. At the time in the UK, there were the four "inkies" all fighting for the readership. *NME, Sounds, Melody Maker* and *Record Mirror*. Although "championed" early on by *NME*, The Clash had over the previous couple of years experienced a "backlash", predominantly because of their success and perseverance with "cracking" the US market. Musical fashions had moved on, and the band were seen possibly to be out of step. There was a lot of "white boy funk", pop and electronic music and the latest fashion movement New Romantic.

I could never have pictured any of The Clash sporting a floppy fringe, standing behind a synthesizer dressed in a kilt and matching accessories.

Much of the coverage of the tours came from the "inkies", and indeed the Joe AWOL incident fueled the news pages over a number of weeks (Job Done Bernie) even if the reality was a little different than might have been planned. Alongside the "inkies" were colour pop and style magazines like *Smash Hits*, *The Face* and *Flexi Pop*.

In the US, the music press was dominated by *Rolling Stone* magazine and *Creem* as well as *Trouser Press*. There was no weekly music press as in the UK with "inkies".

In Japan there was *Music Life* magazine, *Ongaku Senka Music* magazine, *Rockin' On* and *IN Rock*. Many of the articles from Music Life have reappeared in "Clash specials" which appear in the Japanese magazine *The Dig*. These are well worth getting hold of for the pictures alone. Watanabe from The Strummers could not remember clearly what advertising there was for the album.

Australia and New Zealand also had their share of Music Magazines, in Australia, the band were interviewed and featured in the likes of *Rolling Stone*, *RAM* and *Juke*.

Touring

The main promotional tool for a rock band was the tour, and boy did The Clash tour. You could look at the live show album promotion starting in 1981. With the band playing new tracks at the French Mogador Theatre dates, this carried on through 1982 and into 1983, particularly with tours of the US and The Who Stadium support slots. A full list of their tour schedules for these years in included in the *Pink* Clash book (Joe Strummer Paul Simonon, Topper Headon, 2008)(Joe Strummer 2008) and for more detail go the fantastic *Blackmarket Clash* website. dl.dropboxusercontent.com/u/77994754/Blackmarketclash/index.html

Always considered as a loss making exercise, and identified as an issue by Bernie in his decision to book a number of nights in one venue to cut down on transportation and logistical nightmares. By the time the band were playing the stadiums, they would actually be demanding a big enough fee to allow them to make money.

Touring at this time was a way to promote an album, trying to maximize the audience to interest them enough to seek out the latest tunes. Over the last few years, touring has become a money maker. Bands are reforming to play special tours "Performing their hit album in full", making money from the sometimes outrageous ticket price, and a healthy dose of merchandise.

Merchandise

The great spin off from touring, although not exclusively was the merchandise stall. The Clash were definitely a "T-shirt band", I should know, I have a wardrobe shelf full of them. There was money to be made on the tour merchandise, and free promotion.

During my regular internet trawls for information, particularly for international merchandise, I came across a number of posters for the US shows on the *Combat Rock* Tour. Usually large sizes to promote the shows in each city. I have encountered In-store promotional material, mainly *Combat Rock* album cover posters.

Please go to the colour section of the book for some of the *Combat Rock* merchandise.

Jules Blame also remembered designing the *Rock The Casbah* flash graphic which appeared on posters and t-shirts. When I interviewed him he did mention that there had been many "re-interpreted" versions of some of the t-shirt designs over the years.

The now legendary *Fifth Column T-Shirt Company*, produced many of the shirts which were sold, I was told on an *ad hoc* and informal basis. You can still buy the *Know Your Rights* and *Straight To Hell* shirts from them via mail order.

www.fifthcolumn.co.uk/

Sadly, my own Casbah Club T-Shirt bit the dust decades back, a limited run were reprinted in the US. This was another design by Jules Balme with his favoured "retro feel". The original image he explained was from "Stag Mags" from the 1930's onwards which were marketed as "Magazines For Men".

Graphic – Jules Balme

There was a particularly nice "Tour Program" produced for the Japanese tour, filled with some great black and white band shots by photographer Konno.

Design – David Corp, Japan

Clash Clobber

I've included this section, perhaps for the real Clash *Combat Rock* era fanatic. Without a doubt, the stage clothes that The Clash wore for the *Down at the Casbah* and *Combat Rock* tours were received with mixed reviews, as was the album. "Pop star fatigues" was one description I read, and the review from Cartwright from the Australian tour already mentioned, "colour coded sleeveless outfits resembling more a camp dance troupe than radical rockers". In *The Clash – The Only Band That Mattered* (Egan, 2015) the author noted that the "Red Angels" dress code was paramilitary, and not dissimilar to the military fatigue look of the band.

Personally, I think they were very cool, some that Mick and Joe wore were on display at the 2013 *Black Market Clash Exhibition* in London and at the various Mick Jones *Rock and Roll Library* shows. I can certainly remember well the "sleeveless" fashions of that time period, particularly among rockabilly and Clash/Theatre of Hate type bands. Lots of photo opportunities on line to view these, including visualise.com/virtual-tours/the-clash-pop-up-store-soho-london

During my research, I came across a Clash *Combat Rock* Camouflage sleeveless top on the Bonhams auction site (accessed 20/07/2014) www.bonhams.com/auctions/17973/lot/241/ expected to sell for between £400 and £600.

In 2014, I came across a *Combat Rock* Promotional jacket on the popular online auction site. Jules Balme recalled that these were the brainchild of Pete Winkelman, the CBS product manager for the band. A very limited quantity were made and given to CBS promotional staff and "competition winners" amongst the record shops for their presale orders of the album. This was confirmed by Pete Winkelman in a later interview. Please have a look at the colour section of the book for this and some of the commercially available "Clash Clobber".

Singles

Let's not forget that the single back in the day was seen in some ways as a loss leader issued to promote an album. The Punk explosion of the late 70's had made the single something a little different. Record companies and artists took much more time and effort with singles. Picture bags, coloured vinyl, and picture discs all started to appear. *The Cost of Living EP* by The Clash comes to mind, with its four tracks and gatefold sleeve with inner bag. This was quite sophisticated, and presumably expensive to manufacture. The Clash didn't necessarily follow the "rules". Clash singles were often not album tracks. *Complete Control*, *Clash City Rockers*, *White Man*, *Cost of Living EP*, *Bankrobber* and *This Is Radio Clash* were not taken from their standard UK Released albums. The A-sides of the singles released from *Combat Rock* were all album tracks, and seemed like a conscious effort to promote the album, but at the same time not ignoring the novelty and collectability of them.

The singles charts in the UK were based on sales over the counter in record stores. At the time, the official chart compiler was the British Market Research Bureau. The data was collected using diaries of sales filled in by record stores. Gallup took over data collection at the end of 1982, using electronic data capture techniques.

In the US, the charts were compiled through a combination of sales over the counter and airplay on the many radio stations. The charts were compiled by *Billboard* magazine and sales data was collected fairly crudely from stores.

In *The Clash – The Only Band That Mattered* Egan wrote that the *Combat Rock* album had "spawned multiple singles" which as he wrote came with "gimmicky free gifts, like stickers and stencils". I can see this, but personally I was fan, the singles were great, I would have bought them with or without the extras, they just added a value to them.

Know Your Rights

The first single never performed particularly well, too abrasive for daytime radio, but I think an important "announcement with guitars" to Clash fans that they hadn't lost their edge or aggression. Released as Joe took a walk… and a run in Paris, it would have been a difficult time for band and record label. An album in the pipeline, a single and UK tour lined up, but no singer.

Jules Balme remembered an incident prior to the release of the single. While working in his studio one Sunday near St. Pauls, he heard a knock on the door. At first he thought it was someone complaining about the noise, as he usually cranked up the record player pretty loud especially during the weekend when the rest of the city district was pretty dead. On opening the door, he was confronted by Bernie and Joe, clutching a copy of *Anarchy In The UK*, and an acetate pressing of *Know Your Rights*. They proceeded to play both records back to back to establish which the "loudest" cut was, and gather an opinion from Jules.

Released in the UK as 7" Only single in full colour picture sleeve, initial copies included a round *Know Your Rights* Yellow sticker. The single was only in the Top 100 in the UK for three weeks. Not an encouraging start, but when you consider the probable confusion around Joes disappearance, possibly disgruntled fans who wanted to see the band on tour, only to see dates being cancelled one after the other. It was not released in the US, but was released in Japan in full colour picture sleeve. The single was released also in Europe. Spain, Italy and Holland are listed on the Discogs website, and Australia also released the single.

Rock The Casbah

Rock The Casbah was released as a 7" single in full colour sleeve, in the UK initial copies with a free set of related stickers. *Rock The Casbah* was backed by *Long Time Jerk*. A 12" single was also released with *Mustapha Dance* as the B Side. To boost sales along, a picture disc also hit the UK stores with the same tracks as the 7" release but on the reverse side a picture of again the three band members, no drummer. The Credits for the production on the 12" single were for Mick. In The UK, the single had a slow start, getting airplay on both Radio One and the local radio stations.

The single saw release in Spain (with same Arab and the Orthodox Jew sleeve), Japan (with lyrics on reverse), and in the US on 7" and 12" single.

In Canada the 7" release had *Red Angel Dragnet* as the B Side. It also saw release in Holland, Ireland, Australia and Germany with *Long Time Jerk* as the B side.

In discussion with Jules Balme, he explained more about the sleeve design and concept. The background of the "minarets" was actually a painting done by Jules and Eddie King. As he pointed out, today they would probably find a photograph, and drop in other elements on the top of it using computer software. The Jewish and Arab characters were played by "Smart Mart", a mate of Kosmo (The Arab), and Mark Halfont who worked with Bernie backed Jo Boxers (as the Orthodox Jew).

The concept for the sleeve Jules believed came from Pete Ashworth, who was a photographer who worked with the Eurythmics and Adam Ant and Bernie Rhodes. Again, there was a nice set of stickers to be done, and again Eddie King came up with the designs.

At the time of release (June 1982) the band were in the US as the US leg of *The Casbah Club* tour was well underway. By July, The Clash were back in the UK on the UK Leg of the *Casbah Club* Tour. So, combining the touring, the radio play, the singles chart life was extended.

The US Mix and the remix B Side *Mustapha Dance* were Mick's mixes, not Glyn Johns. Largely seen as a "sweetener" for Mick after the "controls" had been taken over by Johns.

You can't deny that the sweet smell of success must have wafted in Mick's direction as the single performed so well, particularly in the US. The mixing was done at the Powerplant in New York, not Electric Lady, with Bob Clearmountain who amongst many others had recently worked with Chic. Mick had done similar remix jobs on *The Call Up* as the *Cool Out*, and *Radio Clash* as *Outside Broadcast*. In *The Clash – The Only Band That Mattered* (Egan, 2015) , Egan made the comment that the remix by Mick made the "splendid" *Combat Rock* original , pale in comparison.

Adverts for the singles appeared in the *NME* on 5th of June, two small adverts one featuring the *Rock The Casbah* Orthodox Jew and the other the Arab. The main strap line was *Mustapha Dance*. A week later in the same paper, an advert appeared telling readers that the 12" was OUT SOON. The same issue advertised the forthcoming July Brixton Fair Deal shows. The following week 19th June, more adverts appeared for the single in *NME*. A wait of a couple of weeks, and 3rd July saw and advert for the single "at last, strictly limited edition 7" picture disc OUT NOW!". The Picture disc design was again produced by Jules Balme.

UK Chart positions of *Know Your Rights* and *Rock The Casbah* in the Singles Chart, and *Combat Rock* in the album Chart.

US Chart Positions of *Rock The Casbah*

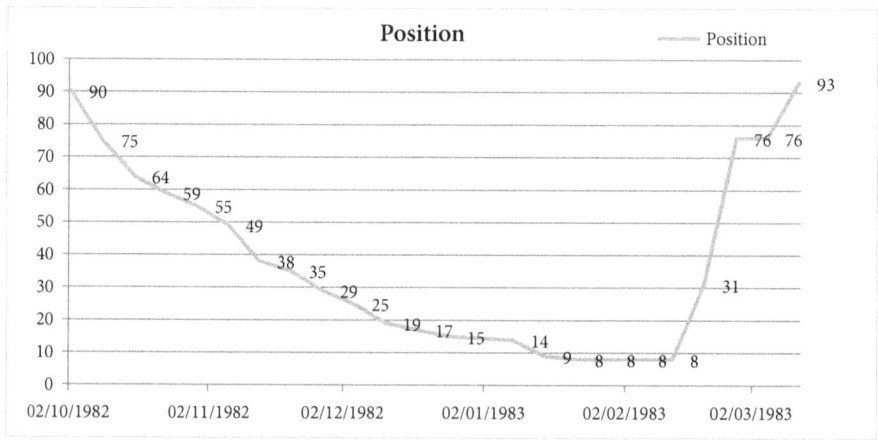

With MTV playing the video, and the band playing huge shows in the US, the single continued to sell and sell.

Should I Stay Or Should I Go

Should I Stay or Should I Go was released both in the UK and the USA. In the UK it was released as a double A side with *Straight To Hell*. The single charted at #62. It was also listed that same week on the Radio One Playlist. Over the next few weeks, the single rose to #17, it was dropped from the Radio One playlist, but was back on the air the following week. It was *Should I Stay or Should I Go* that got the airplay, even though the release was a double A side

Initially released as a 7" single in full colour picture bag, initial copies contained a "tattoo" sticker of the artwork on back cover. The 12" single also came in a full colour picture sleeve. Initial copies had a *Straight To Hell* stencil made of yellow card. A picture disc 7" single was released as the single held at #24 in the charts, which helped push up the following week to a high of #18. The design of which was the work largely by Eddie King.

The artwork for the sleeve again has a story to tell. Again in discussion with Jules Balme, he recalled that when the job came in for the "double A side". He was extremely busy, then working on the Tears For Fears and Blancmange albums. Eddie King picked up on the design work, and between them produced what Jules referred to as the most "sophisticated" sleeve. Eddie King found a sheet of metal which he generally abused over about three weeks, including leaving it out in the rain to rust and bashing with a hammer. The logo again took long hours, the skull and helmet with cross machine guns. The intricate Dragon Tattoo which graced the back of the sleeve and the free sticker. The type for the credits took its influence from *The Dogs of War* and *Soldier of Fortune* magazine.

The twelve inch included the stencil mentioned earlier, which got a mixed response when Jules took over sleeves for Bernie and the band to look at in New York. Bernie wasn't impressed. Joe and Gaby however loved the stencil and proceeded to start making their own t-shirts with them. The idea Jules believed came from the then product manager for The Clash at CBS, Pete Winkleman, now chairman of the MK Dons Football Team in the UK.

The Tom Robinson Band had given a free stencil away with the striking clenched fist back in 1978 and that went down well the politically motivated fans.

Airplay was for *Should I Stay or Should I Go*; *Straight To Hell* was probably not considered daytime radio friendly. By this time, *Combat Rock* was out of the album Top 100 and did not make reappearance on the back of the single release in the UK.

UK Chart Positions of *Should I Stay or Should I Go*

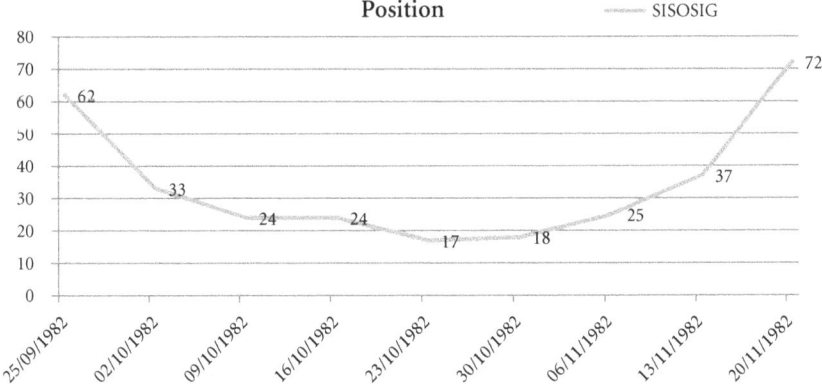

In The US the single charted in the *Billboard* Singles Chart at #92 17th July 1982, peaking at #45 in September 25th, so quite a run. The release strategy was a little different. The single was released in four 7" formats.

There were two picture sleeve versions, one with a band image (minus Topper) and Ladbroke Grove map, the second with a yellow sleeve graced by a picture of Ronnie Reagan, complete with Clash armband (painstakingly added to the picture by Jules Balme).

So we had *Should I Stay or Should I Go* backed with *Cool Confusion*, the Reagan sleeve *First Night Back In London*, a third release appeared in plain blue Epic house bag with *Inoculated City* as the B Side. The final version was a one sided (possibly promo only) single of *Should I Stay or Should I Go*.

US Chart Positions *Should I Stay or Should I Go.*

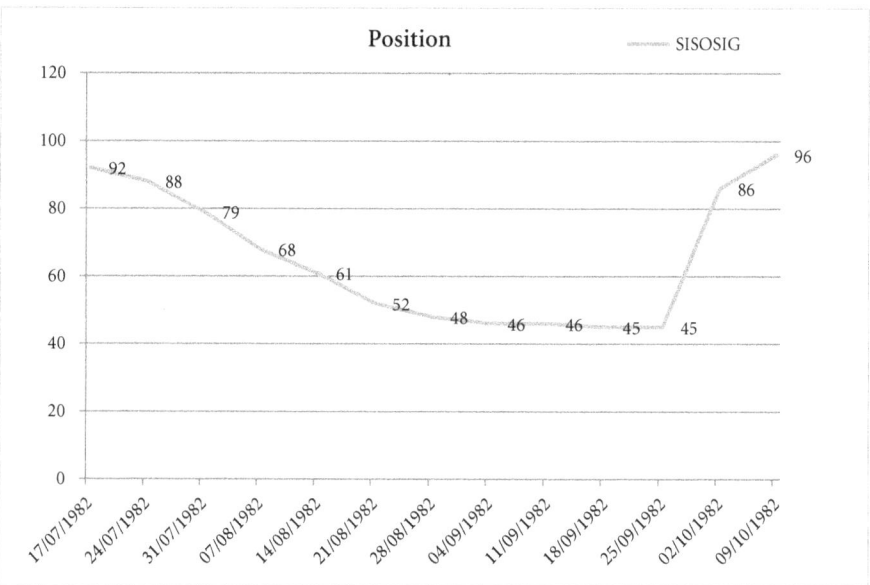

The single was also released in a picture sleeve in Spain (*Should I Stay* being pushed as the A Side, *Straight To Hell* B Side. The cover featuring a picture of the band with Terry Chimes as part of the group. The Japanese release was a picture sleeve as the US release (Three band members and Ladbroke Grove map) and lyrics on the reverse sleeve.

In the US then, the singles possibly helped the Sales of *Combat Rock* By October 1982, the album went Gold in the US (Half a Million sales), the band were in the US on the *Combat Rock* Tour, and in November 1982 the album peaked in the Hot 100 Chart at # 7. By February 1983, US Sales had hit 1 Million as the album went Platinum. By then they were back in the UK.

Overpowered By Funk

I came across this release through a "popular online auction website", and was intrigued as to its origins. The single is a CBS Especial which features *Overpowered by Funk* on the b-side of a 33 ⅓ Rpm 7" single. The A side is Neil Young *Computer Age*.

The single seems to translate as "the world was better with lycra", and trusty Google translate seems to indicate that it the track or tracks were from a DuPont "Lycra" advert from Argentinean TV. The single comes in a full colour 7" sleeve and insert. It originally appeared as the B side of *Rock The Casbah* release in Argentina. It looks as if the single was issued in 1982, which bearing in mind the then "situation" between the UK and Argentina at the time is a little bizarre! This single version appears on the "Singles Box Set" on CD 17 (Rock The Casbah).

VINYL

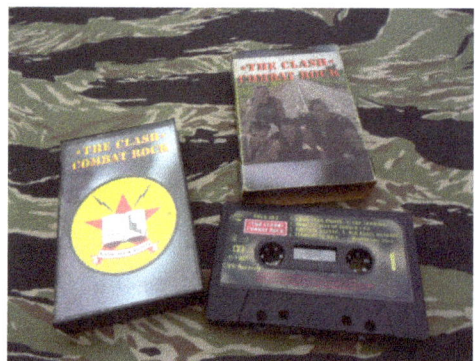

CASSETTE

8 TRACK

Original Photographs by Pennie Smith /Poster Tinting Paul Simonon / Design Jules Balme / CBS Records/EPIC Records

Free Poster Sticker from Album Sleeve – Designed by Jules Balme

There were two interesting picture disc albums of *Combat Rock* released in 1983, used as promotional tools by the US label EPIC

 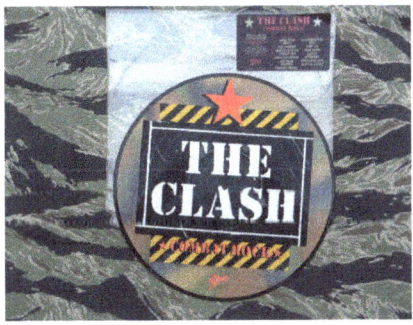

Designer Unknown Epic Records USA/Band Shot Bob Gruen

Below – South African Vinyl Version (Picture Provided by Ant Davie)

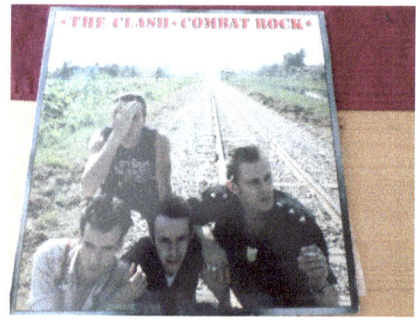 

Original Photographs by Pennie Smith/Design Jules Balme/CBS Records

In the US, the album was released with band member stickers on the cover. So to get the set, you would need to get one with Topper, one with Paul, One with Joe and one with Mick, another four copies.

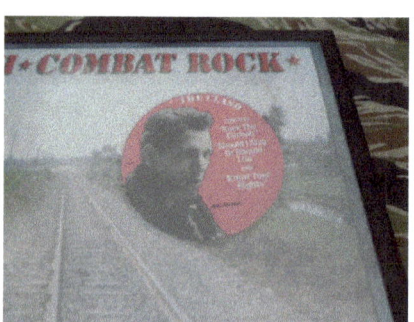 

Original Photographs by Pennie Smith / Design Jules Balme / Epic Records / Sticker Design Unknown

For real collectors, the various territories issued the album with different label designs. The UK with a camouflage style label, other countries used their standard label colour red and variants.

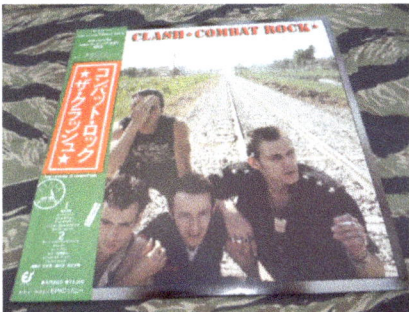 

Above – Japanese Vinyl Release

Below – Japanese Vinyl with Inner

Below – Mexican Vinyl Release

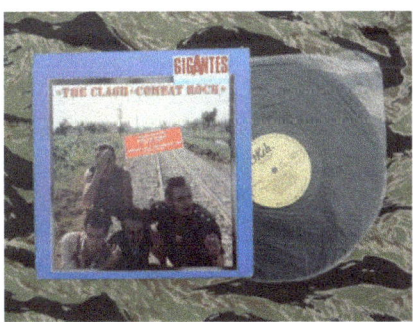 

Above – Malaysian Vinyl Release with hit song titles on cover

Below – Greek Release with reversed out lyric sheet

There was also a three track "Promo Only" sampler released in Japan in 1982.
The keyboards are credited to Polly Maxwell!!

Later releases of the album have presented us with CD versions in jewel boxes, paper/cardboard album sleeve replicas, Re-masters, Japanese imports with obi and double and triple pack collections with *Combat Rock* included. Sadly, the old side one and side two track listings are merged to the twelve track version.

Below – Original US CD Release – Epic Records

 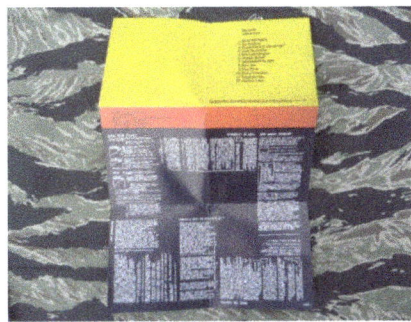

Below – Restored CD UK Version

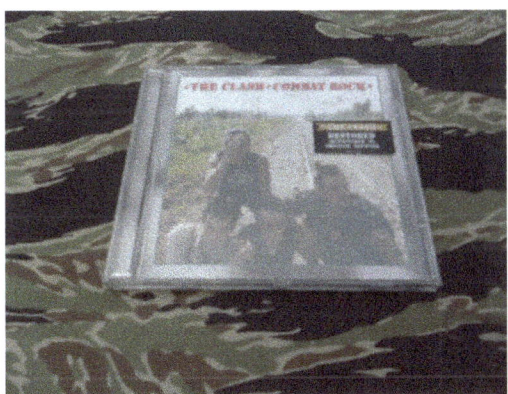

Below – Russian Two On One Version of *Combat Rock* and "Super Blackmarket Clash"

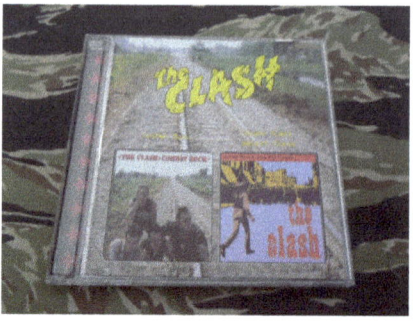

Below – Japan "Blue Spec CD2" Release

Below – Japanese "Vinyl Replica" Release

Below – UK Mini Disc Release

Below – Far East – Cassette Version Original Photographs by Pennie Smith/Design Jules Balme/ CBS Records /Himalayan Records

MERCHANDISE

The first shirt is from Canada, the second, a late reproduction of the *Combat Rock* Tour shirt from the US. Both feature the *Know Your Rights* graphic.

Other variations included the *Straight To Hell* design. The black white and red on the left was designed by Jules Balme, and was based on the stencil design from the 12" single.

Logo – Eddie King/Jules Balme

Combat Rock Era Tour Badges

Design – Casbah -Jules Balme/US Tour-Unknown/Joe-Unknown/Let That Raga – Eddie King

CLASH CLOBBER

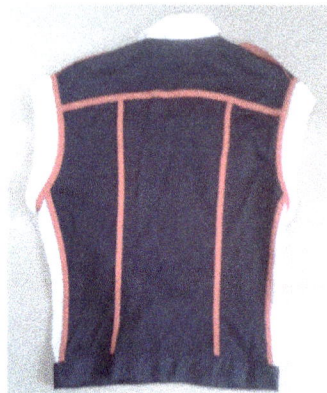

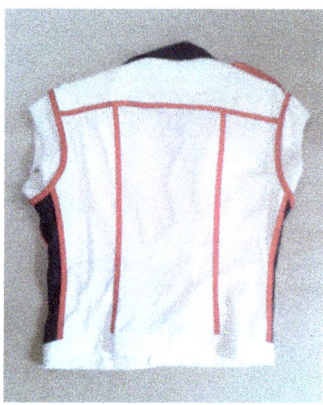

In 2004, Japanese clothing company 666 produced some "tribute" cut off shirts in the style of the Alex Michon designs, complete with "Luggage Clips" fastenings as Paul described them. I am sure now highly valuable and collectable, certainly in Japan. They are "shirts of great beauty", my own quote here.

From the pages of the NME in 1982, in the small ad there was an advertisement for *Combat Rock* gear. Amongst the items a customised cut off combat shirt, picture below.

Below - *Combat Rock* Promotional jacket

RAT PATROL FROM FORT BRAGG

Combat Rock Outakes – Unofficial Release

Combat Out Rock Band Photo: Pennie Smith – Unofficial Release

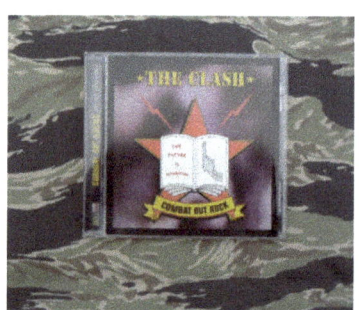 

Another Combat Rock Band Photo: Pennie Smith – Unofficial Release

Rat Patrol Topper Photograph – Source Unknown - Unofficial Release

Rat Patrol From Fort Bragg – Band Photo: Pennie Smith - Unofficial Release

Topper backstage at Bonds Casino 1981

Picture by Joe Streno

Joe backstage at Bonds Casino 1981
Juggling balls and beers

Picture by Joe Streno

Mick outside Bonds Casino 1981
With Joe Blaney

Picture by Joe Streno

Paul backstage at Bonds Casino 1981

Picture by Joe Streno

Joe on stage at Asbury Park 1982

Picture by Joe Streno

Mick on stage at Asbury Park 1982

Picture by Joe Streno

Paul on stage at Asbury Park 1982

Picture by Joe Streno

Terry at *Combat Rock* launch party Asbury Park 1982

Picture by Joe Streno

Paul and Pearl at *Combat Rock* launch party Asbury Park 1982

Picture by Joe Streno

Kosmo and Friend at *Combat Rock* launch party Asbury Park 1982

Picture by Joe Streno

Bonds, New York 1981: This is a public service announcement ... with(out) guitar!

When it came to photographing The Clash, I was a fan first. Getting into Bonds was not through my doing. My then girlfriend Dorothy, had a girlfriend Brenda, who worked for The Clash. It was Brenda who got Dorothy and me into that Saturday show. Brenda also got us backstage passes. With my pass came the ability and privilege to watch and photograph the show from the side of the stage; something I had never done before. Being allowed access backstage was pure magic — for a fan or a photographer. To this day I am very proud of the photographs I took backstage at Bonds, and thankful to Joe, Mick, Paul, Topper, and even Pearl Harbor for letting me photograph them — posed or candid. These moments were historic; for them and for me.

Asbury Park, NJ 1982: Should I Stay Or Should I Go

I met with Kosmo Vinyl at Electric Lady recording studio in New York City, while Joe Strummer was finishing production on Combat Rock. My meeting was to show Kosmo my Clash portfolio, consisting of my Palladium NY, and Bonds photos; live, backstage, and street. It was a great feeling to see how much he appreciated the photos. At one point Strummer comes out of the control room and into the lounge. Kosmo holds — over his head — my 11x14 print of my favorite backstage Bonds photo of Strummer, "From Behind The Curtain", and shows Joe. Joe smiles a huge toothy grin, gives a energetic thumbs up, and says: "Who's that ugly git?" He cracks a big smile again, grabs his drink and walks back into the control room. Shortly after that little exchange, Kosmo tells me he loves my photos and The Clash will be playing the U.S. and wants me there to photograph the band. That was my ticket in, and I loved it.

The shows were incredible! The energy was as electric as the stage lighting was stunning, in Convention Hall those three nights in May 1982. Even Joe's "disappearance" before the start of this tour, and the "sacking" of Topper couldn't douse the fire and energy of these shows.

I always thought this was the beginning of the end; especially with this statement appearing on the private party invitation: "Joe's Back And Topper's Gone. What Else Do You Want To Know?" It may have been a foreboding omen of what was to come. But in the moment? Those shows were hot! The Clash were hot! And the party thrown at the Asbury Park Amusement Casino was a fan's and photographer's wet dream!

The amount of accessibility to the band, as a group and individually was typical — in a great way. If I thought backstage at Bonds was amazing, we were all kids in a candy store in Asbury! To see Joe, Mick, Paul, and Terry playing games, riding rides, and having so much fun, was at once incredibly humanizing and so very joyous.

For me? An event of a lifetime!

Joe Streno - 2016

11. Fort Bragg's revolt from the post-apocalypse 12. Rat Patrol 13. All the covers and controversy 14. Covers and cultural effect 15. Bragg's bombshell 16. Reading list 17. Conclusions 18. Those who served 19. References

11. RAT PATROL FROM FORT BRAGG

So, what happened to those unloved mixes that Mick spent hours and dollars sweating over in the run up to release of *Combat Rock*. Much had been rumoured about the album that was not to be. Was it too clever for its own good; was it commercial enough, had Mick lost the plot? Whatever your opinion, Uncut magazine named *Rat Patrol From Fort Bragg* the 6th best bootleg in 2011. This was a reference to the 2 CD Set which we will look at shortly.

www.stereogum.com/830851/uncuts-50-greatest-bootlegs/list/

Over the years, and a number of bootleg releases, you are able to judge for yourself.

Please refer again to the colour section of the book for sleeve shots.

My first personal contact was via a CD bought in the US called *Combat Rock Outs*, previously I had only been aware of an Italian Vinyl bootleg called Combat Rock Outtakes More information available in the fantastic *The Clash Retrospective Book*. (Provocateur UNKNOWN). Ten tracks were listed on the vinyl album. The album sleeve itself lists the tracks in a completely mixed up way, and *Man In a Box* and *R.A.D.* are on the track listing, which actually turn out to be *The Beautiful People are Ugly* and *Inoculated City* respectively.

Please see the *Rat Patrol From Fort Bragg* section in the colour pages of this book for cover pictures.

Tracks.

Side One

Straight To Hell

Know Your Rights

Rock The Casbah

Ghetto Defendant

Side Two

Sean Flynn

Car Jamming

Atom Tan

The Beautiful People

First Night Back in London

Inoculated City

As we moved in to the CD age, there is no longer any side to take!

Combat Rock Out boasted 15 tracks, two listed simply as "unreleased song". These were studio outtakes of good quality, and you certainly get an idea of how much polish was applied by Glyn

Johns for the *Combat Rock* release. That is not to say that *Rat Patrol* does not stand up as a good album. As time has gone on, there have been more appearances of the *Rat Patrol* album with different tracks and artwork. This album may also have hit the record fairs as *Combat Out Rock* which is reviewed on the very wonderful website

www.sharoma.com/clash/combat_out_rock.

The reviewer believed that these recordings did date back to late 1981, and that the recordings did sound a little "muggy". Interestingly, there is no sign of *Overpowered By Funk*

Tracks

1. Know Your Rights
2. Car Jamming
3. Rock The Casbah
4. Red Angel Dragnet
5. Should I Stay Or Should I Go
6. Ghetto Defendant
7. Straight To Hell
8. Inoculated City
9. Atom Tan
10. Cool Confusion
11. Sean Flynn
12. Death Is a Star
13. First Night back In London
14. Unreleased Song #1 The Beautiful People Are Ugly Too
15. Unreleased Song #2 Kill Time

The web article writer looked at each track in turn, noting the differences between the more polished *Combat Rock* tracks and these early mixes.

After these, I got hold of *Another Combat Rock* boasting another Pennie Smith Shot from the railway line in Thailand, with perhaps a more sympathetic band shot, but not a great advertisement for an anti-smoking campaign. More information online

100greatestbootlegs.blogspot.co.uk/2013/06/flac-clash-another-combat-rock.html

Billed as the original Mick Jones mix of *Combat Rock*, it includes the twelve album titles plus three previously unknown tracks and a version of *First Night back In London* which got an official airing as a single B side.

Tracks

1. Know Your Rights — 5:07
2. Car Jamming — 3:53
3. Should I Stay or Should I Go — 3:03
4. Rock the Casbah — 3:46
5. Red Angel Dragnet — 5:13
6. Straight to Hell — 6:55
7. Overpowered By Funk — 7:00
8. Atom Tan — 2:43
9. Sean Flynn — 7:28
10. Ghetto Defendant — 6:17
11. Inoculated City — 4:28
12. Death Is a Star — 2:37
13. The Beautiful People Are Ugly Too — 3:43
14. Kill Time — 4:52
15. First Night Back in London — 3:00
16. Walk Evil Talk — 7:31

Next up was *Rat Patrol From Fort Bragg* featuring a cover on which only Topper appears, as well as a small comic strip picture of the war time *Rat Patrol* from the TV series.

Tracks

1. The Beautiful People Are Ugly Too
2. Kill Time
3. Should I Stay or Should I Go
4. Rock The Casbah
5. Know Your Rights
6. Red Angel Dragnet
7. Ghetto Defendant
8. Sean Flynn
9. Car jamming
10. Inoculated City

11. Death Is A Star

12. Walk Evil Talk

13. Atom Tan (Edited)

14. Inoculated City (Uncensored Combat Rock Version)

15. First Night Back In London

16. Cool Confusion

17. Straight To Hell

Billed as the original version of *Combat Rock*, produced by Mick Jones and includes a previously unknown track *Walk Evil Talk*.

In 2003, perhaps the "ultimate" bootleg edition made an appearance, in something along the lines of what record labels are doing with "classic album" releases, making a nicely packaged double album. The CD set was made in Italy on the Red line label. The packaging is so believable; you would think it was an official Sony release. Same band cover shot as *Combat Rock*, but the album title changed to *Rat Patrol From Fort Bragg*. It is like the legacy edition version of *London Calling*, with an extra album of works in progress and remixes. I consider it to be an important document of the way the album could have been made.

The albums list a staggering 38 tracks. Disc 1 is made up of the 12 songs that appeared remixed on *Combat Rock*, with the addition of the previously officially unreleased tracks *The Beautiful People are Ugly, Kill Time, Walk Evil Walk*, an *Overpowered by Funk* demo, and unedited versions of *Inoculated City* and the extended mix of *Straight To Hell*. Two tracks that were dropped from the final mix but made it as B sides, *Cool Confusion* and *First Night Back In London*. The second disc has instrumental versions of tracks, remixes and edited and alternative versions, including *Rock The Casbah* with Ranking Roger from The Beat toasting over it.

Tracks

1. The Beautiful People Are Ugly, Too

2. Kill Time (Idle In Kangaroo Court W1)

3. Should I Stay Or Should I Go?

4. Rock The Casbah

5. Know Your Rights

6. Red Angel Dragnet

7. Ghetto Defendant

8. Sean Flynn

9. Car Jamming

10. Inoculated City

11. Death Is A Star

12. Walk Evil Talk
13. Atom Tan
14. Overpowered By Funk (Demo)
15. Inoculated City (Uncensored)
16. First Night Back In London
17. Cool Confusion
18. Straight To Hell (Extended Mix)

1. Should I Stay Or Should I Go? (Shea St.)
2. Rock The Casbah (Instrumental)
3. Know Your Rights (Instrumental)
4. Red Angel Dragnet (Instrumental)
5. Overpowered By Funk (Instrumental)
6. Ghetto Defendant 1 (Instrumental)
7. Ghetto Defendant 2 (Instrumental)
8. Atom Tan (Instrumental)
9. First Night Back In London (Instrumental)
10. Cool Confusion 1 (Instrumental)
11. Cool Confusion 2 (Instrumental)
12. Straight To Hell (7 Inch)
13. Overpowered By Funk (No Flushes)
14. Hell W10
15. Cool Confusion (Remix)
16. Know Your Rights (Alt Version.)
17. Cool Confusion (Full)
18. Red Angel Dragnet (Edited)
19. Ghetto Defendant (Edited)
20. Rock The Casbah

The track *Walk Evil Talk* is a strange one. Just jazzy drums and a tinkly jazz piano. There are no vocals or guitars. There is no evidence that The Clash even played it. The drumming could easily be Topper in full jazz wig out mode, but who played the piano parts? Seven Minutes and thirty seven seconds in length, it ambles along, not really going anywhere. Maybe it was an idea for a soundtrack piece; it does sort of align itself to *Death Is a Star*.

More Vinyl versions of *Rat Patrol* make an appearance, the next one I came across was a single coloured vinyl version, again called *Rat Patrol From Fort Bragg*. The album features a post Topper lineup photo (Terry Chimes in his place)

Tracks

1. Know Your Rights
2. Car jamming
3. Should I Stay Or Should I Go
4. Rock The Casbah
5. Red Angel Dragnet
6. Straight To Hell

1. Overpowered By Funk
2. Atom tan
3. Sean Flynn
4. Ghetto Defendant
5. Inoculated City
6. Death Is A Star

This version keeps true to the *Combat Rock* running order, but uses the Mick Jones produced recordings instead of the Glyn Johns tracks.

It serves very well as a comparison to what was and what might have been.

The most recent Vinyl edition was a double coloured vinyl version of *Rat Patrol From Fort Bragg*, which follows the formula of the 2 CD set mentioned earlier.

Although the sleeve is totally out of time and context with the *Combat Rock* era Clash, it features a front picture of The Clash around *Give 'Em Enough Rope* era, and a back photo from the Belfast photo shoot.

Tracks

1. The Beautiful people Are Ugly
2. Kill Time
3. Should I Stay Or Should I Go

4. Rock The Casbah

5. Inoculated City (Uncensored)

6. Know Your Rights

7. Red Angel Dragnet

8. Ghetto Defendant

9. Car Jamming

1. Sean Flynn

2. Death Is a Star

3. Atom Tan

4. Cool Confusion (Remix)

5. Rock The Casbah (With Ranking Roger)

6. Know Your Rights (Instrumental)

7. Red Angel Dragnet (Instrumental)

8. Overpowered By Funk (Instrumental)

9. Ghetto Defendant 1 & 2 (Instrumental)

10. Atom Tan (Instrumental)

11. First Night Back in London (Instrumental)

12. Cool Confusion 1 & 2 (Instrumental)

13. Hell W10

In 2014, I came across *Rat Patrol From Fort Bragg* available as a "fantasy 8 track". I think a one off customized version of the bootleg album. Even the box is "aged" and the care and attention to detail is extraordinary. In the same way as the "deluxe" version of *Rat Patrol*, it is totally believable that it is a genuine release.

Tracks

1. The Beautiful people Are Ugly

2. Kill Time

3. Should I Stay Or Should I Go

4. Rock The Casbah

5. Know Your Rights

6. Red Angel Dragnet

7. Ghetto Defendant

8. Sean Flynn

9. Car Jamming

10. Inoculated City

11. Death Is a Star

12. Walk Evil Talk

13. Atom Tan (Edit)

14. First Night Back In London

15. Straight To Hell

16. Overpowered By Funk

17. Hell W10

18. Cool Confusion (Remix)

19. Mustapha Dance

Again in 2014, another CD variation came to my attention, not an "official", unofficial bootleg called *Cool Confusion - The Combat Rock Demos*.

Tracks

1. The Beautiful People Are Ugly Too

2. Kill Time

3. Should I Stay or Should I Go

4. Rock The Casbah

5. Know Your Rights

6. Red Angel Dragnet

7. Ghetto Defendant

8. Sean Flynn

9. Car Jamming

10. Inoculated City

11. Death Is A Star

12. Walk Evil Talk

13. Atom Tan (Edited)

14. Inoculated City (Uncensored)

15. First Night Back In London

16. Cool Confusion

17. Straight To Hell

So, what about the songs that would have been on the Mick Jones produced album, which never made the final cut on *Combat Rock*. There were a number of edits made to the original tracks, which then appeared on *Combat Rock*. *Straight To Hell* in particular was cut down.

In the *Mojo* article *Who Killed The Clash* (Snow, 2008) The writer looked at the *Rat Patrol* album in more detail. Needs pointed out that *Rat Patrol* was "little more than a rumour". He also said that the title came from Mick, and was reference to the Rat Patrol 60's TV series, as discussed earlier. *Combat Rock*, said Needs was "pruned down from 65 to 48 minutes" and that intros, codas and whole tracks were culled. It seemed that *Overpowered By Funk* was initially dropped from *Combat Rock*, but then reinstated. Personally, I'm glad, it is a fine track!

The *Rat Patrol* Bootleg was believed to have originated from a tape cassette that was "found in a record company execs desk" and it was leaked out. Clearly, there is much, much more to this, the quality and range of material doesn't strike me as recordings on a cheap and cheerful cassette.

For some great thoughts, theories and insights into the *Rat Patrol* album, I would strongly recommend the Chris Knowles book *Clash City Showdown*, which covers the tracks, suggests better track running orders. He also noted that if you compared the two albums, "Joe went in and recorded a lot of extra guitar", especially on *Know Your Rights*, *Car Jamming* and *Should I Stay*. Knowles also added that "It has been said that Joe didn't do a lot of playing on the last two albums, and that it was a major factor in the essence of the energy levels" He also felt that "Joe wasn't a guitarist per se, but a weird kind of percussionist". This was backed up by Mick Jones when he appeared on the "Telecaster 60 years" TV show in 2012, Mick pointed out that when Joe played the Telecaster, he was left- handed, but played a right handed guitar. He was therefore using his more dexterous hand to strum, which gave him a more rhythmic style.

So, I think it is worth looking at these tracks and some opinions!

TRACK 1: THE BEAUTIFUL PEOPLE ARE UGLY 3:45

Kris Needs noted that this was "Joes Broadside against the hip elite of New York"; it is a kind of calypso style song, but with a synthesized melody, with shared vocals from Joe and Mick. The (amazing) Sharoma Clash website www.sharoma.com/clash/ thought it was a great song, which is very catchy, and in keeping with some of the other album tracks. Also known as *Fulham Connection W11* and *Man In A Box*. In *The Complete Clash*, Topping wrote that this track was recorded at Electric Lady in 1981. Some of the guitar is played in the same funky style as *Overpowered by Funk* and there is a bass break/instrumental break that is certainly funky! Chris Knowles found the track to be "an updated samba track flavoured rock tune, inexplicably cut from *Combat Rock*". He believed that perhaps the master tapes were lost for this track and second track *Kill Time*.

TRACK 2: KILL TIME 4:58

This is in a similar vein to *The Beautiful People*, a synthesizer with a kind of Caribbean Steel Drums sound, and a lot of percussion. The Sharoma web site again felt this was a great song, commenting that the quality of the recording is very good. This track was also listed by Topping as being recorded in 1981 at Electric lady. It also reveals that it had two other possible working titles *(Licence To) Kill Time* and *Idle in the Kangaroo Court*. Kris Needs commented that the "flute noises" came from Mick's "synth guitar" aka "the Dalek's handbag". Lyrically it appears to be another comment by Joe on the "hip party" scene in New York. There is a definite sense of relationship between these two tracks, but both were dropped from the *Combat Rock* Album.

TRACK 3: SHOULD I STAY OR SHOULD I GO 3:06

Kris Needs noted that the original version had Gary Barnacle playing saxophone, but this part was "trimmed" from the *Combat Rock* Version. Also revealed on this alternative version are more "Spanish vocals" from the two Joes, and the original not clean lyrics. This summary is echoed by the Sharoma website review. "The mix is very clear, a little less 'bright' than the *Combat Rock* version, but the saxophone is a nice addition."

TRACK 4: ROCK THE CASBAH 3:47

The *Sharoma* website noted that the introduction is a little different from the *Combat Rock* album version, and there are added sound effects. The intro starts off with "Toppers Bongos", and follows pretty much the same route as the *Combat Rock* version, but possibly the guitars are a little more subdued.

TRACK 5: KNOW YOUR RIGHTS 5:04

Kris Needs wrote that the original version is 90 Seconds longer, and that a mid section of the song was cut. The *Sharoma* website noted that the original version also seemed a little slower. There are possibly three versions, the bootleg version, one that appears on *Clash On Broadway Outtakes* bootleg and the *Combat Rock* Version. Rather than the loud ranting "this is a public service announcement", this part is more spoken. It lacks the energy and immediacy that the *Combat Rock* version has.

TRACK 6: RED ANGEL DRAGNET 6:12

Kris Needs noted that two and a half minutes of this track were cut from the *Combat Rock* version, most of it Kosmo's "Travis Bickle" part. The *Sharoma* web site noticed that the instrumentation seemed a little louder on the final version, particularly the organ part. Also noted was that there were extra background vocals from Mick and Joe.

TRACK 7: GHETTO DEFENDANT 6:17

Another song which was chopped by about 90 seconds observed Kris Needs, and that Mick had wanted to allow the music to "stretch" to create an atmosphere. The *Sharoma* view was that some of Ginsberg's lyrics appeared in different places from the *Combat Rock* mix, and that Joes vocals were sung differently. Again it lacks the polish of the Glyn Johns version.

TRACK 8: SEAN FLYNN 7:30

Needs mentioned the Mick Jones "stretch", and this extended version was cut by about three minutes for *Combat Rock* version. He referred to this track as an example of Mick's "expansive mixes". *Sharoma* noted that the bootleg version has a longer "spooky" introduction, but that overall, not too different from the final *Combat Rock* mix. Mick has mentioned a 15 minute version of this, but 7 minutes is probably "ample".

TRACK 9: CAR JAMMING 3:53

Needs identified this track as one of the few that was built on a "straight rock beat" *Sharoma* picked up on the extra sound effects and extended version here. More car horns certainly!! There is quite a difference in the volume level of the keyboards in the *Combat Rock* version.

TRACK 10: INOCULATED CITY 4:32

Sharoma website picked up again on the extended version here, and how the *Combat Rock* version felt a little short. The "2000 flushes" advert is present as well as more sound effects. Kris Needs called it a "classic Clash strut" also noted that Glyn Johns took 2 minutes off the original. It does seem a little less intensely sung by Mick. The "2000 flushes" sample seems a little further back in the mix, less obvious compared to the *Combat Rock* mix.

TRACK 11: DEATH IS A STAR 2:39

Needs identified this as "Joes poem about seeing movies to watch people die". I wonder what Joe might have made of the new generation of computer games like *Call of Duty*, now that's *Combat Rock*! The *Rat Patrol* version does sound to me more demo like, with extra background effects and keyboard /synths.

TRACK 12: WALK EVIL TALK 7:37

"The most far out gem of The Clash" said Needs, "buried for years". This is piano and drums only and has been the subject of some controversy as there is no proof that it is The Clash playing. I can certainly believe that Topper could cook up this jazz rhythm, but who played the keyboards? You could say it was a soundtrack piece, and possibly a relation of *Death Is a Star*. A bit of a wig out, I would say.

TRACK 13: ATOM TAN 2:45

Needs noted that *Atom Tan* was only cut by 13 seconds for the *Combat Rock* album. *Sharoma* felt there was little difference between the versions, perhaps just a little slower. In places it sounds a "little Rolling Stones".

TRACK 14: FIRST NIGHT BACK IN LONDON 2:56

Tony Fletcher wrote that this track was recorded in 1981 at Ear Studios, and felt that it was "little more than half a song". Finished, said Fletcher at Electric Lady. It did get released as a B Side after being dropped by Glyn Johns from the *Combat Rock* album. *Sharoma* have both this and the next track as the same versions which appeared on the *Super Black Market Clash* album.

Fletcher likened the Mick "echo saturated guitar" to the Police hit *Walking On The Moon*. It is a half sung/ half rap kind of song with electronic percussion with synth keyboards and some spooky background echo/dubby effects. Almost like they were from Scooby Doo, or the *Forbidden Planet* Sci-Fi movie. It appeared as the B side to *Know Your Rights*.

TRACK 15: COOL CONFUSION 3:10

With no real verse/chorus structure, *Cool Confusion* is a kind of Reggae downbeat guitar with keyboard filling and sound effects. It would be a weak track to include on *Combat Rock*, and made an appearance as a B-side on one of the US Versions of *Should I Stay or Should I Go*. Topping believed it was recorded at Electric Lady in November/October 1981. The lyrics may have been partly inspired by a visit to the New York Studio 54, and reference to big celebrities who "swanned in" and "swanned out "again. Joe referred to this in *The Clash On Broadway* Booklet. Tony Fletcher said the track had "all the focus of a *Sandinista* out-take". There are a couple of versions of the track in circulation, another on The Clash D.O.A compilation bootleg. In *The Clash – The Only Band that Mattered*, Egan lumped this track together with the other single B-sides as being slight, and not helped by what he referred to as "electronic farts" which Mick included.

TRACK 16: STRAIGHT TO HELL 6:56

The *Rat Patrol* version is longer than the *Combat Rock* edited version, which according to Needs lost 86 seconds! But was restored to full glory on the B-side (or AA side) of *Should I Stay or Should I Go* 12" version, and again of *Clash On Broadway*.

The *Deluxe Fort Bragg* 2 CD set includes the second disc of mainly instrumental versions of the *Rat Patrol* Tracks, in some cases, two versions. The live Shea Stadium *Should I Stay or Should I Go* also makes an appearance. *Overpowered By Funk* is listed with *No Flushes* in error. The "demo" version of the track has no keyboards, and instrumental only with an incredibly funky feel to it, choppy guitars and a bass line to die for. The instrumental version which is slightly longer at 3:12 is more developed, still without keyboards, but a definite refinement. Another addition, *Hell W10* is a short instrumental piece. It is not clear if this was written specifically for the *Hell W10* film which the band and associates later filmed in 1983, or just a demoed idea. It is only about one minute long.

The last track on the second disc is *Rock The Casbah* Featuring Ranking Roger from The Beat. The backing track with some Clash vocals is used as Ranking Roger toasts over the top, very effective. This has appeared on bootleg compilations and recently was released as a 7" single on Go Feet Records (Red Vinyl) along with a version of *Red Angel Dragnet* again featuring Ranking Roger.

I think safe to say that these various formats cover the bases in terms of the unofficially released works of the band at the time of *Combat Rock* What is very clear is that Glyn Johns work certainly cleaned up, tidied up some perhaps "rough edges", which admittedly have their charm, and place. Whether *Rat Patrol* would have had such a huge commercial success as the Glyn Johns produced *Combat Rock*, is open to debate. I would think not. *Rat Patrol* would have kept Clash fans entertained, I'm not sure happy applies here, but as for winning over new fans and new world territories, I don't think it would.

However, thirty two years or so later on, how might the "Mick Jones mix" be received? Traditionally, song length was restricted by the limitations of the "medium", the technology available at the time. The vinyl 45 for example imposed a maximum playing time, well optimum playing time of about three and a half minutes. Similarly an album playing at 33 ⅓ had a physical limitation of time. At release time, we were still in "the good old days" of vinyl records and analogue cassettes. Was Mick actually "ahead" of the game in some respects? CD was just being introduced in the early 80's, and again there were physical restrictions to how much digital data you could store on a compact disc, but playing time was dramatically increased, physical size of the media decreased. Perhaps Mick was making music for the "next generation of formats". As the 80's developed, if memory serves me well, it became the era of the extended mix, the "dub" mix, the remix of the remix, largely perhaps because there was more room to fill on the new medium, and possibly, because of the initial high price of CD's, somebody actually thinking that CD buyers should get a little extra for their money.

12. POST APOCALYPSE

So what happened after the stormy release date of The *Combat Rock* Album?

At the end of chapter three, we left the band "Topper less", but with Terry Chimes substituting at the very last minute. Gilbert noted that having Terry back on board, did give the band some continuity. The band hit the US for the next leg of their world-wide campaign. Under the banner The *Casbah Club* tour, the US dates kicked off with three nights in New Jersey 29th – 31st May. *Combat Rock* had been released in the US already. The New Jersey shows particularly the first night were seen as a return to form. Despite the absence of Topper, the reviews for the show were highly complementary. In *Melody Maker*, under the *Caught in The Act* live section, David Fricke reviewed the New Jersey Convention Hall show, the second night. Joe opened by commenting about the fog they had imported from London, and how they wanted to show groups like Styx and Foreigner how to "do it". Fricke pointed out that they were in Springsteen's back yard. The warm up song was *Running Scared* by Roy Orbison, and Fricke reported that the band were at their tightest, most aggressive and most committed. Terry Chimes "played the show like he had been rehearsing the set for a year". Joe was singled out for particular praise, and the band played "not just for their reputation, but for their very lives as a rock and roll band"

Joe sported his "Travis Bickle" Mohawk haircut, and wore some of the new range of Clash Clobber. In Kris Needs book, he wrote that "for the *Combat Rock* world, The Clash adopted a stage look, half Vietnam half "Juvie Street Gang". The clothes were militaristic, camouflage, sleeves "torn from jackets" and "shirts at the shoulders". Apparently, just before the New Jersey shows, according to Salewicz, the band were mistaken for British soldiers on their way to the Falklands.

It has been said that the set was "weighted" towards the first album, which Terry was more familiar with. This doesn't seem to ring true if you look at the set lists on the bootleg albums. Sure, we get *Police and Thieves* and *Career Opportunities*, but they also played *Car Jamming*, *Ghetto Defendant*, *Should I Stay or Should I Go* and *Straight To Hell* from the *Combat Rock* album. Roadie "Digby" felt that "they were winging it, seriously winging it without Topper".

You can view some of the Asbury Park performance, which night I am not certain, but a bootleg DVD is available with eight songs, including *Straight To Hell* and *Should I Stay or Should I Go*.

The Asbury Park show also acted as an album launch party, and the record company took over a local fairground for the evening, and guests rode free. There are a number of photographs from the evening doing the rounds, Mick in the bumper cars, Joe and Paul looking cool and casual. What is apparent is the lack of pictures of Terry Chimes at the launch party. Either he wasn't included for promotional purposes, possibly feeling a little out of place, or possibly exhausted after the first night onslaught!

Amongst the audience on the first night was photographer Joe Streno, who has some amazing live shots of the bands performance. www.go2jo.com - absolutely worth a visit.

The first night had gone extremely well, but could have been quite different. During the set fireworks were thrown at the stage. A second one was thrown as the band finished at the end of the first encore, and exploded as it made contact with Joe's knee. The show came to an end, with Joe being taken to hospital and treated for minor burns. Joe later told Dave McCullough in a *Sounds* article that the firework had gone up the trouser leg of the one that keeps time, and showed the writer the scar.

After the show, according to Marcus Gray, Joe had said "I don't think we played a good gig after Topper was fired" but later conceded that maybe there had been one good show… "this one".

In the *Q Classic Clash Special* magazine, Kris Needs noted that by June 1982, the band were out of debt with the record company for the first time. *Rock The Casbah* had scraped the Top 30 and *Combat Rock* had "hit the US Top 10".

In the UK, there was still criticism aimed at the band. In *Melody Maker Backlash* section, Andrew Harris wrote that "It appears that the band that everybody loves to hate now is The Clash". Accused of "going further away from what I liked about them in 1976", by Adrian Borland of the band The Sound. Harris posed the question, did he "expect them to continue making the same music on and on for the rest of their career" He pointed out that a change in direction did not mean to say that it was worse, and that they had to adapt to new musical styles.

As the US tour moved to Atlanta, there was another incident outside the Fox Theatre, where "neo Nazis started a rowdy protest during the show" The local Atlanta media had a field day with this, although The Clash themselves were not involved. Unlikely that this was a Bernie inspired PR stunt!

The support act for some of the dates was The Beat (AKA The English Beat), and this was the start of a lasting relationship, Ranking Roger providing toasting duties on an alternative mix of *Rock The Casbah* mentioned earlier, and Mick assisting with guitar duties of later Beat incarnation General Public.

The Casbah dates rolled on with dates in Texas at two venues. The band filmed the *Rock The Casbah* video discussed earlier in the best next thing to a desert. The tour moved to the West Coast, including five sold out nights at the Hollywood Palladium. Bob Dylan was present for one of the shows. Along with Bob was 12 year old son Jakob, who was "awestruck" by what he witnessed, and was thereafter intent on being in a band. Years later, Jakob would make The Clash connection when Mick Jones collaborated with Jakob and his band The Wallflowers on tracks on their 2012 album *Glad All Over*. Worth tracking down *Reboot The Mission* with Mick sharing vocals, and a Joe Strummer name check.

In *Sounds* dated 17th July 1982 (McCullough, 1982) in a fittingly entitled piece called *Sten Guns in LA*, the writer talked about arriving in the US to cover the tour and dates at The Palladium. He had arrived and "stepped in to 'The ClashMobile'", as he said "alongside a series of young men dressed in combat gear with shorn hair, looking cool sure, but more The Clash of '77 than the fashion idols of '81". He felt that *Combat Rock* had "sharpened them up", and had "made them all of a sudden alive again on record". It was during McCullough's various interviews that Bernie had told him that "I own the group".

Joe and McCullough discussed The "return of Terry Chimes", and what he thought about it Joe was pleased that it was seen in a positive way. "I'm glad about that" said Joe, "it's a hell of a thing, after five years to come in". Joe also emphasized that they had only five days to find a drummer before the US dates commenced. Joe was also asked if Topper would return, to which Joe replied that he didn't really think so, and that he was "getting himself together right now".

While the band were touring, the US label released *Should I Stay or Should I Go* as a single. Towards the end of June, the band hit another territory, this time Canada for three shows in three cities.

In the UK, it was announced that the Falklands War was over, the band returned to the UK, not exactly received as War Heroes, but they had certainly been on an exhausting campaign. *Rock The Casbah* had been released in June. To some, a testing time was ahead. The first UK dates in the UK since the "Sold Out" Lyceum shows of Autumn 1981.

The UK Leg of the *Casbah Club* tour began on 10th July at the Fair Deal in Brixton. Two nights, before taking the *Casbah Club* around the UK until early August. The plan was to "take over" the venues and make it a club night, with the band, entertainers and "public figures" making an appearance. The tour was replacing the earlier *Know Your Rights* Tour which had been abandoned when Joe had disappeared.

On the day of the first Brixton show, a Clash Manifesto was published in the Tour news section of The NME 10th July

"In order to get away from the predictable rock industry formats, The Clash will be presenting the *Casbah Club* in a number of towns across the country on their UK tour" It was to be a celebration of "lowlife and Clash fans" On The Terry Chimes DVD Interview, Terry recalled that the dates "had Keith Allen and Fire Eaters, and even Burundi Drummers at the Brixton show. It was a way to challenge the audience a bit".

The opening night was in front of 4300 people. Kris Needs had reported that it was a "consummate Clash show, with the *Combat Rock* songs starting to sound great". For once, the *NME* seemed to be impressed, remarking that the band had reinvented their roots. The result of the dates was a two record set bootleg *The Clash down at The Casbah Club* (or *The Return of Tory Crimes*). The album sleeve has some interesting takes on the song titles, *Carry on Julie* and *What Have I Done*, but captures *Rock The Casbah*, *Should I Stay or Should I Go* and *Straight To Hell*. It does however list the date of recording as 17th July, when the band were actually playing in Bradford St. Georges Hall that night.

The show was reviewed by Simon Steele in the Music Industry Trade paper *Music Week* 17th July 1982 in the performance page. Starting with the comment "with every year that passes and every album that gets released, The Clash become less profound and less dangerous". He picked out Terry and his "none too sophisticated, violent style" as "perfect for The Clash". He also added that Paul's "sturdy bass lines were becoming more that just the backbone of their live sound, but increasingly the basis of compositions like *Radio Clash*" Mick he reported "tortured his guitar, in a style he had made his own over the last six years". Joe again was singled out for his "wit and hard work" which had made the show such a success. More interestingly, as it turned out, Steele commented that Joe's recent "vacation" showed that he had a deep concern about not becoming a "cog in the Music Business machine".

In an *NME* Review of the Fair Deal show dated 17th July, the writer contrasted their career point with the Rolling Stones, commenting that the Stones had "floundered their way through their "Satanic majesties", and were mired in indecision". The Clash they said, had already recorded their *Exile on Main Street* (Sandinista). The review also said that they had learned to "channel their sound like never before" and that "one of the years greatest songs is central to this". The song was *Know Your Rights*.

In true to form generosity, the band played a "charity show" at the Stoke Mandeville Hospital sports stadium in their old stomping ground of Aylesbury. Kris Needs attended, but found the dressing room backstage atmosphere a little different than previously. The sound had not been good and the ritual of "gobbing" had returned. Needs noticed that the band seemed to "gravitate away from each other".

As the tour proceeded, weaving their way north and south of the country, the band bashed away, returning again to the Brixton Fair Deal on 30th July. Another bootleg resulted from this show *A Fair Deal in Brixton*, single album edited set, with only *Know Your Rights* from *Combat Rock* making the final vinyl album.

At the Brighton Centre show, according to Salewicz, two models, Daisy and Tricia attended the gig and made their way backstage. Daisy was apparently on a mission to "snag" Joe, but ended up leaving with Mick, staying together for eight years. Paul met Trica, but it was five years later that they would start a relationship and eventually marry.

The last two dates of the *Casbah Club* tour were at the Bristol Locarno on 2nd and 3rd August. They turned out to be the last UK dates that Mick played with The Clash, and by fate and circumstance I was present at both. I can't say I remember too much, the shows were absolutely packed, but I remember walking away with my "Join Pimps, Punks and Good Time Girls Down at The Casbah Club" sleeveless T Shirt, which I wore with pride and a cut off sleeve army shirt. COMBAT READY...

Six days after the last *Casbah Club* shows in the UK. It was back to the US for the *Combat Rock* US Tour. This would run pretty continuously from August until late October. The band had been touring since the end of January '82 (In Japan), March and April was free of touring, but still an album to mix, and touring picking up again in May, through to October '82. This stage of the promotional tour took in more of the East Coast venues that were not covered on the *Casbah Club* dates. They kicked off at the Red Rock Amphitheater in Colorado on August 9th, covering Chicago, Detroit, Akron and Pittsburgh. They played three nights at Hyannis on Cape Cod (Great town, worth a visit, I hope that record store is still there, that's where I picked up my first *Combat Rock Bootleg*).

Then, on to Philadelphia and three rainy nights at Pier 84 in New York, and according to Needs, Alan Ginsberg made an appearance on the second night and recited his piece in *Ghetto Defendant*. Into September, they hit Boston with the Beat as support. Another nice bootleg was the result of the two shows, *The Boston Tapes* with selected track from both nights. This is a single album of mainly old material, with *Straight To Hell* being the only *Combat Rock* track.

The collectorsmusicreviews website www.collectorsmusicreviews.com/the-clash/the-clash-the-boston-tapes-viva-zapata-vz006/ felt that some of the show was a little uninspired, possibly down to the "tensions" between the band, or general fatigue! Terry Chimes definitely remembered "terrible tensions" between the band members, not about politics when he was in the band first time round. There was he felt a Mick vs. Joe and Paul battle, with Kosmo siding with Paul and Joe. On one memorable occasion for Terry, Joe actually went and deadened Mick's guitar while he was off on an effects driven wig out on stage. It was an uncomfortable moment, and Mick was most unhappy after the show. Mick had often used the live situation to experiment a little, certainly on the Bonds residency; you can hear more effects being used on the guitar. A CBS executive from the UK, Kit Butler, attended at least one of the Shea shows, and in *Last Gang In Town*, had described the atmosphere within the band as "open warfare". He also noted that the band did not speak to each other, but he could have put this down to nerves.

The original plan was for the tour to end in Boston, but along came another surprise. The Who were on a round of "farewells" in the US, and Pete Townsend offered The Clash the chance to open up for them on their stadium tour of the US. Much has been said about this gesture; although I'm sure it was a business decision as much as anything else.

Some saw the support slots as the "passing of the mantle" from an "old school UK rock band" to the "new school UK rock band". The Who, retiring and handing over their crown. In *Last Gang In Town*, Gray wrote that there had been a proposal that the Rolling Stones go out together with The Clash, in a similar "contest" of "upstarts vs. established rockers".

The Clash were "hot" at this time, and had pulled in thousands of punters each night on their US tour. The Who didn't need the numbers, and from what I can gather, the support slot was announced after most of The Who shows had sold out. Ironic really that The Who are back out of retirement (not for the first time) and still tour and perform (be it without Keith Moon and John

Entwistle). There was a rumour circulating at the time (according to Gray) that Topper might step up to the drum stool instead of the ex-Faces drummer Kenny Jones. That would certainly have been ironic if it had materialized.

At this point, some critics of the band, be they journalists, or cynical fans interpreted the decision as a "back down" from one of The Clash policies of not supporting any other band, apart from at a charity event or festival show. This had dated back to 1976 according to Kris Needs. The size of venue was an issue, but it would allow the band to reach a bigger and wider audience.

In *The Clash – The Only Band That Mattered*, Egan felt that the band's integrity had been dealt a hefty blow. By agreeing to support The Who, that had gone against their policy. I can see this absolutely, but they were a handful of dates, and the band were still headlining major shows in the US in between The Who dates. Egan was right to point out that none of the dates with The Who were in the UK, where he felt that they would have been "ridiculed" by the UK fans, and that that move might have been commercially "counter productive".

So, from 8,000 people a night to 80,000. That was quite a change for The Clash. The Who tour began on 25th September at the JFK Stadium in Philadelphia, The Clash followed David Johansen, formally of the New York Dolls. Mick admitted to Kris Needs that he wasn't really "into the big ones", but that it was good for them to play with The Who, and that they had sold loads of records and picked up new fans. It was also a chance for the band to fight the "anti AOR battle". The decision to play stadiums must have caused some trepidation amongst the band. It was not the kind of environment they flourished in. Communication is what they thrived on, they were well aware of terrible views for the crowds, bad sound and "cynical business approach".

The set was limited to 45 minutes. Get on, do the "hits" and off again. So in terms of promoting *Combat Rock*, the band were limited by time and familiarity. The "hits" included past triumphs, and some of the *Combat Rock* material, it was pretty much down to *Should I Stay or Should I Go* and *Rock The Casbah*.

At one of the Canadian shows, Joe and Mick were interviewed for TV. Mick had said that they were looking forward to The Who shows. Joe was obviously in a very bad mood, and gruffly answered a question after a second time of asking. Mick was asked about the record label business, to which he replied that "it's no worse than any other prostitution business" and that they felt that they "still had some dignity".

In the *Mojo* article *Who Killed The Clash* (Snow, 2008) Pete Townsend commented that the support slot was "like a ceremonial handover from the old bosses of thinking rebels Britrock to the new". Having joined them onstage back in 1980, he had believed that "this quartet of fellow West Londoners were The Who's rightful heirs" He was also quick to point out that it wasn't that easy for them, and that Who fans "pelted them with apples and bottles" at a show in Philadelphia. During the September dates, the UK Record label released *Should I Stay or Should I Go* as a double A side single with *Straight To Hell*.

Among the audiences at these shows was Mick Jagger and Clash fanatic daughter Jade. Were The Clash moving in the circles of the "old rock aristocracy"? Jagger apparently gave the band his advice about playing to such large crowds, and that after one or two shows, it became just like any other. Paul felt that it was a little like miming, as they were so far from the crowd, and there was no real interaction with the audiences. To keep the train rolling, in between The Who dates, the band booked a few shows of their own in New York State, Vermont and Massachusetts. These were Clash shows, and gave them more opportunity to push some of the *Combat Rock* tracks, like *Car Jamming* and *Straight To Hell*.

As the two Shea Stadium shows loomed with The Who, the band appeared on *Saturday Night Live* as discussed earlier, which gave them another piece of great exposure, broadcast the night before the first Shea experience.

Don Letts was in town to film more material, and shoot live video from the shows. In *The Last Gang in Town*, Gray wrote that it was "Business as usual for The Clash". Kosmo Vinyl, "managing to get hundreds of kids into a private enclosure". Kris Needs wrote that Joe was "still getting fans in the backdoor", and recounted the story of Joe missing the band bus from the hotel, and having to go on the subway. By the time he had got there he had 360 people tagging along with him who he had invited. Using the "if they can't come in, the band won't play" approach, they all got in to see the show.

Don Letts filmed the band travelling to the Shea show in the open topped Cadillac and filmed the live performance of *Should I Stay or Should I Go*. As much as anything, this was seen as something of a statement against the behavior of The Who. They would arrive at their shows each in a separate limo, never together. The Clash wanted to be seen as a unit. In the *Who Killed The Clash* article (Snow, 2008) Bernie commented on this, "…never be like that group. They might be successful, but they hate each other. Never be like those people… you are different". In the Snow article, Kosmo added that in The Who "they saw what they didn't want to be, The Clash were a team, which was why they arrived in the one car". Don Letts remembered in *Passion is a Fashion* that they had to keep back within 30 feet from the members of The Who.

The drive and film shoot were no picnic either; it was mid-October in New York, and pretty cold, not a drive through downtown Miami for sure. The original idea had been to arrive in a NY yellow checker cab; it might have been more comfortable!

In an *NME* review 23rd October of the Shea show, there was criticism that the band should have taken the opportunity "to subvert the whole process", rather than "play it safe by playing a predictable shopping list of hits". The *NME* named the show "the Battle of My Generation" and that the "punks meet the godfathers to see who is the angriest, most sincere and relevant of them all". I take their point, the band could have gone on stage and played a set of dub tracks, but it would have been an opportunity wasted. At no point I think did they veer away from the desire to be heard, and heard by more people. You have to hook people in, people get interested in the music, they find out more, they dip into your back catalogue and find the message.

On one of the Shea nights, there was an after show party which saw Andy Warhol in attendance. You can see the evidence in the booklet of the *Live At Shea Stadium* release.

In his book *Sound Man*, Glyn Johns recalled that it was at the Shea Stadium shows that he came in contact with The Clash again. He recalled that Mick seemed to have got over the earlier hurt over the album mixing, and it was "pleasant" all round. He was even asked to record The Clash sets at Shea and The Colosseum in LA, where he was also recording The Who. He understood this was for a possible Live Album for release at some point. He did not seem to be impressed. He recalled "a lot of manic energy, not a good sound, and a bass player that seemed to be on some other non musical planet".

In a second *NME* Review of the Shea shows 6/11/1982. It was reported that as I mentioned, tickets went on sale before the announcement that The Clash would play. The reviewer felt that despite their "flash infatuations with classic American imagery", running through their repertoire "reveals them every bit as English deep down as The Jam". The writer dismissed the idea that it was Pete Townsend's "idea" to get them on board, although talked about "a judicious piece of matchmaking" and "offering an approved substitute, and passing The Clash their inheritance… the mass American market"

In a *Mojo* Article by Charles Shaar Murray (Shaar-Murray, 2003) entitled *Comrade Goodbye*, Joe was quoted about the experience with The Who. "It was like seeing us in 20 years time. I don't want to be the new boss same as the old boss". He felt that no matter what, you were on a huge circuit, "do this phone interview, do a video on top of a building". It was a case of "not living a life that can relate to anyone else's". He also made reference to U2, and thanked God that The Clash didn't do that, because he wanted to "be a person".

In the *NME* review, Pete Townsend had expressed his reservations about whether Shea Stadium and the like were the right kind of environment for a band like The Clash to get their message across. Paul noted that the crowd looked like Dolly Mixtures which I thought was amusing!

In *Relix Magazine* (Orshoski, 2008), Mick was philosophical about the Shea shows, and said "it shows you come from nothing to something, and that's inspiring". In the same article, Tom Morello from RATM recalled that it was a "life changing show", but he didn't remember it being a great show. He had detected tension on stage, and the chemistry he felt was wrong.

Another audience member (Who fan Jim Merlis) saw them differently, as having real swagger and stage presence, "like nothing I had seen before", and "that they looked like a gang on stage who he knew were gonna' kick your ass!!"

The *Should I Stay/Straight To Hell* single was released in the UK, while in the USA *Rock The Casbah* was released, and with MTV playing the video, The Who support shows all boosted the chart position to Number 8. The irony as Joe noted, was that their biggest US Hit single was written by their sacked drummer.

After the Shea appearances, The Clash again filled in some down time with more of their own shows before completing The Who dates with two nights at the Coliseum in Oakland, and the last night at the Los Angeles Coliseum, where Jakob Dylan again attended and met with Joe backstage.

In October 1982, all the hard work, tears and tantrums could be said to have been rewarded, as sales of *Combat Rock* in the US hit half a million, and went "gold". By November, the *Combat Rock* album peaked in the US Album charts at number 7. Depending on your stance, this was either an amazing achievement in the bands career, or a BIG sellout.

As a parting shot to 1982, The Clash flew to Jamaica to play at the Jamaica World Music festival at Montego Bay. Held in the Bob Marley Centre, it was a gala affair with a mixed bag of artists like Rick James, Jimmy Buffet, Yellowman, Black Uhuru, Peter Tosh, Rita Marley and old compadres The Beat. Aretha Franklyn, The Beach Boys and The Grateful Dead also made appearances. Joe made a comment about bringing "The Dead" on if the crowd didn't liven up a bit. The whole event had over run and they hit the stage at either 3am or 4am, I found conflicting information about this. The set leaned more towards the reggae side of the material, *Guns of Brixton*, *Junco Partner*, *One More Time* and *Bank Robber*. But also they got to air *Should I Stay or Should I Go*, *Rock The Casbah* and *Straight To Hell* from *Combat Rock*. There are at least two bootlegs of the show, three vinyl versions and two CD, good quality and again worth a listen. There are some short live clips on YouTube, but sadly the band refused to have the full set filmed by the crew that were there to cover the festival. Terry Chimes felt that it seemed like a bit of a holiday for all the hard work they had put in over the previous months. The band even took their girlfriends along. On the live bootleg album, Joe seems to back this up, mentioning that it had been a very nice holiday there. The festival was the last Clash show that Terry Chimes played; he was quick to make the point that this was his decision.

December saw no live dates or releases by the band, who at this stage must have been pretty exhausted, physically and mentally. There had been tensions throughout the year between Bernie and the band, Mick and Joe, Mick and Paul, and they had lost the "engine room" Topper to heroin addiction, again with tensions and frustrations and regret. Had it all been worth a gold disc? Certainly the band had a much higher profile especially in the US, and could still make their mark politically and tactically. In a year that had seen them play a small town hall in the South Island of New Zealand through to the prestigious Shea Stadium in the US, the band had taken everything on that was thrown at them. At all times, trying to keep their artistic, political and moral integrity, in a rollercoaster of a year.

At some point in December 1982, the band minus Topper or Terry went in to Wessex Studios with some of the Blockheads and Janie Jones to record the Joe written *House of The Ju Ju Queen* single, and a B-side version of *Sex Machine*. It is not clear what the official release date was, but the Discogs website lists as "1983". It appeared on the independent label Big Beat, in another side project for the band. The single does seem miles away from the *Combat Rock* material and sound, more like a *London Calling* era piece, and played with the Blockheads who were so intertwined with band at that time. According to Chris Salewicz, the whole project was paid for by Joe.

In December, Kris Needs interviewed Mick, and recounted that Mick seemed "buoyant" about The Clash, and that they all still believed in what they were doing. Then a disturbing incident took place in front of his eyes. Sitting in a café, Paul and his Dad walked past and looked through the window. Mick waved, but Paul "didn't see him". Mick commented that he saw him but he ran away. Significantly, Kris Needs received a "mix tape" from Mick for Christmas. As Needs said, "Mick was besotted with the sonic revolution, audacious master mixes, and editing and extending tracks into startling mutants". Mick's chosen tracks displayed just how far away from "rock and roll" he was drifting in to, with artists like Vanity 6, The Peach Boys, Sekou Bunch, Indeep's *Last Night a DJ Saved My Life* and Marvin Gaye's *Sexual Healing*. The second side of the tape included Diana Ross's *Muscles* Arthur Baker mixes and ended with Madonna *Everybody*.

As the band entered 1983, the *Combat Rock* fallout was not over. Despite having been reviewed by US magazine *Creem* as a "relative piece of shit", the album was voted 3rd Best in their annual poll for 1982. Despite the criticism, humiliation and aggression in the UK, the *NME* Critics annual poll saw *Combat Rock* at number 4 in best albums of the year.

In the end of year reviews which ran in the UK and US Press, the band were placed in high positions, behind the likes of The Jam in the UK, who seemed to have picked up the "press darlings" mantle and in the US, The Clash featured behind The Who and Van Halen. In The *NME*, they were voted third best band, second best album, third best song writers and third best live act.

It seemed to have been decided that the band would take a few months off to regroup. Terry had felt that internal tensions were a hindrance to the creative process, and the Mick situation was a big issue for the future of the band. Terry did more work with Billy Idol and Hanoi Rocks. Then studied medicine, and went on to become a chiropractor.

The three months were the bands first real break since they had started in 1976. According to Kris Needs, Joe got his first mortgage, and moved in with long time partner Gaby. Paul spent time with his recently bereaved father. Joe also went on the run again, this time officially, being sponsored by The Sun newspaper in the London Marathon in aid of leukemia research.

This was also seen as something of a controversy, as The Sun had a certain reputation especially their readership and content. In *Redemption Song*, Salewicz revealed that Joe had been prepared to be interviewed by The Sun to promote the *Combat Rock* album, much to the disapproval of Mick.

Joe was offered an acting role in a film called "*The Hit*" which he turned down. Instead, he started writing and directing his own film "*Hell W10*" The tapes of this, according to Needs were rescued from a car boot sale by a couple of fans. The movie was shot in black and white, and is perhaps significant on a number of levels. In the plot, Mick is portrayed as the "Bad Guy" a "Mr. Socrates".

Barry Auguste aka Drum Roadie/ Tech "The Baker", wrote an interesting article about the film in 2013

www.thedailyswarm.com/swarm/joe-strummer-film-director-making-and-meaning-hell-w10/

The whole film was directed and conceived and paid for by Joe. At first it appears as a "simple, unpretentious home movie", but as Auguste said "hidden beneath its cops-and-robbers plotline, Joe was cleverly caricaturing the true life roles of everyone in the band". "Art imitating life". Auguste believed that *"Hell W10"* gave us "a premonition of the events to come" and pointed out that Kosmo was cast as "Socrate's double crossing consigliore". Kosmo had always been seen as "Mick's man", but later "covertly switched sides", and "becoming Joe's right hand man". Joe it appears in character was "eager to collaborate with the bad guy", but "willing to turn him in at a moment's notice". Mick portrayed as the "bad guy" and Paul as the "hero", which again is how many saw the situation within the band.

In the *Sounds* article (McCullough, 1982) *Sten Guns in LA*, the writer had asked Joe if he felt like he should be "creative in a different area". Joe had replied, "more and more, half of me wants to cut out and write a book or do a film…I'm very into films now".

Mick was also originally writing music for the soundtrack, believed to be more "hip hop" in nature. The music was rejected by Joe and in the end, what appears on the version included on *The Essential Clash* DVD release, is late Clash instrumentals including *Rat Patrol* tracks *Beautiful People are Ugly* and *Cool Confusion*.

This appeared to be another falling out with Mick, who remarked later, "Maybe it was a bit hip".

By February 1983, in the US, *Combat Rock* hit platinum sales of one million. More proof that their incredible work ethic had paid some dividends. The Clash went in to rehearsals again, perhaps wondering how they could top this, and what direction they could take the music, and who they could get as a permanent replacement for Topper.

During this time, Johnny Green, former Clash road manager, had been going through his own heroin hell, after losing his wife and first child through meningitis. Robin Banks was on hand, but asked Joe for some financial help with funeral costs and to take Johnny to Greece to get away. Joe offered money for both the funeral expenses and air tickets.

For Mick, there was an inevitable split with Ellen Foley. The relative inactivity was blamed by Bernie on Mick's unwillingness to tour, an allegation which Mick denied, saying that he wanted to tour in places they had not been to before, like South America. It was reported that they had previously been offered a show (or two) in Cuba, but Mick had declined "as a requirement was they would work one day in the fields". So it was down to the Manic Street Preachers in 2001 to "make history" and become the first western "rock" band to play there. In fairness, couldn't have happened to a nicer bunch of blokes!

In March, the band were approached to play at the huge "US" festival in the USA. The offer came from the then Apple tycoon Steve Wozniak. In the same month according to Kris Needs, the band moved back to the Rehearsals Rehearsals building which had been refurbished and contained a rehearsal studio and 16 track recording facilities called LUCKY 8.

In April, adverts appeared for the empty drum stool, (23rd April 1983) and after a huge number of auditions, (over 300 according to Kris Needs), Pete Howard was appointed.

The US Festival Tour ran from 18th May until 28th May, with Pete Howard on drums. The four dates prior to the US Festival were "warm ups" for the main event, allowing Pete Howard to "bed in". Three of the dates were in Texas, and one in Tucson Arizona.

The Unite US in Song festival was a huge affair, The Clash being asked to headline on the New Music Day of the event which was of Woodstock proportions, again testing both band and fans in terms of what the band stood for. Especially as they were offered $500,000 to appear.

The US Festival on 28th May at San Bernandino, was also significantly the last show that Mick played with The Clash. There are of course video and bootleg albums in circulation for this show. The DVD is good quality, the show itself is a little fraught with tensions up to the max. The set is varied and career spanning, with *Rock The Casbah*, *Know Your Rights*, *Straight To Hell* and *Should I Stay or Should I Go* all getting a good thumping. The vinyl album mixes the running order and gave us 12 tracks, only *Know Your Rights* from *Combat Rock* is on display. What you don't see, apart from one or two comments made by a highly agitated Joe Strummer, was what had occurred before, during and after the performance. There had been disagreement over the ticket prices, the initial $17 had become $25 with a parking charge included. A press conference was called with mainly Bernie and Kosmo shouting the odds. The Clash would not play unless a donation of $32,000 was made to a local charity summer camp. (Originally they had asked for $100,000) according to *Redemption Song*. There was a two hour delay before the band took to the stage under the banner "Clash Not For Sale", and in front of 140,000 people, the biggest audience they had ever been in front of. They played for 80 minutes.

The drama was not over though, just prior to the start of their set, according to Salewicz, Bernie had called another press conference on the side of the stage, demanding that other acts donate some of their fee to charities. At the end of the show after the third encore, some fisticuffs broke out between Kosmo and a DJ, who had started talking to the crowd, preventing another encore from the band. Mick had got involved and Paul moved in to help him out.

Joe later told US *Creem* magazine that "I'm not going to have some millionaire restoring Woodstock for his own gratification and tax loss in his back yard". He explained his aggression by saying that "there was too much self gratification in the air" and that he was trying to provoke a reaction. The high appearance fee was justified by Joe as they needed the money to set up a club they had promised to start called Lucky 7, and added that if Wozniak was prepared to pay them that kind of money, he was a sucker!! On their return to the UK, there were inevitable disagreements about how the money should be spent.

There was a dichotomy for the band and perhaps for Joe in particular.

After the US dates, there is a real lull in activity and little going on in The Clash world until a Clash Communiqué was issued in September, announcing that Mick Jones had been sacked from the band. Mick issued a counter claim via the CBS Press Office.

In the *Mojo* Article *Who killed The Clash*, Mick remembered turning up for the rehearsals, which were for the next album. Mick had felt under pressure, both creatively and business wise, as there were "contracts" that he would not sign. Mick felt that Bernie was sacking everybody, and he was the only one trying to stop him. Bernie was also suggesting that they made a "New Orleans" album next. When asked what sort of album the next would be by Bernie, Mick had according to Salewicz, replied "rock and roll". The song writing had become posting tapes through each other's doors, although Mick denied this, adding that he would take over the tapes to Joe once he had worked on them.

There was a rumour that the Band were to play at The Notting Hill Carnival in 1983, but that the idea was shelved because Mick wasn't talking to the rest of the band at the time. That would have been a hell of a show, and in many ways would almost complete the circle for the "band from the Westway". A much more dignified exit for Mick if that had been his last show rather than a huge festival in the US.

The story continued, and is amply covered by other Clash Works (*Redemption Song* in particular), and much better than I could cover.

So, as Mick walked away with his cheque and a whole new guitar case of ideas I feel that the 80's *Combat Rock* story is over.

However, the album and hit singles kept rolling, so in the unreleased words of Mick "it ain't over". I want to look at the lasting effects and influence the album has had, and the legacy it left behind.

13. ALL THE POWER IN THE HANDS

Although *Combat Rock* and its "hit singles" are a sensitive issue for some Clash fans, the lasting "power" of the material still resonates today. Still inspiring, still challenging people's attitudes and approaches to making music. In many ways, what The Clash were trying to do, "distilling their music" has been made even more accepted today. Back in 1982, listening to or getting hold of any music involved a whole process of reading about, talking about and actually getting out of your seat to buy a physical chunk of music. Today, everything is available at the click of a button. You can tweet your friends… or even acquaintances, find Facebook contacts, chat or text, get the gossip, see reviews, hear samples, watch videos and download music free or paid for. For a new generation, you can add anything you want in to the mix. You want tribal chanting, or maybe Joe's favorite Cumbian track, just get online. The early 1980's were a major turning point for The Clash, as they were for the way music was served up. The Cassette Walkman had in many ways changed how people listened to their music. Initially introduced in 1980, music became portable, as it had been with transistor radios, but it was also a bit more "private" with full stereo headphones and your own playlist. No longer reliant on the output from radio stations, you could buy pre-recorded cassettes, or make you own compilations. Another example of the music hardware industry introducing a great new gadget, which then the music "software" companies (record labels) realise will mean they will potentially lose money from "home taping" and "piracy". The music companies then proceed to blame the general public for taking liberties, when the hardware companies have presented them with the tools for the job. On top of that, the hardware companies are sometimes owners or strongly connected to the record labels themselves, Sony and Phillips being prime examples. So where does the "blame" lie?

The introduction of the Sony Walkman I would say really kick started the whole "gadget industry". The gadgets become the object of desire and perhaps sometimes not for the right reasons (music playback?), but fashion items, with constant updates and upgrades. In *The People's Songs* (Maconie, 2013), the author seemed to agree, and talked about the iPod, and how it could store thousands of songs on a portable hard drive. The design was "striking and ergonomically brilliant" (I think referring to the original "wheel" version) and that this "ensured the iPod became the most desirable artifact of its time". Maconie also felt that "For maybe the first time, with the possible exception of the Sony Walkman, it was the hardware not the songs that the listener lusted after".

The Sony Walkman of course had to fight off The Clash approved Ghetto Blaster first, which had been around since the mid 70's. David Byrne talked about the "Power of the Boom Box Ghetto Blaster", and the technology that went in to these, which allowed the listener to hear music much LOUDER, and with compressors and circuitry, it allowed some of the quieter sounds to be pushed to the fore.

During my interview with Pete Winkelman, he talked about his thoughts about the record business, especially in today's digital age. He remembered well the Sony Walkman cassette player, and was completely bemused by what had happened to the music industry. How the huge conglomerate companies like Sony could let a non-music company like Apple control the main music distribution platform?

Sony had "software", music and video with the then owned Columbia Pictures, it had a hardware company within Sony which had innovated with the Sony Walkman and assisted with the development of the CD hardware. He felt that instead of spending time and money fighting against Napster, the music business should have embraced the new technology and developed their own hardware and distribution system much earlier, before Apple were able to steam in and dominate the market.

As Maconie pointed out in *The People's Songs*, file sharing developed by Steve Fanning and Napster was a "Pandoras Box" which turned the "whole music business on its head", and that "a generation would grow up thinking that music should be free as air". He also agreed with Pete Winkelman, that by concentrating on criminalising and threatening the audience as they had with the "home taping is killing music" offensive, the "bizz" had missed an opportunity to develop a "workable, paid for download system".

In the online interview with Bill Flanagan (*Talks At Google - Glyn Johns in Conversation*, 2014) Glyn Johns was asked to talk about technology, and how he had probably been through "six revolutions" of technology. Johns was pretty adamant that a lot of technology has actually ruined popular music for him. People playing together always worked better for him, and he also felt that technology had affected the way that people wrote songs today. He admitted that he was a "boring old fart", but recording was originally designed to capture what was going on, he had never been one for recording people individually. Overdubbing was though "forgivable", but often the overdubbed instrument was not "emotionally involved", as the main music track would have already been recorded. He was very insistent that a band or musicians playing together meant that they could influence each other, and it was that interaction was what was important. He felt that "contemporary recording" would not happen anymore. Johns was questioned about the fact that anyone with enough money could buy equipment and software to allow them to record and produce in their bedroom, and whether he felt that it was a "Good Thing". Johns was pretty frank in his reply, it was good that people could afford that type of technology, but he personally wasn't into it. I have to agree, having the equipment, or the money for the equipment does not make you a great "producer", doesn't guarantee that the user is, or will become a great songwriter or musician. Tools for the trade possibly, but you need to have the talents and skills there in the first place.

14. COVERS AND CONTROVERSY

Since the release of *Combat Rock*, there have been a number of covers, tributes and "liftings" of the tracks. Predominantly as you might expect, the singles, particularly *Should I Stay or Should I Go*.

Hunting through my own collection, and online I constructed a list, which will not be definitive, but gives an idea of the time span, and illustrating my point about still being an influence on music today.

MORE INFO

www.secondhandsongs.com

Artist	Song	Format	Label	Year
Long Tall Texans	Should I Stay Or Should I Go	7" Single	Razor	1988
Pato Banton/ Ranking Roger	Rock The Casbah	Burning London - Clash Tribute	Epic Records	1989
Ice Cube /Mackio	Should I Stay Or Should I Go	The Clash Tribute - Burning London	Epic Records	1989
Moby feat Heather Nova	Straight To Hell	The Clash Tribute - Burning London	Epic Records	1989
NC Thirteen	Rock The Casbah	Backlash - The Clash Tribute	Dwell	1990
Super Green	Should I Stay Or Should I Go	Backlash - The Clash Tribute	Dwell	1990
Living Colour	Should I Stay Or Should I Go	B Side To "Type"	Epic	1990
Thee Stash	Should I Stay Or Should I Go	7" Single	Yeah Hupp	1991
Red Letter Day	Straight To Hell	The Clash Tribute - Never Ending Story Part 1	Released Emotions	1991
One Bad Pig	Rock The Casbah	Blow The House Down	Myrrh	1992
Skin	Should I Stay Or Should I Go	Look But Don't Touch EP	Parlophone	1994
The Picketts	Should I Stay Or Should I Go	Euphonium	Rounder	1996
Primal Scream	Know Your Rights	Kowalski EP	Creation	1997
The SKAndalous Allstars	Rock The Casbah	Punk Steady	Shanachie	1998
Kylie Minogue	Should I Stay Or Should I Go	Intimate and Live	Mushroom	1998

Artist	Song	Format	Label	Year
Bloco Vomit	Should I Stay Or Should I Go	Never Mind The Bossa Nova	Trama	1998
Salinas	Should I Stay Or Should I Go	12" Single	Control	1998
Kristian De Beauvoir	Rock The Casbah	Police State - A Tribute To The Clash	Dressed To Kill	1999
Lareplik	Rock The Casbah	The Clash On Parade Volume 2 - A Tribute To The Clash	Stay Free Records	1999
The Solar Twins	Rock The Casbah	Solar Twins/ Brokedown Palace Soundtrack	Maverick	1999
The NC Thirteens	Rock The Casbah	Backlash - Tribute To The Clash	Dwell	1999
Demonspeed	Rock The Casbah	City Rockers - A Clash Tribute	Chord	1999
Demon Speed	Should I Stay Or Should I Go	City Rockers - A Clash Tribute	Chord	1999
Parker	Should I Stay Or Should I Go	Police State - A Tribute To The Clash	Dressed To Kill	1999
Error Type 11	Should I Stay Or Should I Go	City Rockers - A Clash Tribute	Chord	1999
Skinnerbox	Straight To Hell	City Rockers - A Clash Tribute	Chord	1999
Will Smith	Will 2K (Rock The Casbah Sample)	Willenium Album	Sony	1999
Tinnitus	Should I Stay Or Should I Go	Auf Dem Weg	Wolverine	2000
Pussy 2000	It's gonna Be Alright (Rock The Casbah Sample)	Maxi Single	V2	2001
Tica	Rock The Casbah	Unknown	Unknown	2001
386 DX	Should I Stay Or Should I Go	The Best of 386 DX	Staalplaat	2001
The Caravans	Know Your Rights	This Is Rockabilly Clash	Raucous Records	2002
Peter B	Rock The Casbah	A Punk Tribute To The Clash	Cleopatra	2002
Long Tall Texans	Should I Stay Or Should I Go	This Is Rockabilly Clash	Raucous Records	2002
Knox	Should I Stay Or Should I Go	A Punk Tribute To The Clash	Cleopatra	2002
New Rote' Ka	Death Is A Star	The Clash Tribute	Omnibus Japan	2003

Artist	Song	Format	Label	Year
The Caravans	Know Your Rights	White Riot Volume 1 - A Tribute To The Clash	Uncut	2003
Mr David Viner	Should I Stay Or Should I Go	White Riot Volume 1 - A Tribute To The Clash	Uncut	2003
Guitar Wolf	Should I Stay Or Should I Go	The Clash Tribute	Omnibus Japan	2003
Forever Young	Should I Stay Or Should I Go	Water Boys	Unknown	2003
Josh Reuse	Straight To Hell	White Riot Volume 1 - A Tribute to the Clash	Uncut	2003
The Silver Hawks	Atom Tan	Charlie Does Surf	Rickshaw Records	2004
Richard Cheese	Rock The Casbah	I'd Like a Virgin	IdeaTown	2004
Chum	Straight To Hell	Charlie Does Surf	Rickshaw Records	2004
Howlin Pelle & Randy	Rock The Casbah	Joe Strummer Tribute	Unknown	2005
Joe Dolan	Should I Stay Or Should I Go	21st Century Joe	EMI Ireland	2005
The Ukulele Orchestra of Great Britain	Should I Stay Or Should I Go	Anarchy In The Ukulele	Own Label	2005
Steve Ketchen & The Kensington Hillbillies	Straight To Hell	Start Your Own Country (Various Artists)	Loose Recordings	2005
The Tailgators	Should I Stay Or Should I Go	Tailgators	Cherry Red	2006
Makrosoft	Should I Stay Or Should I Go	The First Makrosoft Adventure Stereo Also Playable Mono	Handle With Care	2006
Roman Pushkin (Mixer)	Should I Stay Or Should I Go (Main Mix) (Dub Mix)	Rare UK Mixes	Spirit Records	2006
The Bots	Straight To Hell	Rockers Galore	Time Bomb	2006
MIA	Paper Planes (Straight To Hell sampled)		XL Interscope	2007
Something For kate	Rock The Casbah	Like a Version/The Murmur Years	Murmur	2007
Soncai System	Rock The Casbah	Clashturies	Discos L'Aguañaz	2007
Nouvelle Star	Should I Stay Or Should I Go	B Side to 3esexe	Sony	2007
Die Toten Hosen	Should I Stay Or Should I Go	Learning English - Lesson One	JKP/WM	2007

Artist	Song	Format	Label	Year
The Coltrane Quartet	Should I Stay Or Should I Go	Vintage Café: Lounge & Jazz Blends	Music Brokers	2007
Rachid Taha	Rock El Casbah	Rebel Music - Songs Of Protest and Inserrection	Mojo	2008
The Trust Company	Rock The Casbah	Unreleased Rarities	Released Via MySpace	2008
The Go Getters	Should I Stay Or Should I Go	Hot Rod Roadeo	Goffin/Goofin	2008
Chomsky All Stars	Know Your Rights	Shatter The Hotel - A Dub Inspired Tribute To Joe Strummer	Mojo Brand Music	2009
Dub Spencer & Trance Hill	Rock The Casbah	The Clashification Of Dub	Echo Beach	2009
Nate Wize Feat Ammoye	Rock The Casbah	Shatter The Hotel - A Dub Inspired Tribute To Joe Strummer	Mojo Brand Music	2009
The Bogarts Acoustic Trio	Rock The Casbah	Play It Again	Drycastle	2009
Dub Spencer & Trance Hill	Should I Stay Or Should I Go	The Clashification Of Dub	Echo Beach	2009
The Krewmen	Should I Stay Or Should I Go	Into The Tomb	Rockin Rollin	2009
MxPx	Should I Stay Or Should I Go	On The Cover II	Tooth And Nail	2009
Danny Michael	Straight To Hell	Shatter The Hotel - A Dub Inspired Tribute To Joe Strummer	Mojo Brand Music	2009
Lilly Allen (With Mick Jones)	Straight To Hell	Warchild Heroes	Parlophone	2009
Plays The Clash	Inoculated City	Plays The Clash	Smoove	2010
Plays The Clash	Rock The Casbar (Acoustic Cover)	Plays The Clash	Smoove	2010
Sunshiners	Should I Stay Or Should I Go	Cool Tributes: The 80's Session	Wagram	2010
Plays the Clash	Should I Stay Or Should I Go	Plays The Clash	Smoove	2010
Plays The Clash	Straight To Hell	Plays The Clash	Smoove	2010
The Swing Easy Orchestra	Rock The Casbah	In The Mood For Ska	Swing Easy	2011
Powerman 5000	Should I Stay Or Should I Go	Copies Clones & Replicants	Cleopatra	2011
Anti Flag	Should I Stay Or Should I Go	Complete Control Session	SideOneDummy	2011

Artist	Song	Format	Label	Year
Taryn Szpillman	Rock The Casbah	Rock Bossa	Bossa58	2013
Rob Tex	Rock The Kasbah		EDR	2013
Rockabye Baby Lullabies	Rock The Casbah	Andrew Bissell/ Rockabye Baby	Rockabye Baby	2014
We Are Standard	Rock The Casbah	We Are Standard Plays The Clash	Mushroom Pillow	2014
Rockabye Baby Lullabies	Should I Stay Or Should I Go	Andrew Bissell/ Rockabye Baby	Rockabye Baby	2014
We Are Standard	Should I Stay Or Should I Go	We Are Standard Plays The Clash	Mushroom Pillow	2014
Rockabye Baby Lullabies	Straight To Hell	Andrew Bissell/ Rockabye Baby	Rockabye Baby	2014

Source: Authors Collection/Discogs/Wikepedia/secondhandsongs.com

There are an incredible range of styles with the covers, particularly *Should I Stay or Should I Go*. From Kylie Minogue to the Ukulele Orchestra, via a computer generated voice version from 386DX, country and even lounge versions. In 2014, you could even buy CD of Clash songs done in a "lullaby style". So your baby can "rock" to *Rock The Casbah* and contemplate *Staying or Going... Straight To Hell*.

I guess that is the sign of a classic hit. Looking forward to the Mick and Ellen Foley duet version of *Should I Stay or Should I Go*... à la Elton and Kiki Dee….please!!!

So having looked at the covers, we can look at the controversy. This mainly revolves around the two big singles *Rock The Casbah* and *Should I Stay or Should I Go*

Rock The Casbah has traditionally been misinterpreted, perhaps never more so than when in 1991 it was the first song broadcast by the US Military Radio Station when the Gulf War kicked off, and the Desert Storm began. It was "Good Morning Tehran…"

Joe in particular was appalled by this. Perhaps the unfortunate inclusion of two US "Jet Fighters" going in to land at a Texas US Airbase in the *Rock The Casbah* only fueled the provocative nature of the song. In *"The Future is Unwritten"* film, a friend of Joes recalled him openly weeping when he was told that *Rock The Casbah* had been written on a US Bomb detonated in Iraq.

Following the 9/11 attacks in New York, the track was put on a list of "inappropriate" titles to be played on the radio in the US.

In *Clash* magazine September/October 2008, Simon Harper interviewed the remaining Clash members, and Topper was asked about *Rock The Casbah*. "Everyone knows I wrote it" he said, "and I get money for it". On the issue of the US Forces playing it, he replied, "In 20 years time, they might go to war playing the John Lennon song…you don't know". He agreed it went against what the band believed in, but that the Gulf war was actually 10-15 years after the band had been apart.

As I write this in 2014, The US and allies including the UK and Middle Eastern forces are again dropping bombs between the minarets in Iraq and Syria, in an attempt to halt the spread of the Islamic State ISIS Militant Group.

Should I Stay or Should I Go stirred up a whole different hornets' nest of emotion. Jeans brand Levis had built up a reputation for using old "classic" songs to put in TV commercials to advertise their 501 Jeans brand. These included the "Legendary" Nick Kamen 1985 Launderette based *Heard It Through The Grapevine*. The ad that launched a thousand pairs of boxer shorts, and Nick quite literally got his rocks off (and put these in the washing machine to add the distressed worn in look to his new pair of jeans). In 1986, *Wonderful World* sung by Tony Jackson, accompanied the "Levis Hunk" while he shrink fitted his pair in the bath".

In 1990, we had the jean stealing beach babe advert using Bad Company's *Can't Get enough of Your Love* and in 1991, saw the "Wall Street Biker" advert with Steve Miller's *The Joker*.

So amongst the other classic artists, Percy Sledge, Muddy Waters and Ben E King, Levi's decided in 1990 that *Should I Stay or Should I Go* could move the denim for them. You can see the advert on YouTube, and worth a look. Not the finest Levi's advert in my book, and perhaps the brand should have gone for *Pool Hall Richard* by The Faces. But there it is, a cool guy, a "perspiring 'chick'", and a pool hall bet using Levi 501's as "collateral".

"Quality Never Goes Out Of Style" said the tag line at the end of the advert. I would apply that certainly to the band, and for me, I will probably be wearing 501's when they bury me.

So why, do you ask, am I ranting on about jeans commercials?

As with the previous tracks used, a re-release of the single was on the cards, the "TV advert tie in" and *Should I Stay or Should I Go* was no exception.

So what was the controversy, getting your song placed in an advert could be a huge money spinner, not only from broadcast royalties, repeat adverts and public profile, but opportunities for compilation album appearances and album re-issues, and greatest hits albums re-promotions.

But wait a minute, this is The Clash we are talking about here, they didn't play these types of games, or did they? To some, this was an unacceptable "sell out" and there were some pretty strong reactions to this move. Why did the band not veto the whole project?

Well, the track was Mick's work and ultimately, he had the decision, he also very cleverly insisted that the release included a new Big Audio Dynamite track *Rush* from his second incarnation of BAD, BAD II. Was this clever, manipulative? Denying any more royalty benefits to other Clash band members by not using a band or Strummer/Jones track? I guess you have to decide. The 12" single did include *Protex Blue* as the third track (a song about "Rubber Johnnies"). Mick I recall justified its use by pointing out that jeans had been associated with rebellion, and what could be more rock and roll than Levis jeans.

What the release did give The Clash was their first and only number one single in the UK which could not have harmed sales of their album back catalogue. The re-released singles also charted highly in Europe and outside (number 2 in New Zealand).

Whatever your opinion, a certain Wild Billy Childish was provoked enough to release a "protest" single under the band moniker Thee Stash *Should I Suck Or Should I Blow* backed with *We're selling Jeans for the USA* It was released complete with pastiche picture sleeve based on the *Remote Control* single, it is well worth a listen, buy the 7" single?

In an interview with Jules Balme, he recalled that everyone seemed to be against the inclusion of *Rush* as the double A-side. Mick was adamant, and apparently used the argument that Paul had done the re-issue/Jeremy Healy remixed *Return To Brixton* aka *Guns Of Brixton*, and used a more contemporary photograph of himself on the sleeve. If I recall correctly, the release was a reaction to the use of the *Guns Of Brixton* bass line in the Beats International Hit *Dub Be Good To Me* in 1990.

In 2012, controversy continued, this time it's One Direction and their track *Live While We're Young* The mega star boy band were accused of "ripping off The Clash". It was a TWITTER campaign that broke out, accusing the band of copying the opening bars of *Should I Stay or Should I Go*. On the BBC Newsbeat program, band member Harry Styles admitted that the riff was a great one and that using it was "kind of on purpose".

Another band member Louis added that it was "almost impossible for people to create music nowadays without copying something else", and that "surely there's only so many riffs you can pull out?"

Without a doubt, *Should I Stay or Should I Go* has an amazing unforgettable guitar riff, but back track to the earlier chapter on the *Should I Stay or Should I Go* track in chapter 6, and re-access the comments above.

As I write in 2014, in the UK, Scotland makes its mind up about whether it will vote for independence from Britain. News coverage of the subject on the Newsnight TV programme is preceded by that famous riff. Not the chorus, not the first few lines of the verse, just the riff. It's like everyone knows that it means "Should I Stay or Should I Go?"

August 12th 2014, and the news was that Lauren Bacall had died, for me, it was a natural step side one, track 2 *Car Jamming*. I say again "Quality Never Goes Out Of Style".

15. CONCLUSIONS AND CULTURAL EFFECT

The Clash as a band are still a huge influence on many people (myself included), but also to musicians who may not have even been born when the first album was released, or even the *Combat Rock* album.

Its 2013, I'm sitting watching late night TV... *Alan Carr Chatty Man*... not my usual choice of viewing, but his musical guest Fallout Boy is announced... am I dreaming... is it intentional... what is going on... the band are garbed out like The Clash in the *Rock The Casbah* video. The Lead singer in cut off army shirt, the bass player had the Simmo beret and fatigues, the drummer à la Terry Chimes and the guitarist ala Mick... only with helmet not cap... but the same face veil/scarf, I am freaked out, could it be after all this time, The Clash can still influence younger, newer artists? Well yes and here was my proof. "A visual homage to The Clash" said one of the sadly removed posts on YouTube. The band had recently reformed after a career break of a couple of years 2010-2012. Ever wonder...???

During my interview with Pete Winkelmann (CBS Product Manager for *Combat Rock*) in hindsight, he made some observations about The Clash. He believed them to be highly intellectual, and felt that they would have existed without the advent of the punk movement. They, like Bernie had by this time become highly focused on what they were doing, and where they wanted to go. They wanted very much to sell records, and they seemed very focused on the US, backed up by the amount of time they spent there. He believed that they were "global", not just another "act" on the record label. They were global in their outlook, politics and worldliness, with an extraordinary knowledge of political situations in other countries. In *The Clash – The Only Band That Mattered*, Egan took the view that the band went beyond "practical", into the "realms of mercenary", in order to make up what you might consider lost ground.

In a 2015 Radio Six Music documentary about "Riot Girl band" Sleater-Kinney (BBC 6 Music, 2015), the producer John Goodmanson talked about the *One Beat* album, which the band recorded in 2002. The album includes a track *Combat Rock*, and Goodmanson explained that the band had used the whole *Combat Rock* album as a kind of reference point. Not, he emphasized, a kind of copy, does this track sound like this track of their own, but as a guide. The US was experiencing a similar political climate as they had when *Combat Rock* was being written and produced, particularly with the Bush administration and the Iraq war under way. So twenty years on after release date, the album was still inspiring and influencing newer acts.

I don't think you can underestimate the cultural effect of the *Combat Rock* release, and tied in with that the singles released from it. I looked at the use of Clash songs in media, that is TV, Film and yes even Computer Games. This covers an amazing variety of programs and films from about 1994 until the present day.

Just looking at the *Combat Rock* material, the tracks are dominated by *Should I Stay or Should I Go* and *Rock The Casbah*. Also present, *Know Your Rights, Mustapha Dance, Straight To Hell* and *Ghetto Defendant*.

Should I Stay Or Should I Go

TV

Shows that have included this are US HBO series "*The Hitchhiker*" (1983-1991), "*The Sopranos*" (1999-2007) and "*Waking The Dead*" (2000 onwards), cartoon series "*Beavis and Butthead*". In the UK, "*Top Gear*", and the compulsive legal drama, "*This Life*" (1996-1997)

Film

The track appears in "*Rugrats go Wild*" (2003), "The *Royal Tenenbaums*" (2001), "*28 Days*" (2000), "*Taking Lives*" (2004) and "*Iron Man 2*" (2010) and "*Divorcing Jack*" (1998). And Mick's very own karaoke version in "*Code 46*" (2003)

Computer Games

Yes, the track even made it to "*Sing Star Pop*" (2007), so you can sing away on the console of your choice, from the safety of you bedroom. (Extra points if you can master the "Spanish" backup vocals). You can even "air guitar" your way through the song, with a plastic guitar and the "*Rockband*" console game (2007)

Rock The Casbah

TV

The UK "Blokes with Cars Show" – "*Top Gear*" also included this track on one show, "*Chuck*" (2007-2012), "*American Dad*" (2005 onwards), "*The Simpsons*" (1989 onwards) and featured in one episode of an interesting Australian series called "*20 To 1*" (2005-2011), which counted down an undefined "Top 20" of "elements or events of popular culture, such as films, songs and sporting scandals".

Film

Thinner on the ground film wise, the track appears in "*Rogue Trader*" (1999) and "*The Royal Tenenbaums*" (2001)

Others

A short film (5 Minutes long) from 2003 called "*Cosmopolis*", included *Ghetto Defendant*, based strangely enough, in New York, maybe in a "Slam Dance Cosmopolis".

Know Your Rights appears in "*American Splendor*" (2003), and a Video called "*Embedded*" (2005).

Straight To Hell appears on *"Kevin & Perry Go Large"* (2000) and *"Complicity"* (2000) (based on the very fine Iain Banks novel of the same name). You could say that it makes an impressive appearance (in a way) in the Danny Boyle blockbusting *"Slum Dog Millionaire"* (2008) via *Paper Planes*. In *33 Revolutions Per Minute* (Lynskey, 2010) the author talked about the MIA interpretation using the *Straight To Hell* Sample. He contrasted how the "Third world citizens who are downtrodden" in Joes lyric are "newly empowered" in the MIA lyric. Lynskey also pointed out that MIA suggested that the *Paper Planes* track is a celebration of Immigrant Culture and at the same time a "critique of the arms industry".

Mustapha Dance made it into the *"History Boys"* in 2006, a film set in the 1980's, with a younger looking James Corden.

Source: imdb.com/Wikipedia/authors collection

Mick Lewis – Combat Rock
BBC Books 9780563538554

I came across this book on my routine trawls through the internet, and investigated a little further. The novel was written as part of the many *Dr Who* series of novels published by BBC Books. The stories are written around a particular "Doctor", and are not scripts or stories from the hugely successful TV Series.

I was intrigued enough to get hold of a copy, and discovered that the writer Mick Lewis was a Clash fan of old, and in his acknowledgments wrote that he "better thank The Clash, really … Complete Control, even over this book".

The story is based around the Patrick Troughton era, although the bulk of the story revolves around a bunch of mercenaries, one who is called "Bass" and is partly based I suspect on Paul Simonon (light brown hair, slicked back with oil, cigarette tucked behind one ear, who always wore sleeveless army shirts). Is this conjuring up any pictures for you? I'm not sure if Simmo could "take a man's head off with one slice of a Bowie knife", but I don't think I would want to put that theory to the test.

The story takes place in a jungle, "Vietnam" type country, but with added cannibalism and spooky goings on, mercenaries and political shenanigans, which takes it even more into *Combat Rock* territory.

So, if like me, you like The Clash mixed with a bit of Doctor Who, worth checking this out for some light reading.

Facts and Figures

I'm indebted to Bob MacDonald who I worked with at Gallup in their Charts Department between 1989 and 1994, for his encyclopedic brain for some facts and figures on *Combat Rock*

Combat Rock is the only album by The Clash to be certified double platinum in America, getting to No.7 on the Billboard album chart.

Should I Stay or Should I Go spent 20 weeks in the rock airplay top 60, reaching No.13, and got to No.45 on the Hot 100.

The real hit, though, was *Rock The Casbah*, which entered the Billboard Hot 100 in October 1982 and became an early beneficiary of the second "British Invasion" spending four weeks at its No.8 Hot 100 peak in January and February 1983; it got to No.6 in rock airplay.

In 2010 Rolling Stone published their "500 Greatest Songs Of All Time" special issue, and placed *Should I Stay or Should I Go* at No.228

The Clash only had one Top 10 single each in Britain and America, but *Combat Rock* was responsible for both of them. *Should I Stay or Should I Go*, originally No.17 in the UK in October 1982 as part of a double A-side with *Straight To Hell*, eventually spent two weeks at No.1 in March 1991 thanks to a Levi's commercial, sandwiched between chart-toppers by the Simpsons (*Do The Bartman*) and Hale And Pace And The Stonkers (*The Stonk*).

Ironically, *Combat Rock* was kept off the number one album spot in the UK by the Paul Mc Cartney album *Tug Of War*. It equaled the high chart position of *Give 'Em Enough Rope* on release, but lasted much longer in the UK charts, 23 weeks in all, making it their most successful album.

Some words about Mick.

Looking through the stormy lifespan of *Combat Rock*, and perhaps after, you might get the impression that Mick as he was portrayed in *"Hell W10"* was the "BAD GUY" in all of this. Much has been made of his liking of the "rock star" lifestyle, his "Elizabeth Taylor" style bad moods and mercenary attitude towards the Levis adverts. In a short film *Wot No Bike* (Walsh, 2015) Paul Simonon referred to the "Elizabeth Taylor" references again, and said of the band split, "I don't wanna put Mick on the spot, but it was Mick's fault".

It was interesting reading *Clothes, Clothes, Clothes, Music, Music, Music, Boys, Boys, Boys* (Albertine 2014), Viv talked about how Mick was always on the payphone at Art School for hours and hours, trying to get people/musicians together, arranging rehearsals. He was absolutely driven as far back as the mid seventies. Viv explained, "Mick is that person in a band- and there is always one- who does all the organising" and "who takes the pain and the losses of the band to heart".

Mick had wanted the "rock star" life, and pretty much got it. I don't think you can take that away from him. He wanted it; he worked hard to get it, crafting songs, developing his playing, and managing the band at times. In the *Downbeat* magazine article (Goldberg, 1982),the author wrote that The Clash had now found themselves "in a bind", treated like stars when they toured America, "despite everything they can do to prevent it". Mick had said "I find it humiliating; I try not to be anything other than a human being. But you can't just say I don't want to sign autographs if there's a hundred people there".

In a *Radio 4a* broadcast, from the Brighton based radio station *The Joe Strummer Special* (Unknown, 2012), Chris Salewicz spoke about Joe. He felt that Joe liked anonymity, but he also loved being Joe Strummer too. Salewicz felt that Joe did have a big ego, but it was well balanced because of his experiences. He referred to it as "sufferation", and that he had had to live with the pressure of being the "front man" of The Clash. So Joe and Mick were perhaps no different in that their goal was to be a "rock and roll star", it was just the way the two characters dealt with this. In the same way that Mick was driven, in the same Radio 4a documentary, Julian Yewdall recalled that before Joe had joined The Clash they had a discussion about what they wanted to do in life. Joe had said that he wanted to be in a rock and roll band, and be a "rock and roll star", and as Yewdall said, "that's what he did!"

Mick is probably not down on the list of "Great Guitarists of Our Time"; I think especially during the eighties, the rock world became much more "Widdly widdly" obsessed, with the likes of Eddie Van Halen, Joe Satriani and Richie Sambora. But when you look at Mick's contribution, he can write great songs, some "pop", some not. He is a great arranger, and willing to probe the advances in technology and new genres. The first Big Audio Dynamite album was for me, absolutely ground breaking in its use of samples, beats, both human and machine, and of course … Tunes!

Akito Watanabe from The Strummers band in Japan when asked about the influence of *Combat Rock* on himself and others felt that the album itself did not really impact on him directly, he received a great deal of influence from Mick Jones as a guitarist. "Such skills to copy" as he put it. Watanabe remembered that he wanted to "jump in front of his guitar hero" at the Tokyo shows.

Despite the differences between Mick and Joe, especially how Joe found the fame and fortune difficult to handle and justify to himself, and perhaps Mick was better able to deal with it. David Byrne in *How Music Works* produced a great statement. "Being a musician is a good job, but it doesn't mean its ok to go broke doing it"

In *The Clash – The Only Band That Mattered*, Egan talked about an interview that Mick had done in 1979, in which he explained that he had given up everything for The Clash, who were at the time being called "The Greatest Rock and Roll Band in the world", but that he was actually skint. Egan also took the view that the "business minded" approach that Bernie brought to the band over the '82-83 period was not necessarily a "betrayal" of their values, but trying to claim what was rightfully theirs, and enjoy the "fruits of their labour".

In 2012, Mick appeared on *The Telecaster 60 Years* TV Show, and made the comment that "All music was connected", and it was about finding out how other people put their music together. When he was playing with The Gorillas, he felt that it took him back to his BAD and late period Clash times. He took his music very seriously, and if you look at his own personal success around the *Combat Rock* album, it is impressive on a commercial level. Not for the first time did Mick write a highly successful song in the shape of *Should I Stay or Should I Go*, but he mixed and was asked to mix the second huge hit from the album, that being Toppers work *Rock The Casbah*, a song which Joe felt Mick treated as a bit "jokey". Mick was passionate about the music. A kind soul who emailed me was Jeremy Vanes, with some thoughts about *Combat Rock* and the UK Tour of 1982. He had followed the band around, and became a regular at the show, building up a relationship with the group. Jeremy wrote that "Mick really kept to himself, but was a deep, romantic thinker who loved to play well".

All credit to Mick for picking himself up after being evicted from his own band for the second time. (First time, early in his career when ousted from Violent Luck).

The initial ideas in TRAC (prior to the creation of the magnificent Big Audio Dynamite) took ideas and techniques he had been refining over the years, and tried to take the music forwards. You can find these early recordings on a bootleg album, and again for historical purposes, these are worth a listen. BAD really refined these ideas into slick well constructed sample heavy pieces, but always with tunes and melody.

So what is my point?

My point is that even though *Combat Rock* was released in 1982, and theoretically was a "spent force" really by the end of 1983, it lives on and continues to sell today. As recently as 2013, the whole Clash back catalogue was re promoted alongside the *Sound System Box Set* compilation and the pop up shop extension of the Mick Jones's *Rock and Roll Library*, which became the *Black Market Clash Pop Up Shop*. The Box set included a CD of previously unreleased tracks, including *Combat Rock* Track *Sean Flynn* from Marcus Music studios, and the previously unavailable (except on bootleg) *The Beautiful People are Ugly Too* and *Idle in Kangaroo Court*.

I pick up again from a comment made by Joe Schalit in *Let Fury Have The Hour*, about *Combat Rock* being the most politically overt album to chart. It is strange how the US really took to the *Combat Rock* album. In the *Downbeat* magazine article (Goldberg, 1982) the author mentioned that he had spoken to Joe and Mick, and how they were "no more enchanted with the US and the complacency of Americans". (I would think than they were when they were writing *I'm So Bored with The USA*). Goldberg also quoted Kosmo who said that "nobody in America wants anything to question or upset what they might personally be". Much of the *Combat Rock* material, as with some of *Sandinista*, was knocking the US, it's Government, International Policy and culture!

In *The Clash – The Only Band That Mattered*, again the author picked up on the fact that the album climbed up the "most conservative" album chart in the world. Despite the fact that it had highly political subject material, English accents and "avant garde" instrumentation.

In the *Sten Guns in LA* article, McCullough talked to Joe about America. Often accused of "selling out" to the US and being obsessed by it, Joe made the point that America (in 1982) was different "now that the Romanticism had gone." Joe explained that the first two times they visited, he had come with "a head full of Kerouac and Tom Waits and Woody Guthrie", but that was "all out of the window now". He complained about the fact that America had become plasticized, "horrific – all the same from New Jersey to wherever." Joe was also well aware that England had given them the "big brush off", and that the band probably wouldn't have gone to the US if it hadn't.

In true Clash tradition, Joe felt that if the band had "made it" that they would have had it, as they always seemed to be struggling. As he said, "I like to feel we have a constant struggle on our hands, although it was a great feeling to be number 2 in Good Ole Britain you know."

Goldberg posed the question "can political rock and roll actually accomplish anything?", and believed that The Clash were trying to be realistic… "if not optimistic". Mick was quoted as saying that "maybe it won't change anything, but I still believe in it, as something worth doing. But it ain't gonna tell Politicians what to do, and it ain't gonna save people from wars."

So, looking back now at *Combat Rock*, how relevant is it today? The world is still full of conflict, the US, and others, are still involved and exerting their influence, particularly in the Middle East.

Combat Rock was a great achievement, whether you are a fan of the music on it, or not. It was a rock soap opera unfolding before you. Only now, over 35 years later, am I aware of, I was going to say the full story, but I doubt I am, or ever will be. We had creative disagreements, inter band politics, power plays between members and their dominant, outspoken manager, Joe goes missing at a crucial point, drug addiction issues, a business financial crisis, legal actions, and a small scale "war" in the Falkland Islands.

The band took on the world, touring Europe, The Far East and the USA on their mission to prove they were "The Best Rock and Roll Band in the World".

Possibly overlooked by some Clash fans as a "sellout" or "too commercial", it was actually a natural evolution or progression for the band that refused to stand still and play the formula game. They had now distilled their wide and varied influences into a sound that they could call their own.

It was the bands biggest selling album, and as usual with The Clash, it was not straight forward. The "hits" were enough to get the album into the homes of a wide audience around the world, particularly the US. Once there, like a Commando Undercover mission, the songs, particularly Side 2 were set to work amongst the minds of the listeners. No need for three chord protest, subtlety is the game. The track order for me runs like a movie soundtrack. *Know Your Rights* kicks off with a loud "shouty" opening, you move into the more up-tempo tunes as the plot unfolds. By the end of Side 1 *Straight To Hell*, you hit melancholy and the message.

Side Two *Overpowered by Funk* snaps you out of this, if only temporarily, before the drama continues, leading to the finale that is *Death Is a Star*.

In the 2015 aired film *The Clash – New Years Day '77* (Temple, 2015), what was so interesting was that even in 1976/77 the band realised how powerful films were. Joe kicked it off by saying that you could tell when a film was good, because people came out acting the part. Like a western…he would come out and walking "like bow legged" down the street. Mick picked up on …"*Taxi Driver*" (Released 1976), and how people came out of that film all with their collars turned up. Obviously this made a lasting impression on the whole band! Paul chipped in with the Bruce Lee Kung Fu films and how people would come out of those chopping and kicking (complete with sound effects!!!)

Over the period of my research, a phrase seems to pop up more than once, "we went in, did our job and left." *Combat Rock* perhaps more than any other Clash album fulfills this so well.

In *How Music Works*, David Byrne looked at "contemporary music venues", he talked about "Contemporary Hip Hop", and how he felt that the music is written to be heard in cars. He felt it had "morphed" into music "that sounds better in cars". Massive volumes allowing "sharing your music with everyone gratis".

This got me thinking about *Combat Rock*, and where it was written to be played, in a club, a football ground or Shea Stadium? Well for me, it has got to be the… "Dark Cinema".

16 READING LIST

I have read huge quantities of material for the research on this book, and I am tempted to list everything I came across. Most of the books relate to the whole career of The Clash, but you can extract the relevant sections easily if you wish. Failing that, read the whole thing, it's worthwhile. Some of the material was background, and so in direct relation to *Combat Rock*, I would recommend the following:

Tony Fletcher – *The Music That Matters*

Pat Gilbert – *Passion is a Fashion*

Marcus Gray – *Last Gang In Town - The Story and Myth Of The Clash*

Chris Knowles – *Clash City Showdown*

Joe Strummer, Mick Jones, Topper Headon, Paul Simonon – *The Clash* (Pink Book)

Kris Needs – *Joe Strummer and The Legend Of The Clash*

Agent Provocateur – *The Clash Retrospective*

Chris Salewicz – *Redemption Song* - The Ballad Of Joe Strummer

Keith Topping – *The Complete Clash* (Blackmarket Clash)

Michael Herr – *Dispatches*

For a comprehensive list of Clash books go to the Blackmarket Clash website.

www.blackmarketclash.co.uk

17 WATCHING LIST

As with reading matter, I have spent many hours watching video footage, official, unofficial, online, on DVD and VHS tapes. As with the reading list, they cover the whole Clash career, so if you don't want the whole story, dip in as appropriate. If you haven't seen them already, I would recommend the following, and take it from there.

The Rise and Fall Of The Clash - The Inside Story – Danny Garcia

Westway To the World – Don Letts

The Essential Clash – Various

Hell W10

The Clash In Tokyo – 2nd January 1982

The Clash - Live in Asbury Park NJ – 1982

The Future Is Unwritten – Julian Temple

Taxi Driver

Apocalypse Now

The Deer Hunter

18. THOSE WHO SERVED...
ACKNOWLEDGMENTS

The British Library	UK
Anthony "Ant" Davie	UK
Blackmarket Clash	UK
Paul Wooff	NZ
Anne Oliver	NZ
James Braithwaite	NZ
Eric Beaumont	US
Philippa Hayes	UK
Bob MacDonald	UK
Russell Baillie	UK
Richard England	UK
Andrea Rehman	NZ
Garth Cartwright	AUS
Neil Pearce	NZ
Robyn Collins	AUS
Nick Bollinger	NZ
Murray Cammick	NZ
Junko Kiriya	JAP
Nob (Nobuya Suzuki)	JAP
Lucy Spencer	AUS
Toshiyuki Tsujiguchi	JAP
Fe Skoufa	AUS
Patricia Egan	AUS
Rusty Deluce	CAN
Pennie Smith	UK
Douglas Kean	UK
Julian "Jules" Balme	UK
Akito Watanabe (The Strummers)	JAP
Pete Winkelman	UK

19. REFERENCES

Albertine, V. (2014). *Clothes Music Boys* (p. 421). London: faber and Faber.

Alex James. (2007). *A Bit Of A Blur* (pp. 101–104). Abacus.

Astor, P. (2014). *Richard Hell and the Voidoids' Blank Generation* (33 1/3) (p. 144). UK: Bloomsbury Academic.

Banks, R. (1981). The Clash. *Zig Zag*.

Bateman, S. (2003). *Ay Hinterview. Repeat Website, Rants*. Retrieved from www.repeatfanzine.co.uk/Rants/Penniesmith.htm

BBC 4. (2015). *The Sound of Song*.

BBC 6 Music. (2015). *The Story of Sleater Kinney*.

Blackmarket Clash/Topping. (2003). *The Complete Clash* (p. 271). UK: Reynolds and Hearn.

Bohn, C. (1982). No Title. *NME*.

Bowe, B. J. (2011). The Clash - Punk Rock Band. Enslow Publishers Inc.

Byrne, D. (2012). *How Music Works* (p. 346). Edinburgh: Canongate.

Campbell, D. (1982a). Jones In Vain Part 1. *Unknown*. New Zealand.

Campbell, D. (1982b). Mick Jones Part 2 - Politics. *Unknown*. New Zealand.

Cartwright, G. (1982). *The Clash* - Logan Campbell Centre. New Zealand.

Chimes, T. (2013). *The Strange Case of Dr Terry and Mr Chimes* (p. 228). UK: Wilkinson Publishing.

Christgau, R. (1994). *Christgau's Record Guide To The 80's*. New York: Da Capo Press.

Clerk, C. (1982). News. *Melody Maker*. UK.

Crosthwaite, R. (1982). The Clash Have Us All taped. *Daily Telegraph Sydney Morning Daily*. Sydney Australia.

Doane, R. (2012). *Stealing All Transmissions* (p. 99). Custos.

Dudanski, R. (2014). *Squat City Rocks* (p. 233). CreateSpace Independent Publishing Platform.

Du-Noyer, P. (1981). The Clash Answer Back. *RAM*.

Du-Noyer, P. (1982). Singles Reviews. *NME*. UK.

Egan, S. (2015). *The Clash - The Only Band That Mattered* (p. 154). Rowman & Littlefield.

Farren, M. (1981a, June). News Section. *NME*.

Farren, M. (1981b, June 20). How The Clash fed the Wonderbread Generation and made the mountain come to Mohammed..and other Miracles. *NME*.

Fletcher, T. (2012). *The Clash - The Music That Matters* (p. 112). Omnibus Press.

Fricke, D. (1982). The Clash - Combat Rock. *Rolling Stone*.

Garcia, D. (2012a). *The Rise and Fall Of The Clash* (1st ed., p. 196). London: Thin man Press.

Garcia, D. (2012b). *The Rise and Fall Of The Clash - The Inside Story* (p. 101 Minutes). Epic Japan.

Gilbert, P. (2004). *Passion Is A Fashion - The Real Story of The Clash* (Paperback ., p. 404). Aurum.

Gilmore, M. (2011). The Fury and The Power of The Clash. *Rolling Stone*, (1125), 8.

Gimarc, G. (1997). *Post Punk Diary 1980-1982* (p. 374). New York: St Martins Press.

Goldberg, M. (1982). Downbeat. *Downbeat*.

Gorman, P. (2006). *The Look* (p. 223). Adelita.

Gray, M. (1995). *Last Gang In Town - The Story and Myth of The Clash* (p. 512). Fourth Estate Limited.

Hall, P. (1982). The Year Of The Clash. *Rolling Stone*, 62.

Harrigan, B. (1982a). Fast Forward. *Melody Maker*.

Harrigan, B. (1982b). News Review. *Melody Maker*. UK.

Harrington, B. (1982). The Clash…Have You seen this Tour? *Melody Maker*. UK.

Harris, J. (2003). Combat Rock Review. *Uncut*.

Harrsion, F. and. (2014). *Punk Rock Warlord* (Faulk and ., p. 195). Ashgate.

Hayashi, Y. (1981). No Title. *Crossbeat The Clash Special Edition*, 4.

Herr, M. (1977). *Dispatches*.

Hewitt, P. (1981). The Clash. *Melody Maker*, 1.

Humphries, P. (1982). Singles Review. *Melody Maker*.

Hutcheon, D. (2010). What's My 'Nam. *Q Classics The Clash - The Inside Story*, 1(8), 2.

Joe Strummer Paul Simonon, Topper Headon, M. J. (2008). *The Clash* (p. 384). Atlantic Books.

Johns, G. (2014). *Sound Man* (p. 320). Blue Rider Press.

Johnstone, N. (2006). *The Clash "Talking."* (N. Johnstone, Ed.) (p. 128). Omnibus Press.

Kelly, D. (2005). Mick Jones Remembers - Once Upon A Time In West London. *The Word*, (33), 14.

Knowles, C. (2003). *Clash City Showdown* (p. 264). PageFree Publishing.

Konno, Y. (1982). New Music Matters.

Law, M. (1982). No Ordinary Joe. *Melody Maker*. UK.

Lergessner, J. G. (2013). *Cloudland - Queen Of The Dance Halls* (p. 252). Australia: Boolarong Press.

Letts, D. (2001). *Westway To The World*. UK: Sony .

Letts, D. (2011). *Clash On Broadway Video*.

Lewis, A. (1981). *Was It really Worth It?* Sounds, 5.

Lynskey, D. (2010). *33 Revolutions Per Minute*. Faber and Faber.

Maconie, S. (2013). *The People's Songs* (p. 380). Random House.

Majewski, L., & Bernstein, J. (2014). *Mad World* (p. 320). ABRAMS IMAGE.

Manning, J. (1982). The Clash - Capitol Theatre Sydney. *Juke*.

Martin, G. (1999). Combat Rock. *Uncut Magazine*, 19.

Martin, G. (2010). Bringing Back the Glory Days. *Uncut*.

McCullough, D. (1982, July). Sten Guns In LA. *Sounds*, pp. 27–30.

McSporran, M. (1982). The Clash Want To Be Number One. *Rolling Stone Magazine*.

Metzer, R. (1982). Overpowered By Mere. *Creem*.

Meyers, B. (2007). *The Clash- Music In Review* (p. 50). London: Edgehill Publishing.

Michon, A. (2004). No Title. *Arty Magazine*.

Miles/Tobler/Peachy. (1992). *The Clash - The New Visual Documentary* (p. 112). London: Omnibus Press.

Minakami, H. (1982, March). Clash In Japan. *Sounds*, 14–15.

Molloy, S. (1982). Four Rude Boys who like to Clash. *Sydney Daily*. Sydney Australia.

Moore, X.-. (1982). Blows Against The Empire. *NME*.

Muirhead, B. (1984). *The Record Producers File 1962-1984*. UK: Blandford Press.

Mulholland, G. (2011). The Clash Combat Rock. Clash. *The Ultimate Music Guide*, 4.

Needs, K. (1982). The Goat Lies Down on Broadway. *Flexipop*, 13–15.

Needs, K. (2005). *Joe Strummer and The Legend Of The Clash* (p. 351). Plexus.

Needs, K. (2010). Press Stop. *Q Classics The Clash - The Inside Story*, 1(8), 7.

Needs, K. (2013). Stay Free. *Vive Le Rock*, (10), 13.

Ogg, A. (2006). *No More Heroes A Complete History Of Punk Rock from 1976-1980* (p. 728). London: Cherry Red Books.

Ogg, A. (2008). The Clash Life and legacy - Death Or Glory. *The Big Cheese*, (104), 5.

Orshoski, W. (2008). The Battle Of Shea Stadium. *Relix The Magazine For Music*, 8.

Panel, V. U. (2003). Clash City Rockers - The Clash Their Greatest Songs. *Uncut Magazine*, (December 2003), 30.

Perry, A. (2013). The Real Mick Jones. *Q Magazine*.

Quantick, D. (2000). *The Clash. The Music Makers* (p. 136). Unanimous.

Rai, A. (1982). Alas Poor Kirk - Theatre Of Hate Sheffield Polytechnic. *NME*. London.

Reines, R. (1982). Tropic Of Clash. *NME*.

Robbins, I. (1983). *Four Sides Of The Clash - A Listeners Guide*. Trouser Press, (April 1983), 7.

Salewicz, C. (1981). Home On The Range. *The Face*, 10, 5.

Salewicz, C. (1994). The Clash On Broadway. *Mojo Magazine*.

Salewicz, C. (2006). *Redemption Song - The Ballad Of Joe Strummer* (p. 628). Faber and Faber Inc.

Schalit, J. (2012). Clash Of The Titan. *In Let Fury Have the Hour.* US: Persus Books.

Shaar-Murray, C. (2003). Comrade Goodbye. *Mojo Magazine.*

Shannon, E. A. (2014). Don't Call me Woody. In F. and Harrison (Ed.), *Punk Rock Warlord* (pp. 17–18). Ashgate.

Sharr-Murray, C. (1982). Strummer …Why I ran out on The Clash. *NME.* UK.

Silverton, P. (1982a). Albums. *Smash Hits,* 1.

Silverton, P. (1982b). Strummertime and the living is easy. *Smash Hits*, 2.

Simonon, M. J. and P. (2003). A Riot Of Their Own. *Uncut Magazine*, (December 2003), 5.

Smith, P. (1980). *The Clash Before and After.* Eel Pie.

Smith, P. (2011). *Just Kids.* UK: Bloomsbury.

Snow, M. (2008a). Death Or Glory - Who Killed The Clash. *Mojo Magazine*, 19.

Snow, M. (2008b). Who Killed The Clash. *Mojo,* 19.

St John, B. E. and E. (1982). Mammals Babble: The Flying Sydney Press Conference. *Rolling Stone Magazine.*

Sweeting, A. (1981). The Clash and Cocktail Culture. *Melody Maker.* UK.

Sweeting, A. (1982). Combat Rock. *Melody Maker.*

Swift, D. (1982). Unknown. *New Zealand Herald.*

Talks At Google - Glyn Johns in Conversation. (2014).

Taylor, J. (1982). Singles Review.

Temple, J. (2007). *Joe Strummer - The Future Is Unwritten* (p. 124 Minutes).

Temple, J. (2015). *The Clash - New Years Day '77.*

Thompson, D. (2013). The Clash - The Ultimate Listening Guide. Amazon Kindle.

Tickel. (1982). Stations Of The Cash. *NME.*

Townsend, P. (2013). *Who Am I* (p. 554). London: Harper Collins.

Uncredited. (1982). Bitz - News Pages. *Smash Hits.*

Unknown. (1981). Win A Week In New York With The Clash. *NME*, 4.

Unknown. (1982a). Clash Blow Last Dates. *NME.* UK.

Unknown. (1982b). Clash Mystery - Joe Goes AWOL. *NME.* UK.

Unknown. (1982c). Clash Postpone Dates – Bring Me The Guitar of Joe Strummer. *NME.* UK.

Unknown. (1982d). Clash Shock - Sydney press Conference. *Roadrunner*, 5(1).

Unknown. (1982e). Combat Rock. *NME.*

Unknown. (1982f). News . *NME.* UK.

Unknown. (1982g). News Pages. Melody Maker. UK.

Unknown. (1982h). Still No Show Joe. NME. UK.

Unknown. (1982i). The Clash. *The Press*. New Zealand.

Unknown. (2006). *The Clash's London Calling. Rock Milestones* (p. 70 Minutes). Edgehill Publishing Ltd.

Unknown. (2012). Radio 4A Joe Strummer Special.

Unknown. (2014). *Crossbeat The Clash Special Edition* (p. 175).

Walker, J. (1982). "Clash Brutal Rock Wows Fans." *Courier Mail*. Australia.

Walsh, B. (2015). *Wot No Bike!*

Winterbottom, M. (2003). *Code 46* (p. 87 Minutes). Verve Pictures.

Zanhorn, F. (1982). Total Recall - Lochem Festival. Q *Classics The Clash - The Inside Story,* 1(8), 2.

BIOGRAPHY

TIM SATCHWELL

Tim Satchwell grew up in Shropshire and was sucked into the '77 Punk Revolution. (If a little behind kids from the major cities.) He loved the music and the creativity that went with it and followed it. Anyone could do it, and so he did, taking up bass guitar and being drafted into a band a couple of weeks later.

He left Shropshire to go to college in Bristol and then a couple of years later to London to "follow the dream" of getting into the music industry, be that making the tea, working at a record company or playing in a band. The way in he hoped was working in a record shop. (He had worked in record shops part-time while still at school and carried on even after getting a full-time job). That gave him a great grounding in how things worked in music retail, maybe not the glamorous side. (Although some of those Virgin Megastore cashiers had a damn good try at making it so.)

After working for Our Price and Virgin Music and getting involved in developing a computerised stock system in Virgin, he got bitten by the IT bug. (Barcodes?... Music became tins of beans?) This led to several years working at Gallup on the UK Music and Video Charts, a perfect combination of his interests. (Although "chart" music didn't exactly excite him)

Everything was a learning process, and he headed back to Bristol to work at an independent distributor who were expanding, followed by a return to London to set up and run a UK Music warehouse for US label Rykodisc. A call out of the blue took him to what he thought was the golden fleece... a small record label... but it wasn't, he was no Jason or an Argonaut, and so moved back into a more IT based job with... Books. The pieces all fitted together.

Tim has written three books, with a fourth now in progress, each of them about one of The Clash albums, a band which seemed to take up an important place in his life over the years, and by the late nineties had become something of an obsession. With no previous experience of writing anything "long form" prior to this, he took on that same punk philosophy, anyone can do it, and so he did.

Tim also still dabbles in a little bass playing, but more recently has moved into poetry in the guise of *The Bard of Bicton Heath*.

Tim Satchwell's books; *Combat Ready (Combat Rock)* was originally published in 2016, followed by *All the Peacemakers (Give 'em Enough Rope)* 2019 and in 2021 Move Up Starsky *(First Album)*, were all self-published, (on his own Stay Free imprint) and each one a labour of love. Now they will see the light of day again through Earth Island Books.

Tim is currently working on the long process of researching and writing his fourth book, as yet untitled, which will take a closer look at the story around the writing, recording and promotion of 'Sandinista'.

DEDICATION (IS WHAT YOU NEED...)

This book is dedicated to my wife Pauline and "Sun" Hal, and all the wonderful people I have met, played music with, and worked with over the years…

ALSO BY THE AUTHOR...

Combat Ready was Tim Satchwell's first book about The Clash. He had no previous experience of writing anything of length, let alone being 'published' before this. The book finally saw the light of day in 2016, published independently with help and encouragement from a number of people. Tim's and our thanks go out to them all, it would never have happened without you. That's the punk d.i.y. spirit right there.

Since *Combat Ready* was published Tim has written two more books about The Clash; ***All the Peacemakers*** (About *Give 'em Enough Rope*) 2019, and *Move Up Starsky* (About the First album) 2021. Undeterred, he is currently working on his fourth.

Combat Ready is now generally available through Earth Island Books and the others will follow soon.

www.ingramcontent.com/pod-product-compliance
Lightning Source LLC
Chambersburg PA
CBHW041306110526
44590CB00028B/4264